Short Walks for Inquiring Minds

Canmore &
Kananaskis Country

Disclaimer

There are inherent risks in hiking in wilderness and semi-wilderness areas. Although the author has alerted readers to locations where particular caution must be exercised, trail conditions may change due to weather and other factors.

Walkers use this book entirely at their own risk and the author and publisher disclaim any liability for injuries or other damage which may be sustained by anyone using any of the trails described in this book.

Short Walks for Inquiring Minds

Rocky
Mountain Books
Calgary-Victoria-Vancouver

Canmore & Kananaskis Country

Gillean Daffern

We acknowledge the financial support of the Government of Canada through the Book Publishing Industry Development Program (BPIDP) and the support of the Alberta Foundation for the Arts for our publishing program.

Published by Rocky Mountain Books
108, 17665-66A Ave., Surrey, BC V3S 2A7
Printed and bound in Canada by
RMB Kromar Printing Ltd., Winnipeg

National Library of Canada Cataloguing in Publication Data

Daffern, Gillean, 1938-
  Canmore & Kananaskis country / Gillean Daffern.—2nd ed.

Includes index.
ISBN 1-894765-41-9

1. Walking—Alberta—Kananaskis Country—Guidebooks. 2. Walking—Alberta—Canmore Region—Guidebooks. 3. Trails—Alberta—Kananaskis Country—Guidebooks. 4. Trails—Alberta—Canmore Region—Guidebooks. 5. Kananaskis Country (Alta.)—Guidebooks. 6. Canmore Region (Alta.)—Guidebooks. I. Title. II. Title: Canmore and Kananaskis country.
GV199.44.C22K34 2003   917.123'32   C2003-910611-X

Contents

Area Trails

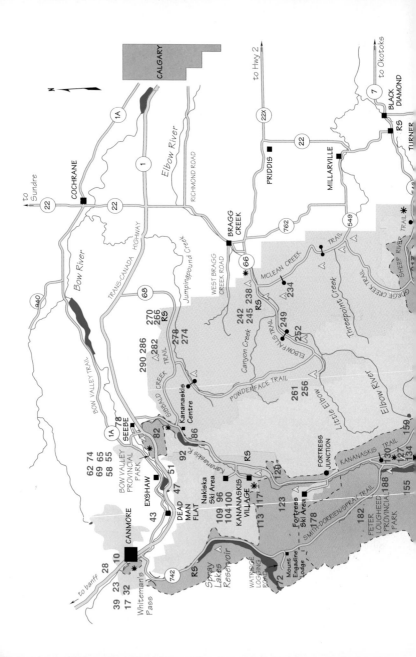

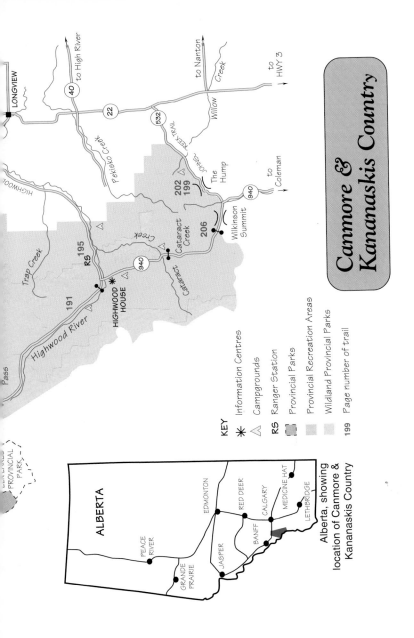

Canmore & Kananaskis Country

KEY

✳	Information Centres
△	Campgrounds
RS	Ranger Station
▨	Provincial Parks
	Provincial Recreation Areas
▨	Wildland Provincial Parks
199	Page number of trail

Alberta, showing location of Canmore & Kananaskis Country

About this Book

- The walks in this book are suitable for tourists, motorists, campers, seniors, families with young children, school groups and other organisations; for anyone with an hour or more to spare who wants to learn more about the area. Some, as noted, are accessible to wheelchair users.

- Space allows only a brief introduction to topics of interest. The purpose of this book is to whet your appetite for further research.

- All walks are less than 10 km return and last from a half hour to half a day.

- Walks follow well-established trails with signposts except where noted.

- Runners and light boots are suitable footwear except where noted.

- Bring an umbrella or light rain coat and a sweater/wind jacket for higher elevation trails.

- Carrying field guides (listed at the back of the book) will add to your enjoyment.

- All sketch maps are orientated with north facing the top of the page. Numbers beside small black circles indicate interpretive signs. Red letters are cross referenced with letters in the text.

- In Kananaskis Country and provincial parks nothing should be removed or harmed except for fish for which you need a license. Dogs must be kept on a leash.

Foreword to the second edition

Four trails from the first edition have been dropped because of flood decimation, road closure and urban development. Canmore is in a growing phase and it's a matter of waiting to see how trails on the benchlands and in Three Sisters will be affected by development and new trail regulations. Four new trails have been added, one in Canmore, two in the Bow Valley and one in the Kananaskis Valley.

Acknowledgments

Thanks are due to Bruce Bembridge, Bill Baxter, Dales Judd, Jean Greig, Mrs. Andy Shellian, Gill and Pete Ford, Dawn Jones, Don Cockerton (as always), Mike O'Reilly, Rowan Bonser and Kim Belloglowka. In particular, I want to thank John Martin who corrected the errors in the first edition.

Photos are by the author, except where noted. A special thank you to E. Jones, Dave Elphinstone, Don Beers, Pam Doyle, H. Barry Giles and Julie Bauer.

Front cover: Chester Lake.

Title page: Plateau Mountain.

Contents page: Upper Kananaskis Lake trailhead near North Interlakes parking lot.

Opposite: Elbow Lake and Mt. Rae.

The Trails

Policeman Creek
3.8 km loop

early spring
summer
late fall

This easy loop follows creeks and ponds where you're sure to see lots of waterfowl, to a viewpoint at the Bow River. End where you began: in the heart of downtown historic Canmore.

Start: Canmore. NWMP barracks on 8 Street near the bridge.

🅰 NWMP Barracks

It wasn't until 1892 that the Northwest Mounted Police had their own permanent barracks in Canmore. It was no big deal, comprised of stables and a mud-chinked log structure, big enough to house two constables at a pinch. Now a Provincial Historic Site, it operates as an interpretive centre and tearoom. The barrack's park features a flower garden and picnic tables. Open from 8 am to 4 pm Wednesday to Sunday.

From the barracks, cross 8 St. to the bridge over Policeman Creek.

After reading the plaque, follow Policeman Creek Trail running along the west bank of Policeman Creek— a mallard hot-spot.

At 10 St. turn right and cross the bridge. Turn left onto the trail. Walk between apartments and the creek where there are sure to be lots more mallards especially at the point where the creek divides.

© *Michael Vincent*

B Spawning Trout

In the fall the pool in front of you is full of fish. This creek and others in the area like Spring Creek and Bill Griffiths Creek in particular are important spawning grounds for the Bow River's Brook and Brown trout population.

Naming of Canmore

'The prairie where they shot the little pine', 'shooting at an animal in the willows'. According to the Stoney Indians this is where a hunter fooled himself into believing a piece of burnt tree stump was a black wolf. Since Chuwapchipchiyan Kude is a bit too difficult for white tongues, another name was needed. CPR's Donald Smith likely came up with the name Canmore for what at that time was only another divisional point on the railroad. Malcolm Canmore III (CEANN MOR = great chief) killed Macbeth the usurper in the fight for the Scottish throne in 1057. He was rather tolerant in other ways. When William the Conqueror invaded England in 1066 he welcomed English refugees to his court and later married the English princess Margaret who later became a saint.

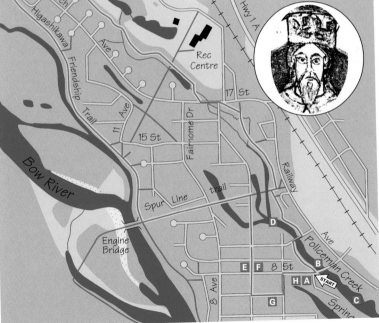

Policeman Creek from first junction with Spur Line Trail

C Policeman Creek

was formerly called Carey Creek after a CPR locomotive engineer. Thomas and William Carey and their families lived across from the NWMP barracks at the location of the Bow Valley Motel. The name was very short-lived. It was renamed Policeman in 1988 when the NWMP came to Canmore and erected log barracks on the opposite side of the street.

D Mallards

Because Policeman Creek never completely freezes over, it attracts hundreds of Canmore's unofficial 'bird' who overwinter in the spring-fed creek with a little bit of help from residents.

Mallards are puddle ducks. That means they feed off the surface or go bottoms up to reach aquatic plants just under the surface. They aren't much good at diving, but are excellent flyers once they get started. Because mallards have legs in the centre of their body they have to almost jump off the water. They always seem to be preening themselves. This is not vanity. The plumage must be continually waterproofed and to do this the bird frequently rubs its head and bill at the base of its back where a special preen gland secretes an oily waxy substance not yet looked into by the manufacturers of rain gear. While males are the silent beautiful type whose sole purpose in life is to attract females, the females do most of the quacking, the building of nests and the bringing up of the young.

Turn right onto Spur Line Trail, then immediately left. Continue along the trail.

Keep left. Cross a picturesque bridge in the Japanese style. Surrounded by pine forest it's hard to believe you're in the middle of a town.

Keep right over a small bridge. Turn immediately left. Emerge at the corner of 17 St. and 8 Ave.

Cross 17 St. and turn left. After the bridge turn right onto a trail. Shortly you recross the creek below a pond.

Keep straight (left leads to 15 St., right to the Rec. Centre which is haunted by the ghost of a little girl lost in the muskeg long before any of these houses or roads were built). Continue beside another pond, then cross a bridge. Now follows a long section through the back yards of houses next to the fenced-off golf course.

Keep right. Arrive at the Bow River viewpoint and take a break. You'll notice that Policeman Creek, a channel of the Bow River is controlled by a sluice gate.

Backtrack to the last junction and turn right onto the Higashikawa Friendship Trail. It runs atop a dike between Larch Ave. and flood channels.

Just after a left-hand bend keep left on the main trail (option to right).

OPTION

The narrow trail bridging the channel to your right crosses an island to the Bow River opposite the Georgetown Trail viewpoints. The trail, wet and rough in spots, can be followed all the way to the Bow River viewpoint at Policeman Creek.

Shortly after reaching the Bow you arrive at Engine Bridge and a 4-way junction with Spur Line Trail.

Turn left at the 4-way junction. Follow Spur Line Trail, the old CPR railbed you crossed earlier.

Cross Fairholme Drive. Pass between two ponds (west fork of Policeman Creek) and reach 7 Ave.

E Centennial Museum

Open daily 12-4 pm, Tues-Sat

801-7 Avenue, tel: 678-2462

Coal mining artifacts, Lawrence Grassi memorabilia, fernleaf fossils in coal, Andy Shellian's 1500 bird house, 400 dolls donated to the museum by Mavis Mallabone, slide presentations, photo albums.

Museum shop. Ask about guided walks to historic points of interest.

Cross 7 Ave. and turn right. Walk down 7 Ave. sidewalk alongside the west fork, another mallard hot spot.

Cross Mallard Alley, 10th and 9th streets into downtown Canmore. On your right is the Centennial Museum, the always popular Coffee Mine and Altitude Sports. Opposite is the historic Canmore Hotel.

Cross 8 St. Continue down 7 Ave. Turn left onto 7 St (Veteran's Way). On the right is St. Michael's Anglican Church.

Turn left up 6 Ave. At 8 St turn right past Sinclairs. Opposite is Marra's, Canmore's oldest grocery store that opened its doors in 1945, and a number of eateries including the tiny Crazyweed Kitchen and the Grizzly Paw Pub, Restaurant & Brewing Company. Pass the United Church and arrive back at the NWMP Police Barracks.

Main Street (8 St.) looking east to Grotto Mountain.

Some Canmore characters

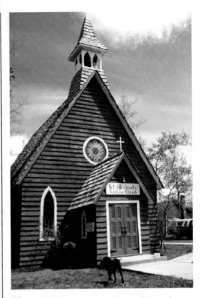

G St. Michael's Anglican Church
Under the brown siding hides the original log church built in 1895 and consecrated in 1897 by the Bishop of Calgary. It's said that in high wind, the structure rocks.

F Canmore Hotel
Built in 1890 by the Count De Rambouville, it is the only one of four large hotels catering to railway workers to survive to this day.

People who have called Canmore home include many artists and musicians such as Kelly Jay, a well-known figure from the 1970s rock 'n roll scene. Crowbar's single went gold and had the distinction of being banned on the US airways by the Nixon administration. Mountaineers include Sharon Wood, first North American woman to reach the summit of Mt. Everest, and Pat Morrow, the first person to climb the highest peaks on all seven continents.

H Ralph Connor Memorial United Church

In the 1890s Presbyterian missionaries from Calgary made regular calls to coal-mining communities along the railroad. Under the direction of one such minister, the Rev. Charles E. Gordon, a simple frame building was put together in 1891 in the fledgling town of Canmore for the cost of $1,200. Arched gothic windows and small belfry with a CPR engine bell were the only concessions to decoration. The new manse built in 1921 beside the church came from parts of several Georgetown residences which had been floated down the Bow River. On May 11, 1942 Canmore United Church was renamed the Ralph Connor Memorial United Church.

(NA 4887-6 Glenbow Archives).

So who was Ralph Connor?

The Rev. Charles E. Gordon! One of the most successful novelists of the day who became a millionaire, but died penniless. His books were part of the High School curriculum in the U.S. His fans included President Woodrow Wilson and Henry Ford.

Because fiction was not considered respectable for a minister he decided on a pen name. He had already decided on a name like Canmore. Cannor sounded about right, but his publisher misread it as Connor and came up with a christian name to fit. Under his nom de plume, Gordon wrote nearly 30 novels, the first being 'Black Rock: A tale of the Selkirks' written in 1898 at Morley and inspired by the nearby mountain in the Ghost River. Into each book went personal experiences and characters he had known, the net result a remarkably successful combination of adventure and religion.

Grassi Lakes
4 km return

late spring
summer
fall

A moderately strenuous walk (height gain 300 m) to two exquisite blue lakes. Interpretive signs, splendid views of mountains and waterfalls, flowers and benches at strategic points, makes this a most enjoyable trail to walk. Ignore the roads, penstock and powerlines. A more difficult option exists to view the petrographs.

Start: Spray Lakes Road. Beyond the Canmore Nordic Centre turn-off, turn next left onto a road signed 'Spray Residences.'.Keep right and park a few metres on at the trail-head parking lot on the right.

Follow the trail into pine forest.

Cross the TransAlta access road to the penstock . The trail built by Lawrence Grassi climbs gently at first. Detour left to an overlook with interpretive signs and a grand view of Ha Ling Peak and the waterfall below the lakes. In winter, seepages to the right of the main fall freeze into what ice climbers call 'The Junkyard'.

A bench signals the steeper section which uses steps with railings to get you up a rocky slope. Note 'Fred Marra 1932' carved into the rock face above the steps. (The Marra's run the oldest grocery store in Canmore on Main Street.) Pass more benches and interpretive signs. The trail zigs then makes a long sweep to the left, crossing the lakes' outlet via a log bridge. Arrive on the TransAlta access road again. Should you follow it to the left you'll arrive at the penstock.

A Spray Plant
"Nestled in a niche blasted in the hard rock wall at the base of Chinaman's Peak" is how Calgary Power's brochure describes the main plant of the Spray Development. Water is diverted from the upper Spray River to Goat Creek "while maintaining its elevation to a point above the Bow River where a vertical drop could be concentrated in a short horizontal distance." From Whiteman's Pond (reservoir) in the pass, the water drops 300 metres through a pressure tunnel called a penstock to the turbine. Enough water trickles into and out of Grassi Lakes to produce this magnificent waterfall below the lower lake.

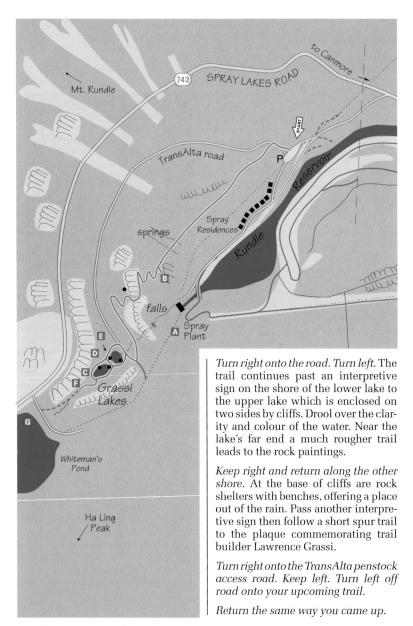

Turn right onto the road. Turn left. The trail continues past an interpretive sign on the shore of the lower lake to the upper lake which is enclosed on two sides by cliffs. Drool over the clarity and colour of the water. Near the lake's far end a much rougher trail leads to the rock paintings.

Keep right and return along the other shore. At the base of cliffs are rock shelters with benches, offering a place out of the rain. Pass another interpretive sign then follow a short spur trail to the plaque commemorating trail builder Lawrence Grassi.

Turn right onto the TransAlta penstock access road. Keep left. Turn left off road onto your upcoming trail.

Return the same way you came up.

Viewpoint Topics

Over 70 years old!

Lawrence Grassi and his buddies built this trail way back in 1921 to what was then known as Twin Lakes. Grassi was best known as the master trail builder at Lake O'Hara, and this little gem went unnoticed by the general public until it became part of Kananaskis Country. Before improvement, Grassi's stamp was very evident in the rustic seats, ladders and steps. The trail started from his house on Three Sisters Drive and took in the Canmore Creek waterfalls, and the sulphur spring. This was before the Rundle Canal cut the trail into two halves.

B How Ha Ling Peak got its name

It happened this way. Ha Ling, a Chinese cook working at the Oskaloosa Hotel in the summer of 1896, was bet $50 he couldn't climb the mountain east of Whiteman's Gap and return within 10 hours. Obviously, Ha Ling must have done a recce up the relatively easy-angled backside, because he readily agreed to the bet, and taking with him a small flag to set on the summit, set off at 7 am breakfast time on a Saturday morning. When he returned at half an hour after noon in time for lunch, claiming to have reached the summit, no one believed him. For a start, they couldn't see the flag with their field glasses, and $5\frac{1}{2}$ hours return seemed a ridiculously short time. Even today, with the help of roads and trails $5\frac{1}{2}$ hours from the pass would be good going.

Ha Ling Peak from Whiteman's Pass.

There was nothing for it but for Ha-Ling to climb the mountain all over again on the Sunday, this time with several of his doubters in tow carrying a flag attached to a 12 foot pole which they felt certain would be seen from down below. In due course they arrived on the summit to find Ha Ling's flag "proudly flapping its tiny form in the breeze." Ashamed of their doubts, they proclaimed, "As the peak has no name, let it henceforth be called 'Ha Ling Peak' in honour of his daring intrepidity."

It wasn't. For 101 years it was called Chinaman's Peak. Then, during the Great Canmore Influx, newcomers perceived the name as derogatory and in1997 the mountain was officially re-christened.

C Coral reefs once under the ocean

Note the size of the figure.

The pockmarked cliff on the north side of the upper Lake is a Devonian reef of the Cairn Formation. Most of the fossils are not easily recognisable corals but things called stromatoporoids. Living from Cambrian to Cretaceous times, Stroms were marine invertebrates of varying shapes and sizes, the dominant organisms in Devonian time. Some were branched and some had a central canal. It's said they're related to present day sclerosponges found in the Caribbean. Without going into names like eurvamhipora which you'll never remember, the layman can recognise the various types by their shapes which vary from thin wafers, through flying saucers to bulbous circles. The centres of bulbous stroms are often leached, and form large cavities called vugs which are sometimes filled with white calcite. When calcite is absent it gives the rock the pitted appearance you see here.

A colony of violet-greens (*Tachycineta thalassina*)

Photo Don Beers.

In late Spring, violet-green swallows begin arriving in their hundreds from Central America, always in the same week year after year. How they do this without a calendar is a mystery. This summer quarters has everything, a wide choice of nesting holes in the cliffs and nearby water with insects. The latinized name of the species *Thalassina* is Greek for 'like the sea' and refers to the colour of the plumage.

D Rock shelters

Not bona fide caves, these underhangs below the Devonian cliffs were most likely used by the Indians who did the rock paintings. They were improved by Lawrence Grassi who built dividing walls and dry-stone walls on the outside, smoothed out the floors, and constructed benches and fireplaces. What with the raspberry bushes and a raft on the lake, this was an incredibly popular lunch spot in the 1920s. Of course, in those days people would start walking from near Grassi's house on Three Sisters Drive via the sulphur spring swimming pool, so it was a full day's trip all right.

E "Lawrence Grassi is a superman"

Born in Felmenta, Italy, in 1890, Grassi came to Canada in 1912 and found work as a CPR sectionman in the Lake Superior area which was too far away from the mountains for him. He got a transfer to Hector in the middle of the Rockies, then in 1916 came to Canmore and found employment as a miner. But first and foremost Grassi was a mountaineer and guide, making over 20 ascents of Mt. Louis, his favourite mountain. Though small in height, his prodigious strength is legendary. Perhaps his greatest feat was carrying in the cast iron stove to the Elizabeth Parker Hut at Lake O'Hara. No access road and two buses a day then. On his retirement, he worked as a warden between 1956-60 at Lake O'Hara, an area he particularly loved. There, he built trails—masterpieces of construction never equalled—to places formerly inaccessible to the average hiker.

Left: Lawrence Grassi (Whyte Museum of the Canadian Rockies)

Upper Grassi Lake.

DETOUR TO ROCK PAINTINGS

Near the end of upper lake turn left.
Climb a steep trail through trees, then
on scree into the rocky confines of a
canyon. When the ground levels,
search the first large boulder you
come to for petrographs of a caribou
and a figure of a man. You might also
see the odd marmot sunning himself
on the rocks.

⬛ The Rock Paintings

are believed to have been painted
by ancestors of the Kootenai Indians over a thousand years ago,
likely as part of a vision quest. As
an initiation to adulthood, a youth
was sent to some remote place for
several days, usually a canyon or
hilltop, where he would fast and
meditate. Out of this would come a
dream which was recorded on the
rocks. This dream was later inter-
preted by the Medicine Man who
would give the youth a new name
and his own set of symbols for his
hunting or warring equipment.

⬛ Whiteman's Pass

Everyone important heading to Oregon went via Whiteman's Pass
from Indian Flat (Canmore) via the
Spray River to White Man Pass on
the BC border: Father Pierre Jean
de Smet in 1945, James Sinclair
and settlers in August 1841 and
1850, and on July 25th 1845 British
officers Henry James Ware and
Mervin Vavasour pretending to be
gentlemen of leisure but actually on
a secret spying mission for the British government (who said Canadian history is boring?). They described the route as one of great
difficulty: "a rapid ascent is made of
about 1,000 ft., the trail following the
right bank of a little torrent, near
which, about halfway up the ascent,
a cave occurs." They complained
about the sharp stones and steep
ascents "under a steep and nearly
perpendicular mountain" which
must have been Ha Ling Peak, giving insecure footing for their horses.
All this changed as recently as
1947, when, as part of the Spray
Development, the present road was
started on September 27th 1948
with construction equipment reaching the Three Sisters dam site on
December 17.

Have you read?

The pass is easily recognisable as
Indian Pass in John Stafford
Gowan's two books about the ad-
ventures of a forest ranger at
Spray Lakes during the 1920s:
'Smoke over Sikanaska' and 'The
Sikanaska Trail.'.A third book 'Re-
turn to Canada' published much
later, discloses the true names of
the places he describes.

Canmore to the Nordic Centre
4.2 km return

spring
summer
fall

Sandwiched between two flat sections along the banks of the Bow River is a fairly stiff climb which won't suit everybody. The Canmore Nordic Centre was the site of the 15th Winter Olympic Games for nordic events.

Start: Canmore at 8 St. (Main St.) and 8 Ave.

Walk down Riverview Place, a continuation of 8 St. to its end in a cul-de-sac. Follow the walkway to the Higashikawa Friendship Trail on the bank of the Bow River.

Turn left. The trail enters Riverside Park.

B The Three Sisters
were named in 1883 by the brother of Major A.B. Rogers who discovered Rogers Pass. "There had been quite a heavy snowstorm in the night, and when we got up in the morning and looked out of the tent I noticed each of the three peaks had a heavy veil of snow on the north side and I said to the boys 'Look at the Three Nuns.' ... Later they were called the Three Sisters, more Protestant like I suppose."

A Higashikawa Friendship Trail
When Higashikawa, Japan, named its ski hill the Canmore Ski Resort, Canmore reciprocated in 1994 by renaming the trail along the east bank of the Bow River in honour of its sister city.

Riverside Park and a view of the Three Sisters. Note the riprap.

Canmore – 23

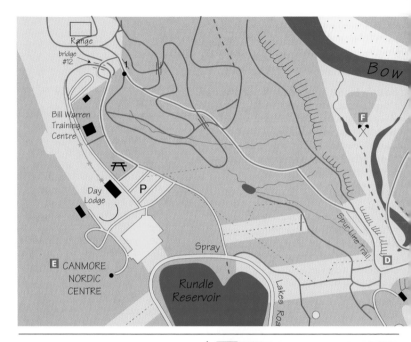

C A Diked Town

After the last glacier receded, the valley floor was covered in drift to a depth of 200 metres. At first, the Bow River cut down through the rubble, but later its energy was transferred from deepening to widening the channel. Migrating from side to side it wore away at valley slopes until the valley floor became very much wider than the channel. Sediments deposited by the river were planed flat, creating a post-glacial flood plain. In hindsight, not a good site for a town. Canmore residents, trying to control the wandering river which floods about once every 10-15 years, have built raised banks called dikes all around the town. Notice how the banks are faced with riprap—large rocks slotted together to prevent erosion.

C The Mine shareholders' Cabin in the 1920s. Photo Daisy Carrol. (NA 4074-4 Glenbow Archives). Note the closeness to the Bow River.

D What happens at the Rundle Power Plant

Discharged water from Spray Plant idles along the Rundle canal to a point close to the Bow River, then plunges 100 metres through an underground steel penstock to this plant. The force of the water on turbine blades drives the shaft of the electric generator which produces the electricity. The electricity enters the substation next door and is transformed into a voltage suitable for transmission along power lines. The used water is freed—temporarily. Still to come are the Kananaskis and Horseshoe Plants at Seebe, the Ghost Plant on Highway 1A and finally the Bearspaw in Calgary.

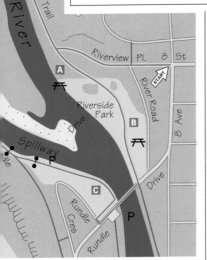

Keep right. Turn right onto Rundle Drive. Cross Bow River bridge.

Turn right onto Rundle Crescent, then turn immediately right. The trail leads back to the Bow River, then turns left, following the grassy west bank along the top of a dike. Pass the historic Mine shareholder' cabin, now Luna Lodge.

Keep right onto Spur Line Trail. You follow the edge of the spillway. To shorten the walk keep straight. If going to the Nordic Centre...

Turn left before Rundle Plant. Climb steps up a steep bank.

At the 4-way junction turn right. A good trail leads to a grassy bench above cliffs of glacial till which is eroding into hoodoos. This is a fine viewpoint for Canmore and the mountains east of town.

Turn next left. Descend slightly then climb a steep hill.

At the top turn right. Keep straight on the main trail. A short uphill brings you to the Georgetown Trail.

Wend left. The Georgetown Trail follows a bank top between Douglas firs and dry slopes of juniper and Kinnikinnick. Cross a small creek.

Cross a ski trail near bridge #3. Cross a ski trail. And another. Join a ski trail near #1 junction.

Turn left, then right at #1 junction. Follow the ski trail towards the Biathlon Stadium area.

Turn left. A descending trail leads under bridge # 12, and turns left uphill.

Turn right. Follow the rising trail behind the Bill Warren Training Centre.

Keep left. Arrive at the parking lot near the Olympic Flame.

Turn right. A minute's walk along the centre's access road brings you opposite the front door of the Day Lodge.

E Summer at the Nordic Centre
Open 9-5:30 pm, 7 days a week

DAY LODGE: Information, Kick N' Glide Cafe and Boutique, showers.

BILL WARREN TRAINING CENTRE: meeting rooms, office space, sports science lab, weight room and Trail Sports rental shop (403- 678-2448, shop@trailsports.ab.ca) which rents mountain bikes and sells accessories.

Group tours, mountain biking trails, roller skiing track, disc golf. Available for banquets, weddings, meetings and other functions by writing Suite 100, 1988 Olympic Way, Canmore, Alta. T1W 2T6. (403-678-2400, Canmore.NordicCentre@gov.ab.ca)

Right: The Day Lodge and cross country stadium.

RETURN

Reverse the route to Rundle Power Plant.

Turn left onto Spur Line Trail. You cross a bridge over the spillway in front of the plant and the substation.

Keep right (trail to left leads to Cochrane Mine). Cross a trestle bridge.

Keep straight (trail to right is for anglers). Five minutes later cross Engine Bridge which carried the spur line over the Bow River from the CPR station in Canmore to Mines No. 1 and 2. It's always a popular fishing spot.

At the 4-way junction turn right. You're back on the Higashikawa Friendship Trail.

Turn left at the houses. A walkway leads back to Riverview Place and the 8 St., 8 Ave. intersection in downtown Canmore. Round about are lots of eateries, antique shops, and picture galleries. Tony Bloom's Stonecrop pottery studio is just around the corner to the left on 8 Ave.

OPTION

After the substation turn left on a trail which ends at the Cochrane Mine site. Apart from subsidence in the trees, two reject piles and small pieces of rusted metal mixed in with contemporary party bottles there's very little to see nowadays.

F Another early mine

Operating between 1888 and 1893, this coal mine was named after British shareholder Lord Cochrane. The fellow who built the trestle from the mine to the tipple was the same William McCardell who discovered the hot springs at Banff a few years previously. Before Engine Bridge was built in 1892, the coal was scowed across the Bow. Seepage from Rundle Reservoir has since flooded the underground passages.

G *Engine Bridge, built in 1892; one year before any road bridge over the Bow River.*

Larch Islands Loop
3.5 km loop

early spring
summer
late fall

A flat easy walk on interpretive trail alongside the Bow River and its channels. Everything that grows here loves moisture, including the beautiful white orchid, Franklin's lady' slipper. Return is via the dike.

Start: Canmore, at the junction of 15 St. and 11 Ave. Use the parking area at the end of 15 St.

A The bridge at the start of the loop. The mountain behind is Mt. Lawrence Grassi, with Ha Ling Peak to right.

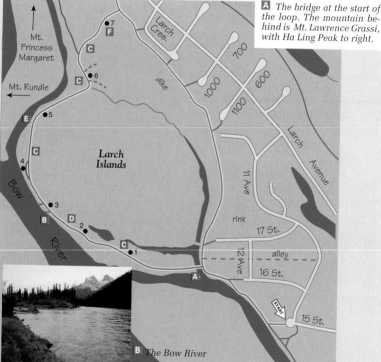

B The Bow River

Flowers of the Islands

Bird's-eye primrose

C **Round-leaved orchid**

A.E. Porsild describes the fully-opened flower as resembling a flying elf-like creature with a head, eyes and mouth and a body and two protruding wings formed by two lateral sepals. Incidentally, this orchid is pollinated by moths.

D **Franklin's lady's slipper**
The Latin name *passerinum* means sparrow-like, some thinking the inflated white sac resembles a sparrow's spotted egg. It is smaller and much less conspicuous than the yellow version and easily missed. Do smell it!

Goldenrod spider, courtesy Ben Gadd, Handbook of the Canadian Rockies.

Masters of camouflage: Goldenrod spiders *Misumena vatia*
Be careful if you bend down to examine the orchids. On more than one occasion I have found myself eye to eye with a goldenrod spider. This little member of the crab family colour co-ordinates on white or yellow flowers, even down to pink streaks on either side of the abdomen in the case of the round-leaved orchid! Take a closer look at the shasta daisies in your garden. Strangely, in this case, the spiders are not white, but bright yellow like the yellow disc florets in the centre.

From the parking area follow the trail out to the Bow River trail.

Turn right. Walk alongside a channel of the Bow River, noting a trail to right leading to 16 St.

Turn left across a footbridge onto Larch Islands interpretive trail. Wander through wolf willow past interpretive signs #1 and #2. Look for round-leaved orchids opposite the slough and Franklin's ladyslipper after #2.

Around sign #3, trails to left lead to the Bow River and it's here on the flats where you'll find elephant heads, false asphodel, butterworts and the birds-eye primrose, and bushes of orange honeysuckle.

At a split go left. Around sign #4 grows rock jasmine. The trail then heads away from Bow River to the willowy bank of a narrow channel and turns right to sign #5. Ahead is a new view of Mt. Rundle and to the right the jagged ridge of Mt. Princess Margaret. The willows are shelter to a large number of birds including the yellow warbler, Wilsons warbler and assorted members of the sparrow family.

On boggy ground keep straight. Do not follow trails down the bank.

At the junction keep left. Come to interpretive sign # 6 — another hot spot for round-leaved orchids.

Keep right. The trail turns away from the channel onto dryer ground with white spruce. Look for dogwood on the right at interpretive sign #7. Come to the dike.

At a T-junction turn right onto Higashikawa Friendship Trail. This trail follows the dike top between Larch Islands and the back gardens of houses with walkways between them through to Larch Avenue. As you will have guessed, the islands are named after the subdivision. At one walkway is a cross with the words "Here he lies, Stiff and Hard, The last dam dog, That pooped in our yard." Shortly after passing open ground and a skating rink, you arrive back at the start of the interpretive trail.

Keep left. Turn second left back to 15 St. parking area.

Missionary Rundle

Cornishman Robert Terril Rundle had only a few months of theological training before being thrown in at the deep end. Before leaving for the wilds of western Canada, he was advised by the Wesleyan Missionary Society to "converse very sparingly" with females "and only for religious purposes". Sir George Simpson, governor of the Hudson Bay Company thought Rundle was "given to frivolous chit-chat" and didn't like the way he visited the Indians at their camps. While over here, Rundle had a go at climbing a mountain and got himself cragfast (not Mt. Rundle, unfortunately). It was James Hector in 1857 who named the mountain after Rundle, recognising the enormous influence he still had on the Stonies 10 years after he had returned to England.

The Rev. Rundle (NA 659-43 Glenbow Archives)

Above: Mt. Rundle and Bruno's Buttress at far left.

F Dogwood Cornus stolonifera

Like willows, the shrub dogwood grows in damp places near to water. You'll also find it in city gardens, prized for its reddish bark, leaves that turn dark purply red in fall and for its attractive white fruit.

E Bruno's Buttress

Legendary storyteller Bruno Engler (1915-2001) came to Canada from Switzerland in 1939 as a mountain guide. Besides guiding VIPS such as Prime Minister Pierre Trudeau and Alberta Premier Peter Lougheed, he worked as a cinematographer and occasional actor for movies starring such notables as Jimmy Stewart and Paul Newman. His lasting legacy, though, is as a photographer of the Canadian Rockies. He had an exceptional eye, not just for landscapes but for portraits and action shots.

In 1955 he set up home in Harvie Heights near Canmore. In his later years, no longer able to climb, he would look out from his balcony to the numbered buttresses of Mt. Rundle and plot routes up the buttress opposite, which is No. 4. In 2001, Chris Perry and Chas Yonge put up the first route on the buttress and named it in honour of Bruno.

Quarry Lake Loop
4.2 km return

spring
summer
fall

A relatively strenuous hike which takes you first to the site of No. 1 Coal Mine, then to a viewpoint for Canmore's unadvertised waterfalls and finally to Quarry Lake Park. Choose a hot day and bring all the paraphernalia for the beach.

Start: Canmore, at the Bow River bridge. Use the parking area on the southwest side.

Heading south, follow the wide Bow River trail to a gravel lane.

Cross. The trail continues in a large meadow.

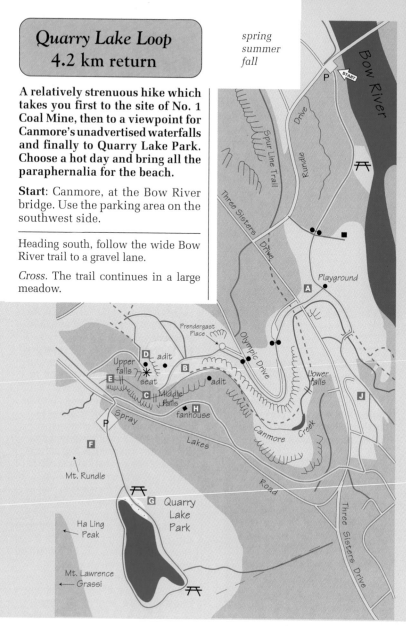

At the 4-way trail intersection (children's playground to left), go right. The trail squeezes between Canmore Creek and Shadow Mountain Estates to Three Sisters Drive. This is the old part of Canmore called Mineside.

Cross the road. The trail continues, climbing to the left of Rummel Place to a gate across the road.

Beyond the gate, walk on the road (now called Olympic Drive) a few metres, then pick up the trail on the left side. Trail and road follow the curve of the bank top above Canmore Creek. Look down to spot Lower Canmore Falls and a cut where the railroad to No. 1 Mine came up the creek. Opposite the gate across Olympic Drive, the trail curves left alongside cul-de-sac Prendergast Place, named after Bert Prendergast whose sod-roofed cabin now resides in Heritage Park.

Continue through a front garden and onto a terrace of spoil. This is the site of No. 1 Mine. Below you was the boiler house and further downstream past the bend, the bath house. On the opposite bank a waterfall spills out of

The Biggest Log Opera House in the World

The Canmore Opera House, a resident of Heritage Park in Calgary, used to face what is now Three Sisters Drive in Canmore. It was built in 1898 from nearby trees cut down and pulled off the hillside with horses. The logs were held together with railroad track braces. Originally earmarked as a band hall, it was later used for concerts, recitals, plays, silent movies and boxing matches—but not operas.

Photo Helena Hoogerheide (NA 3147-1 Glenbow Archives).

Compare this 1910 view of Mineside with the view nowadays from near **A** *. (A2112 Provincial Archives of Alberta).*

opera house

B No. 1 Mine

Canmore's first major mine operated from 1887 in Canmore Creek which was then called Mine Creek or Chinaman's Creek after the Chinese workers who lived down the creek at the bend where the beaver pond used to be.

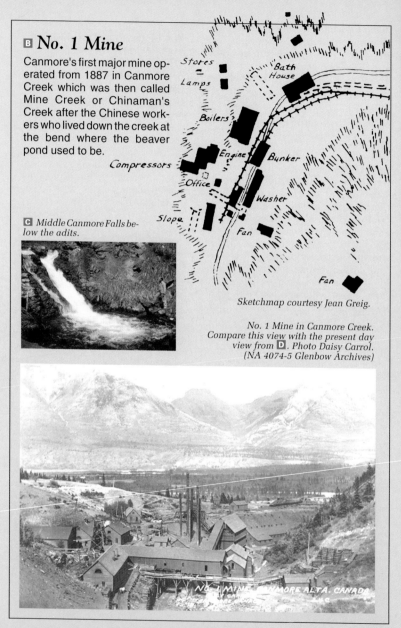

Stores

Bath House

Lamps

Boilers

Compressors

Engine

Bunker

Office

Washer

Slope

Fan

Fan

Sketchmap courtesy Jean Greig.

C *Middle Canmore Falls below the adits.*

No. 1 Mine in Canmore Creek. Compare this view with the present day view from D. Photo Daisy Carrol. (NA 4074-5 Glenbow Archives)

Examining the Hoist House.

a spectacular adit (now blocked off) that was connected to this bank by a trestle bridge. To your right in the trees is the ruin of the hoist house which contained a steam-driven winch for hauling coal cars out of the mine. Continue along the terrace past the steps. The uphill slope led to a later entry now completely filled in and surrounded by a whole hillside of spoil. From here underground passages head north under Rundle View Drive and south to Spray Lakes Road, causing subsidence here and there.

Turn left downhill. A good trail with a handrail takes you down to Canmore Creek and along to Middle Falls.

Return to the terrace. Turn right, then left. Climb the daunting line of steps at the side of a nicer older trail built of railway ties.

E *Upper Falls.*

F Mystery, Alaska

In 1998 Quarry Lake was the location for the Disney movie *Mystery, Alaska*, starring Russell Crowe, Colin Meany and Burt Reynolds. A makeshift town, looking incredibly real, and two hockey rinks sprang up south and west of the parking lot, while the United Church of Mystery, established in 1891, topped the hill to the north of the lake. Hundreds of Canmorites and Calgarians filled the bleachers as extras—maybe you were among them—for the final scene at the hockey rink when, as in all good family movies, the underdogs from Mystery beat the all-powerful New York Rangers.

Keep left (older trail comes in from the right). At the Douglas fir the trail wends left and arrives at a 5-way junction in a meadow.

Turn left (right-hand trails lead to Patrician Street and Rundle View Drive). Turn left at a cairn (right trail leads into a former sandstone quarry). Keep left. Arrive at a grassy promontory with seat, a wonderful viewpoint for Upper Canmore Falls, especially if you wander down the rocky ridge a bit. Look down valley to the site of No. 1 Mine and compare the view to the photo on page 34.

Retrace your steps to the last junction. Keep left. A trail heads through trees towards Spray Lakes Road. On your left, bits of concrete on either side of Canmore Creek are remains of a retaining wall around a small reservoir which fed the generating plant.

Near the culvert, turn left (right trail leads to Spray Lakes Road at Rundle View Drive.) A narrow trail traverses the bank above the culvert.

Keep Right. Cross *Spray Lakes Road into Quarry Lake parking lot.* A trail leaves the lot's far left-hand corner and crosses a flowery meadow to Quarry Lake which features a sandy beach, picnic tables and biffy.

Walk the loop around the lake. Marvel at the views of Mt. Lawrence Grassi, Miner's Peak and Ha Ling Peak—all summits of Ehagay Nakoda. To the north rises the east end of Mt. Rundle, known as EEOR by climbers. And yes, one of the small crags above Whiteman's Pass is called Kangra.

Left top: The Court House.

Left bottom: The United Church of Mystery, established in 1891.

Quarry Lake, looking towards Canmore Wall (left), Mt. Lawrence Grassi, Miner's Peak and Ha Ling Peak.

G Quarry Lake Park

Quarry Lake was once a strip mine that operated in 1970. Notable among those helping in the reclamation was miner Andy Shellian who was responsible for getting a parking lot put in and for arranging with Fish & Wildlife to stock the lake which resulted and for keeping it clean by winching out tree trunks and rusted cars. In winter, you can see methane gas bubbling up from a coal seam on the lake bed but it doesn't seem to bother the grayling who continue to overwinter quite happily in water 17 metres deep.

On becoming a park, grass and flowers were sown: the wild blue flax and, above all, rosy sanfoin which turns the hillside into a riot of pink every summer. You might look to see if Mrs. Shellian's garden seeds, including sweet williams, are still flowering at the far end of the lake.

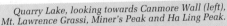

Wild blue flax and Rosy sanfoin (Onobrychis viciaefolia).

RETURN

Return to the parking lot. Cross Spray Lakes Road to the trail you came up on. A few metres along turn right. Shortly the trail heads left onto a broad ridge above Canmore Creek. Look for the remains of a fanhouse for No. 1 Mine on the right side. The trail curves right, nears Spray lakes Road at some rocks, then turns left downhill and becomes a wider track. Follow it down to a 4-way junction.

Go straight (track to left ends in private property). Descend the bank to Three Sisters Drive.

Cross the road. The trail continues.

Go straight, then zig left downhill. Cross Prospects Heights Road. Turn right. Turn left onto a gravel trail. The trail descends a steep bank to a wide gravelled lane, former railbed for the CPR spur line to No. 2 Mine.

Turn left. Walk between houses on Prospect Point and Canmore Creek.

Keep right twice. Cross the footbridge over Canmore Creek into a big meadow. The trail turns left, passing an interpretive sign about the fish stocking of Canmore Creek.

At the 4-way junction go straight. Return the same way you came to the parking lot.

J **The first Prospect**
When No. 2 Mine opened, a new settlement of company houses had to be built. This was Prospect named after a potential site based on preliminary investigation. Two-story ochre-coloured houses lined the northeast side of the rail line beyond Canmore Creek, while smaller houses and duplexes were dotted about the hillsides. Strange thing, though houses were supplied with electricity, no one thought to string up a few street lights, so locals were forced to walk around the streets with a flashlight. Not because they couldn't see, you understand but to scare away wildlife, particularly bears which were prevalent in the area. Even going to the outside biffy could be downright dangerous. None of old Prospect survives today, the last occupant reluctantly leaving only a few years ago to make way for today's Prospect Properties.

H *The map shows this as a fanhouse installed above No. 1 seam. Fans injected fresh air and sucked out stale air.*

Georgetown
7.2 km loop

late spring
summer
fall

A relatively long hike to a meadow, site of the coal mining town of Georgetown. Expect a steep uphill grind on the return.

Start: Canmore. Follow Spray Lakes Road to the Canmore Nordic Centre. Start from the Olympic Flame near the parking lot.

A slightly descending trail leaves the centre's access road to the right of the olympic flame and picnic tables.

Keep right. Pass behind the Bill Warren Training Centre.

Turn left just before bridge #12. Turn right. Go under the bridge and up a small rise. Watch for signs to Georgetown.

Go right. Keep left at #1 on a ski trail. Turn right. A hiking trail signed 'Georgetown' heads through the forest.

Cross a ski trail. And another near bridge #3. Immediately, cross a ski trail below bridge #3. Now follow a stretch above an open bank with Douglas fir trees on your left and a view ahead of Grotto and Pigeon mountains.

Turn left downhill (trail straight on leads to Canmore). Turn left. You're on a wide trail high above the Bow River. At one or two points are views of Canmore, and Mt. Lady MacDonald, named after the Prime Minister's wife. The uphill climb ends when you join the old Georgetown Road at Half-circle Curve.

The trail between the Douglas firs and the open bank. Grotto Mountain and Pigeon Mountain in the background.

B The Meadow

The coal mining town of Georgetown, never destined to become part of Canmore, had a high standard of living for the 1910s. Identical wood houses painted a yellow ochre came equipped with electricity and indoor cold running water. In the winter of 1916-17 after the mine closed, some of the better buildings were removed from their foundations and skated down the frozen Bow to Canmore where they were rolled to their present locations using logs. The store was relocated at the 8th St. and 6th Ave, intersection but is now refaced and taken over by Marra's Grocery.

Boys with pit ponies at Georgetown in 1916. (NA 3333-2 Glenbow Archives).

The meadow's interpretive signs.

A Flood plain Pussy Willows

Have you ever wondered why pussy willows bloom while the plant's roots are still frozen under snow. That's because early sap flow comes from carbohydrates stored in the parenchymal cells of woody stems during late summer and fall. Usually, water evaporation from leaves automatically pulls the water column up the trunk. In early spring there are no leaves of course. So what happens when temperatures rise is that sucrose leaks out of the storage cells into the xylem and phloem vessels, taking some of the cell water with it by osmosis. Under pressure the storage cells send sap upwards into dormant flower buds. This flowering before leafing ensures the leaves don't get in the way of pollen being blown on the wind.

Keep right. The old road descends, winding past interpretive signs to the cool damp valley bottom with its typical flood plain vegetation. A long straight along the railbed blackened by coal dust ends in a meadow, site of the town of Georgetown. Once all grey, it's a pleasant spot nowadays with interpretive signs and mountain views above aspen treetops.

At the signs the trail turns left. A short uphill climb brings you to a T-junction.

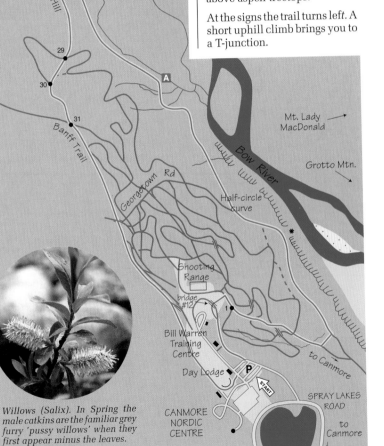

Site of Georgetown

C

B

entry

Killer Hill

29

30

31

Banff Trail

A

Mt. Lady MacDonald

Grotto Mtn.

Bow River

Georgetown Rd

Half-circle curve

Shooting Range

bridge #12

1

Bill Warren Training Centre

Day Lodge

P

START

CANMORE NORDIC CENTRE

SPRAY LAKES ROAD

to Canmore

to Canmore

Willows (Salix). In Spring the male catkins are the familiar grey furry 'pussy willows' when they first appear minus the leaves.

c Georgetown Collieries

Georgetown Collieries (1910-1916) had the steamship bunker trade and, in fact, later changed its name to the Canmore Navigation Coal Company. The mine was financed by British investors, so when World War I started and monies had to be directed towards the war effort, the company ran into financial difficulties and was forced to close down. Trees grown up after 1916 make the surface workings invisible from the meadow. The passages ran under the townsite itself. By searching the meadow and surrounding trees you'll find many telltale slump features.

The entry at Georgetown Mine. (A 2121 Provincial Archives of Alberta).

The entry in 1993.

OPTION TO COAL MINE

Turn right (left is home). Keep left. Keep straight at a trail intersection. Turn left. The grassy road winds uphill to the terrace below the entry. If you search the trees below the spoil you'll find a number of concrete foundations, one with walls nearly two metres-high. A varied assortment of scrap metal litters the ground.

Return the same way to the T-junction.

RETURN

At the T-junction keep right. On the right are more concrete foundations. The angle steepens uncomfortably as you tackle 'Killer Hill' to the ski trail system.

At 29 cross the ski trail. Keep straight. At 30 turn left. At 31 go straight. Join Banff Trail which used to be an access road to a strip mine.

Turn left. Follow Banff Trail. You pass under bridge # 8, then start climbing.

Keep straight on the wide and obvious road. You pass numerous cutoffs to left and right. When the road levels you pass under bridge #14, then over the International Bridge (#13). Look down on the Cross-Country stadium.

Keep left. At the waxing huts cut left off the road onto a trail. The trail half-circles around the end of the stadium to the side of the Day Lodge.

Cross the road to the parking lot.

Grotto Canyon
5 km return

early spring
summer
late fall

Stony underfoot, this is neverthe-less a fairly easy walk through an incredibly spectacular canyon known for its pictographs. You're sure to be entertained by rock climbers and even musicians! In Spring expect running water and stream hopping.

Official start: Bow Valley Trail (Highway 1A) at Grotto Pond day-use area. The pond offers good fishing; hip waders advisable.

The trail kicks off by following the powerline right-of-way access road.

Cross a road to Enviro Enterprises quarry. Ahead is Baymag Plant ll.

Turn right off the powerline onto a trail. It heads across alluvial flat with poplars, water birches and mats of dry crackly avens.

> **A Baymag Plant II**
> is the World's largest and most technologically advanced MgO (magnesia) fusing plant. In other words, it produces high tech raw material for refractory products such as magcarbon bricks used by the steel industry in convertors and electric arc furnaces. The crystalline magnesite isn't local; it comes from the World's purest deposit near Radium Hot Springs.

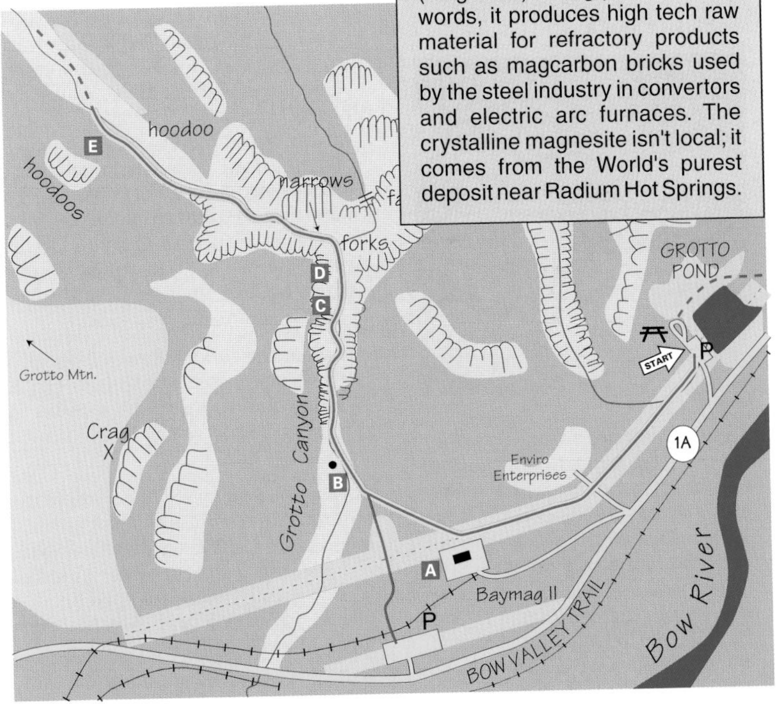

Vertical Dance...

is a mix of rock climbing and dance. In the summer of 2001 the Springboard Dance Company of Calgary gave two performances of 'Corvidae' in Grotto Canyon to appreciative audiences. Suspended 16 m above the ground on Hemmingway Wall, the dancers enacted the raven's "mythical connection to death," accompanied by the haunting strains of a cello. For current performances contact Springboard Dance at www.mcsquared.com/springboard.

Photo Pam Doyle.

B Flash Floods

Grotto Creek in flood.

Sometimes after heavy thunderstorms, flash floods pour down the creekbed, trapping climbers and hikers and spreading rocks and gravel all over the highway. To alleviate the highway problem a settling pond was built a little downstream of here in 2001. Lafarge Canada use the captured material in the production of cement.

Keep right where the alternative start joins in. At Grotto Creek, the trail turns upstream, following the creek bed between vertical cliffs. Watch for the rock paintings on a slab to the left, low down and barely discernible.

Throughout the canyon, sport climbers provide entertainment. In the spring of 1990 this canyon was the scenario for the Canyon Shadows Project for instruments and voices by Robert Rosen and poet Peter Christensen.

Arrive at the forks below a high cliff with seepages that freeze into His & Hers ice climbs. Most of the water in the creek comes from the righthand fork which tumbles over a cliff.

Turn up the left fork. This is where the cliffs on either side attain their greatest height. Suddenly the valley floor widens and the walls on either side fall back just a little. Note a capped hoodoo on the right bank and then the huge block of eroded tillite on the left.

Return the same way.

D In Sport Climbing routes are short, are protected by bolts and have chained anchors at the top. They have been specifically designed for leading, not top-roping.

Sport climber rapelling off near Illusion Rock.

C Pictographs

Recent thinking is that the artists are Hopi from Arizona, who came north some 500-1,300 years ago. By painting the flute player kokapelli, their spiritual leader, they hoped to warm the ground sufficiently to plant corn (unsuccessfully as it turned out). Other badly faded paintings are of deer, elk, a slaughtered moose and stylized humans wearing ceremonial headdresses and holding sticks.

E Hoodoos

Hoodoos always occur in glacial till and are pale-coloured columns composed of sands, gravels and rocks of all sizes glued together by yellowish mud. Truly, a rock fruitcake. Although till is consistently being eroded by water from either rain or run-off, for hoodoos to develop, the slope has to be steep enough, and the till partly consolidated to just the right consistency. The hoodoos on the left slope are still in the development stage. Low down on the right bank is one very small hoodoo capped with a boulder which has protected the column from erosion by rain. Better examples: the hillside above Canmore Cemetery, Tunnel Mountain hoodoos at Banff, and (best example) the Leanchoil hoodoos in Yoho National Park which are capped.

Left: Enhanced image of the flute player by James Henderson.

The developing hoodoos from the end of the trail.

Lac des Arcs Waterfowl Viewing Trail
1.8 km return

early spring
summer
late fall

An easy walk to a bird-watching hot spot on the south shore of Lac des Arcs. Stop often at viewing blinds with interpretive displays and bring binoculars.

Start: The westbound lane of the Trans-Canada Highway (Hwy. 1). Park in a pull-out 2 km west of the Lac des Arcs overpass.

About Lac des Arcs

The lake was named back in 1858 by the Palliser Expedition, the "Lake of the Bows" referring to the Bow River of which this shallow metre-deep lake is merely a widening. In winter, water levels would drop to reveal sand bars that created dust storms whenever the west winds blew through the Gap. To counter this, a dike and inlet and outlet structures were built in 1998 to control water levels.

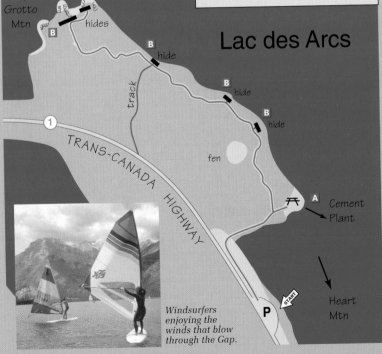

Windsurfers enjoying the winds that blow through the Gap.

From the parking area a trail runs alongside the highway, then heads right onto a promontory.

At a junction go right. A side trail leads to a picnic table overlooking Lac Des Arcs. The view is of Lafarge Canada cement plant, the quarry of Palliser limestone to its left. The mountain to the right is Heart Mountain.

A Lafarge Canada

The Western Canada Cement and Coal Company was established almost 100 years ago, in 1906, and is largely responsible for the development of the town of Exshaw. After numerous mergers over the years, Lafarge is now one of the largest cement producers in North America. As a major sponsor of events in the Bow valley, Lafarge helped fund this interpretive trail.

Return to the junction and turn right. The slightly undulating trail wanders through forest, skirting a fen with willows en route to the south shore of the lake. On your right pass three blinds with interpretive drawings and benches.

Opposite the third blind keep straight (the track to left leads to the highway). A short uphill is followed by a right turn down steps to two more blinds. Here the trail ends above small bays divided by rocky promontories. Across the water rises Grotto Mountain, originally named Pic de Grotto by James Hector and Eugene Bourgeau on August 12, 1858. Farther to the left you can see the mountains about Canmore: Rim Wall, Wind Ridge, The Three Sisters and Ehagay Nakoda.

Return the same way.

Right: Lafarge Canada from A.

How is cement manufactured?

It looks like hell in there. Large rotating kilns transform the ingredients into clinker. The temperature reaches an incredible 1,450-1,650°C.
Photo Tony Daffern

Palliser Formation limestone, mined from the quarry to the left the plant, is combined with shale from the Seebe area, sandstone from the Yamnuska area and iron. The mix is finely ground then burned in kilns where it emerges as clinker. After being pulverized and ground with gypsum, the resulting grey power is—Portland cement. Why the name Portland? Cement was developed In 1824 by Joseph Asdin of Leeds, England, who discovered that by burning limestone with shale, he could made a compound that when mixed with water would "set." The name Portland comes either from the isle of Portland where the stone was quarried or from cement's likeness to the popular building stone called Portland stone.

For thousands of years Lac des Arcs has been a resting and staging area for migrating waterfowl. Spring and fall are the best times to visit.

Tundra & Trumpeter Swans

Tundra swans can be seen in large flocks on the lake, often early in spring while the water is still frozen. Among them you may spot a few trumpeters. It can be very difficult to tell the two apart. Both have black beaks and legs. Tundras may have a distinguishing yellow spot in front of the eye. It can also be distinguished by its smaller size and by its voice that resembles that of a melodious Canada goose. The trumpeter, having a longer and double-looped windpipe, makes a loud, much deeper, trumpet-like call. Both can have orange staining on the head and neck.

Tundra swan. All inset photos by E. Jones.

American coot

B *One of the blinds.*

A family of coyotes take advantage of the spring ice to go birding.

C *Grotto Mountain from the end of the trail.*

CHECK LIST

- ❏ American coot
- ❏ American wigeon
- ❏ Bald eagle
- ❏ Blue-winged teal
- ❏ Bufflehead
- ❏ Canada goose
- ❏ Common goldeneye
- ❏ Common merganser
- ❏ Glacous gull
- ❏ Great blue heron
- ❏ Hooded merganser
- ❏ Killdeer
- ❏ Lesser scarp
- ❏ Mallard
- ❏ Northern pintail
- ❏ Osprey
- ❏ Parasitic jaeger
- ❏ Red-necked grebe
- ❏ Ring-billed gull
- ❏ Surf scoter
- ❏ Trumpeter swans
- ❏ Tundra swans
- ❏ Western grebe
- ❏ White-ringed scoter

Heart Creek
4 km return

early spring
summer
late fall

An easy walk through a lushly vegetated canyon with some unusual plants. After innumerable creek crossings the trail ends at a rock step and hidden waterfall. Interpretive signs along the way.

Start: Trans-Canada Highway (Hwy. 1). At Lac des Arc interchange take the road to Heart Creek parking lot below the rock arch.

At the trail sign a narrow trail leads to the power line right-of-way.

Keep right. Follows the trail around a ridge and downhill to meadows. Cross Heart Creek to a 5-way junction.

Turn right. Shortly the trail enters the canyon between Heart Mountain and Mt. McGillivray, crossing the fast running creek another seven times. En route to trail's end you're entertained by rock climbers and interpretive signs. Keep an eye out for the weeping wall on the left between stream crossings six and seven. A rock step precludes further travel unless you're an experienced hiker. Though you can hear the waterfall, catching a glimpse is difficult unless you're willing to paddle. Much of the water arises from a spring above the rock step.

Return the same way.

A *The arch is best seen from a point farther west on the highway.*

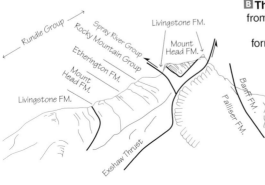

B The name 'Heart' comes from Heart Mountain which has a heart-shaped formation near the summit caused by a synclinal drag (a downward fold in strata). A trough developing between the arms is caused by erosion of softer rocks. Synclinal mountains are very common in the Canadian Rockies.

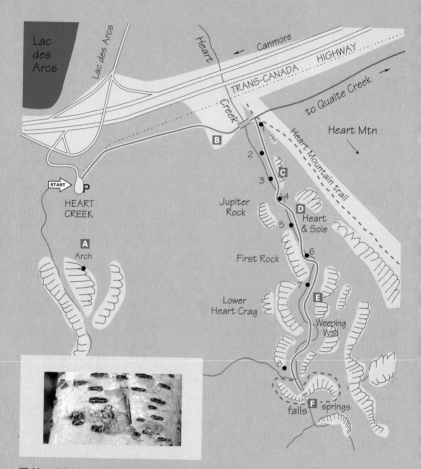

C How birches got their lenticels

In Blackfoot legend they were made by the Old Man who was thoroughly enjoying himself being tossed round by a great wind, up and down valleys and over the mountains. Every tree he caught hold of snapped in his hands which only added to the fun. But the paper birch was tough and did not break. When the wind stopped, he climbed down the birch, very angry, saying, "You spoiled my fun. I was running over the hills and mountains and through the woods until you caught hold of me. Now I am going to punish you." And with that the Old Man took out his knife and gashed savagely at the tree. The marks you see today are the scars made by the Old Man's knife.

D Chinook-hating Trees

Paper birch *(Betula papyrifera)* is not to be confused with aspens. Leaves have a sharper pointed tip, serrated edges, are shinier and a slightly darker green in colour. The bark is girdled with short black lines called lenticels. Unlike aspens which can handle the southern Alberta winter, Paper birch need sheltered valleys like this one and grow in small clumps, not whole hillsides. The problem is that though a thick corky layer of insulation inside the bark protects against cold (they grow successfully up north), warm Chinook winds do them in. Chinooks thaw young branches and buds which refreeze and die when the cold returns.

Incredibly, maples grow in the Rockies but, again, only in sheltered valleys. The Douglas Maple *(Acer glabrum)* is a shrub or small tree distinguished by maple-shaped leaves turning red in fall, reddish stems becoming grey in the mature plant and by pairs of winged fruits called samara.

The Weeping Wall from the 7th bridge.

E Flower Jewellery

In the shady forest are some really neat miniature flowers. To examine the exquisitely designed bishop's cap / bare-stemmed mitrewort (*Mitella nuda*) involves lying down and peering through a magnifying glass.

How Heart Creek got its Stoney name Wichchetha oda hibi Waptan

is not what one expects since it has nothing to do with wind, eagles, bears, porcupines or any other creature of the Canadian Rockies. It means 'arrival of many apes' and it came about like this according to Stoney Elder Gordon Labelle:

"It was in the time of clearing timber for the future Highway 1. The sun had just gone down and Gordon and his crew were sitting sipping tea around a campfire while keeping an eye on burning brush piles when Moses Chiniquay pointed out a dark shape coming over a ridge towards them. Everyone was wondering what it could possibly be since it appeared to be walking on all fours and its front legs appeared to be longer than its back legs. Well, everyone had a good laugh when it got closer and turned out to be Enoch Baptiste come over for some tea, his long black hair hanging down to his knees and sticking out every which way. "Hey, it's an ape," exclaimed Gordon's grandfather John Hunter, to which Enoch replied," well, then, from here on this creek here will have a name." Elijah Hunter asked," Yes, now that is certainly good, what will it be known as?" Enoch answered," It shall be known as Wichochetha ods hibi Waptan. Yes" he said," I thought the same thing about you fellows perched around here, all dark silhouettes by the fire."

F *For everyone who hasn't seen the waterfall above the end of the trail, here it is. This photo was taken from above the rock step looking down into the canyon.*

Story adapted from 'Stoney Place Names" Chiniki Band Council, Morley.

Montane
1.5 km loop

early spring
summer
late fall

This is an easy walk with interpretive signs starting behind the Visitor Centre. It takes you through a patchwork of dry meadows and montane forest to the top of an esker.

Start: Highway 1X at Bow Valley Provincial Park. Follow the park road to the Visitor Information Centre parking lot. Start at the front door of the Visitor Centre.

What *is* Montane?

Montane is an eco-zone like Alpine and Sub-alpine. With clouds spilling much of their moisture farther west over higher peaks, Montane country is much drier, receiving relatively little snow over the winter. Conditions favour pines, Douglas firs and aspens and their associated understory of buffaloberry, kinnikinnick and junipers.

Ⓐ Creamy camas lilies spell death

White camas (*Zigadenus elegans*), a common flower in the Montane, has a bulb which resembles an onion bulb without the distinctive onion smell. It contains an alkaloid called zygadenine which is extremely poisonous to both man and beast. Two bulbs would be more than enough to finish you off.

The big meadow. Goat Mountain (left), Yamnuska (right).

Keep right. Walk around the verandah, following interpretive signs to the side of the building where the trail takes off through an aspen grove and soon enters a large dry meadow, a tightly woven broadloom of kinnikinnick and creeping juniper. In late spring and summer this is the place to look for camas lilies, violets, showy locoweeds, prairie crocus and pasture sage.

Cross the power line right-of-way. After more meadow, the trail climbs a low ridge called an esker where you'll find early yellow locoweeds (photo to left). From the top is a grand view of McConnell Ridge. The trail winds along the esker top then descends through Douglas fir forest back to the powerline.

Recross the power line right-of-way. From here the trail returns through mixed forest to the parking lot. At 'Look and Listen' interpretive stop natural sounds are drowned out by the drone of trains, planes and vehicles on the nearby Trans-Canada Highway.

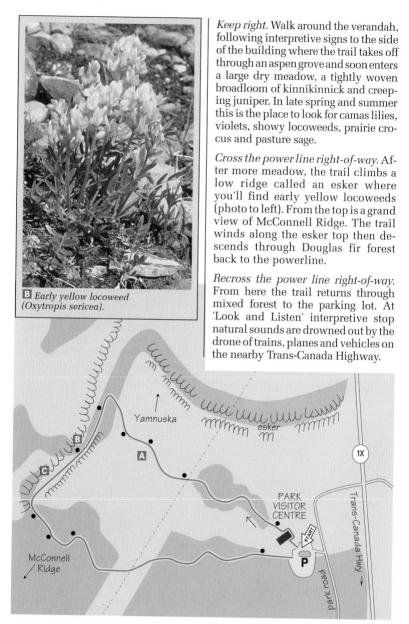

B *Early yellow locoweed (Oxytropis sericea).*

Yamnuska

esker

A

B

C

1X

PARK VISITOR CENTRE

START

P

Trans-Canada Hwy

park road

McConnell Ridge

Walking the esker. The mountain on the extreme left is McConnell Ridge.

☐ How to sort them out

Bow Valley Provincial Park is ideal for looking at glacial landforms, in particular depositional features:

An Esker is always a narrow, winding, steep-sided ridge of stratified gravel deposited by a stream flowing under the ice and left behind when the glacier retreated.

A Kame is an irregular shaped mound formed in a similar manner to eskers. Only what happened here is that the gravel has either been deposited by surface melt streams into holes or low points on the glacier (mounds), or spewed out by sub-glacial streams to form a delta at the edge of retreating glaciers. If returning to Calgary by Highway 1A look to the left side of the road 1.7 km east of Highway 1X where construction has exposed a good example of a kame.

Drumlins are entirely different from Kames and eskers. They are smooth ridges of till or gravel shaped like teardrops with the steep blunt sides facing up-glacier. The axis of the ridges always runs parallel to the movement of the ice, in this case northwest to southeast and there is nearly always lots of drumlins in the same area. What happened here was that glacial till formed by previous glaciers was overridden by the advancing glacier and formed into teardrop shapes by the flow of the ice.

The very best examples are seen on the north side of the Trans-Canada Highway between Morley Flats and Bear Road where the ridges reach an astonishing 25 m in height and 1.5 km in length.

Flowing Water
3 km return

early spring
summer
late fall

An easy loop with one short up-hill. This trail has everything — river flats, forest, ponds, springs, a dry grassy ridge — all exhibiting an astonishing variety of wild flowers and birds.

Start: Highway 1X at Bow Valley Provincial Park. Use the Willow Rock Campground entrance and drive past the checking station to the washrooms/showers/laundry building where you'll find parking spots opposite the trailhead at the start of the campground loop. The trail starts to the right of the amphitheatre trail at the trail sign. Campers at the far end of the loop can pick up this trail between sites # 87 and #89 to the left of the biffies.

Head into the forest.

Keep right. The trail follows the windings of a spring to the top end of the campground loop road.

Cross the road between campsites #87 and #89. At the trail sign pick up the trail.

At the junction with the return loop, keep right. The trail parallels the Kananaskis River on a bank top between wolf willow bushes. Cross a rusty creek draining the swamp. Horsetail groundcover on the left indicates damp ground. A little farther on, steps down the bank to your right let you explore the river flats while keeping an eye on water levels.

Looking up the Kananaskis Valley from near the viewpoint.

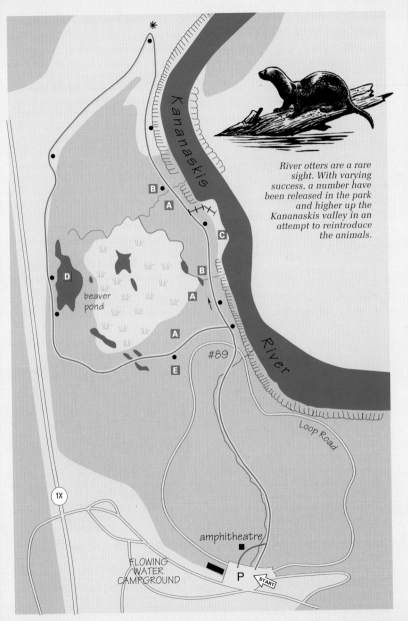

River otters are a rare sight. With varying success, a number have been released in the park and higher up the Kananaskis valley in an attempt to reintroduce the animals.

Kananaskis

River

B
A

C

B
A

D

beaver pond

A

E

#89

Loop Road

1X

amphitheatre

FLOWING WATER CAMPGROUND

P

START

Commentarii in libros sex Pedacii Dioscoridis 1554.

A Horsetails, most ancient of plants

First to appear in Spring is a fertile brown shoot. After the spores have been released, the shoot withers and from the same rhizome appears the green hollow jointed stem about 10-30 cm high. The common horsetail (Equisetum arvense), pictured at left, has jointed side branches, but others like the scouring-rushes look rather like asparagus. Farther along the trail sedge-like horsetail lines the boardwalk. This plant is also called pewterwort, bottlebrush and scouring rush because it contains a large amount of abrasive silica and was actually used at one time as a scouring pad in the kitchen and as sandpaper for polishing arrows or wooden utensils. You should know that bears love the taste.

Imagine. Some 400 million years ago when the climate was warmer and much more humid, horsetails grew to the height of lodgepole pines.

B Rusty Creeks

contain iron, carried there in a dissolved state by waters seeping through marshy soils. Iron combines with oxygen to form actual particles of rust which settle to the creekbed. There's also rust-coloured scum. Take a really close look. The scum is made up of iron bacteria attached one to the other by long strands. It actually gets its energy by making rust. When oxygen combines with iron inside bacteria cells, small amounts of energy are produced and used by the bacteria.

C Prairie gentian (Gentiana affinis). Unlike most other flowers, late August to early September is the time to descend the steps to the river flats to look for the gentians. On the trail above, goldenrods and asters will be blooming.

The trail by the beaver pond.
Inset: Least flycatcher.
Photo E. Jones

Cross another rusty creek. Shortly you enter a meadow where birder Dave Elphinstone often sees a tail-wagging eastern phoebe perched on Douglas fir branches overhanging the river bank. Climb to a viewpoint with bench on the open ridge.

A brief walk among prairie flowers, then you descend back into the woods close to Highway 1X. Stop a while at the beaver pond where birders will have a field day. A chestnut-sided warbler has been spotted near here. The trail continues, crossing beaver canals and the swamp on boardwalk. Birds you're likely to see or hear in the willows include alder, willow and least flycatchers, ovenbirds and calliope hummingbirds.

Turn right.

Return the same way you came.

D *The beaver pond from the interpretive sign.*

E Spruce with wet feet

Although spruce tend to grow in wetter locations that pines, too much water is too much of a good thing. Look what happened to the spruce in the beaver pond and this particular specimen when the beaver dam flooded the area.

Middle Lake
2.5 km loop

*early spring
summer
late fall*

An easy stroll through flower meadows and forest of all kinds with much opportunity for idleness by the lake. Come in early summer when the western wood lilies are blooming, and bring binoculars for viewing ducks.

Start: Highway 1X at Bow Valley Provincial Park. Follow the park road to Middle Lake parking lot.

At the trail sign keep right. The trail wanders through beautiful flower meadows with western wood lilies being the star attraction .

At an intersecting trail detour right. Interpretive signs overlook Middle Lake. Through the Gap you can see the Three Sisters.

Middle Lake from the interpretive signs.

> **C Diving ducks arriving in April**
>
> On arrival, goldeneye females fly through trees looking for nesting sites. First year females don't breed but search for potential holes anyway. Bufflehead females often return to the place where they were raised and nest year after year in the same hole. Not easily flushed, they are sometimes killed in a takeover by the larger and more aggressive goldeneyes which results in a mixed clutch. The young of all three jump-float out of the nest hole to the ground and follow the female to the lake. Learning to fly takes about two months. During egg laying, it's the males you see hanging around in the water.

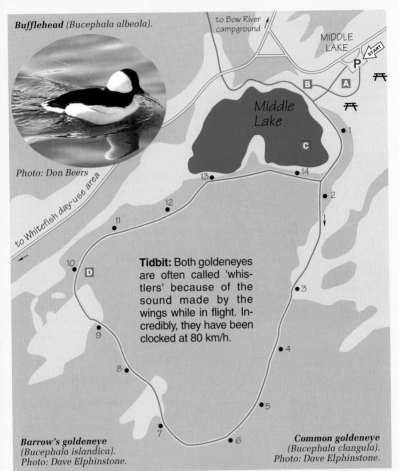

Bufflehead (Bucephala albeola).

to Bow River campground

MIDDLE LAKE

START

P

B A

Middle Lake

C

to Whitefish day-use area

1
14
13
2
12
11
10 D
3
9
4
8
5
7
6

Photo: Don Beers

Tidbit: Both goldeneyes are often called 'whistlers' because of the sound made by the wings while in flight. Incredibly, they have been clocked at 80 km/h.

Barrow's goldeneye (Bucephala islandica).
Photo: Dave Elphinstone.

Common goldeneye (Bucephala clangula).
Photo: Dave Elphinstone.

A Colourful western wood lilies

are worth a yearly pilgrimage to Bow Valley Provincial Park around mid June. *Lilium philadelphicum* (Saskatchewan's floral emblem) grows everywhere, both in the open and in sunny woodlands. Don't even think of picking this flower; the whole plant will die as the bulb cannot generate another set of leaves that season.

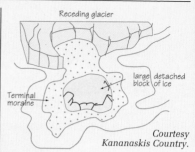

Courtesy
Kananaskis Country.

B Kettles

A long time ago when the glaciers finally retreated from this valley, a large block of ice got left behind. It melted and left a depression in the surrounding moraines. Sand, clay and small rock particles washed down into the bottom of the hole, plugging up the holes in the rubble so the depression could hold water. Actually, the lake bottom is not entirely waterproof. Water seeps very slowly underground.

Return to the main trail. Turn right. At the lakeshore turn left. Keep left. Going clockwise, you follow the loop through clumps of aspen, then spruce forest with a mossy understory and remnants of a Douglas fir stand. Logged at turn of the century, all that's left are the stumps.

Ultimately, you circle back to aspen forest at the south shore of the lake. Watch for trees with clawmarks. Hardly off the prairies and there's bears around? Two benches on either side of a small promontory offer superb views of Yamnuska.

Turn left. Turn right at the lakeshore. Turn right at the intersecting trail. A smaller trail wanders past picnic tables back to the parking lot.

D Logging

Over 100 years ago in 1883, a station along the new CPR line called Kananaskis was used as a supply depot during ongoing survey for the difficult section through the mountains. Entrepreneurs took advantage of its location to open up new businesses like the McCanleish Lime Kilns and the Colonel James Walker Sawmill which had become Walker's under the terms of his resignation as Cochrane Ranche manager. He commuted via train back and forth between Kananaskis and his home in Inglewood, Calgary, wintering his horses over at Soapy Smith's place which is now Rafter 6 Ranch.

Moraine
1.5 km one way

late spring
summer
late fall

Most of the route winds along the top of a moraine offering grand views in all directions. If starting from Bow Valley Campground this trail makes a pleasurable access to Middle Lake where, if feeling energetic you can tack on Middle Lake Loop before returning to your camp site (5 km return including Middle Lake loop).

Start: Highway 1X at Bow Valley Provincial Park. Follow the park road to Middle Lake, then turn right to Bow Valley Campground. Beyond the check-in station, turn left and park at the amphitheatre parking lot on the left side. The trail starts at the trail sign right of the amphitheatre access trail. Note: the park road beyond Middle Lake is open between mid May and mid October.

From the right side of the amphitheatre the trail leads to a powerline right-of-way.

Cross the powerline, keeping right. The trail climbs. You pass a depression sheltered from the wind where the snow lingers longer, the extra moisture encouraging a greater variety of plants like buffaloberry and twining honeysuckle. Further climbing through a forest of pine, Douglas fir and aspen ends on top of a moraine which is exposed to wind and carpeted with kinnikinnick and creeping juniper. Note trees growing on the sheltered lee slope.

Flagged Trees

C This is one of the Rockies' windiest places. Especially in winter. As incipient Chinook winds cross the Great Divide, they lose much of their moisture over the highest peaks. The air mass then descends into Bow Valley where the air warms and gains speed, and—helped by the funnel topography—shoots through the mountain gap onto the prairies. Even at such a low altitude you can see how exposed trees on the crest of the moraine are affected by the strong winds. They have a definite lean to the east and no branches on the windward side.

B Plant adaptation

Most of plants you see here have adapted to both very cold winters, drying Chinook winds, and hot dry summers. For instance, the leathery leaves of kinnikinnick are covered with a thick waxy coating which prevents water loss to drying winds. Thick sap acts in the same way as antifreeze.

E One way to tell a Douglas Fir

The large female cones are distinctive. In common with the larch, the Douglas fir has bracts protruding between the scales. Bracts are three-pronged and often longer than the scales.

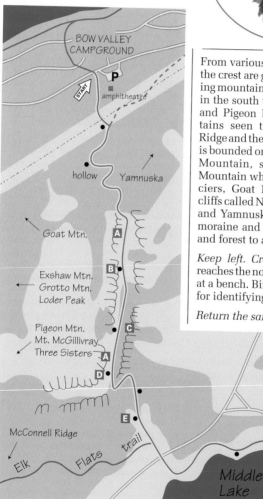

From various interpretive signs along the crest are grand views of surrounding mountains, from McConnell Ridge in the south through Mt. McGillivray and Pigeon Mountain to the mountains seen through the gap, Wind Ridge and the Three Sisters. The valley is bounded on the north side by Grotto Mountain, small forested Exshaw Mountain which was rounded by glaciers, Goat Mountain (with facing cliffs called Nanny Goat and Kid Goat) and Yamnuska. Drop down from the moraine and travel through meadow and forest to a junction.

Keep left. Cross the road. The trail reaches the north shore of Middle Lake at a bench. Binoculars come in handy for identifying birds.

Return the same way.

From the moraine crest looking towards Goat Mountain.

D Dead Ice

From the highway the park appears flat. In reality the terrain is bumpy— an always interesting mix of low hills, hidden valleys, sinuous ridges and rounded depressions, though all of such low relief that walking is no hardship. What happened is that long after the Bow River had eroded the valley, the climate got colder and the Ice Ages started. During the last Ice Age the glaciers advanced four times down the Bow Valley then retreated again, but only the third one called the Canmore Advance got this far. It was reckoned to be about 230-350 m thick, covering Exshaw Mountain and reaching to the base of the cliffs on Yamnuska. During retreat, a sheet of ice larger than the park broke off from the rest and was left here to melt. Kames, eskers, crevasse fillings and kettles which contribute to the bumpy topography are all stagnant ice features. During the retreat it's believed the existing channel of the Bow River was dammed by glacial drift and rerouted from its previous course in the vicinity of Chilver Lake and Rafter Six Guest Ranch.

Moraines are ridgelike deposits of mostly till deposited by glaciers which commonly mark the edge of the ice during stationary periods when the glaciers were neither retreating or advancing. This is an 'end moraine' marking the glacier tongue and is always perpendicular to the direction of the glacier flow. There can be several, the final one being called 'terminal.'

◨ The Carpet

Kinnikinnick

is an Indian name meaning "something to smoke". When you're lost in the Rockies, it's a good emergency food, being available under the snow all winter long. High in carbohydrates and rich in Vitamins C and A, the berries are mealy and tasteless. It's not called mealberry for nothing! Plants are just a few centimetres high, though it's said that if you were to stretch the branches along the ground, then hold up one end, the plant would measure the height of an aspen tree.

Arctostaphylos uva-ursi. The flower is similar to that of heather.

Juniper

Creeping juniper *(Juniperus horizontalis)* grows like a mat out in the open where the wind blows. (The Common or Prickly Juniper is the one you see in the sheltered forest.) A close examination reveals the cedar-like leaves are scaly. And fragrant—Indians burn it as incense during Sun Dance ceremonies. Berries are blueish black when ripe in the second or third year.

Recipes

Stomach ache tea

Add 1 tsp. of dried Kinnikinnick leaves to 1 cup of boiling water. Infuse 5 minutes. Add lemon or honey. Prospectors, apparently, suggested marinating the leaves in whisky first!

Juniper ratafia

Put 3 tsp. ripe juniper berries, 1/4 tsp. coriander, 1/8 tsp. cinnamon and 4 pinches of mace in a mortar and bruise gently. Add the mixture to 1 pt. brandy and let steep for 2 weeks. Them strain the mixture and discard the berries. Boil 1/2 cup sugar in 1/2 cup water for 10 min., then pour into the juniper brandy. Sample when cold. (recipe courtesy Dawn Jones.)

Bow River
2 km one way

late spring
summer
late fall

A flat stroll along the banks of the Bow River between Bow Valley campground and Whitefish day-use area. As you might expect there are numerous connections to camp sites along the way.

Start: Highway 1X at Bow Valley Provincial Park. Follow the park road to Middle Lake. Turn right and drive to Bow Valley Campground. The trail starts in A loop, opposite site #22. Note: the park road beyond Middle Lake is open from mid May to mid October.

Alternate start: drive to Whitefish Day-use area by turning left at Middle Lake.

The trail angles out to the bank of the Bow River at an interpretive sign about brown trout. Downstream is the CPR railway bridge.

Keep straight (access trail to left). After passing interpretive sign "Following the Tracks" opposite an island marking the location of the old river crossing before there were bridges, you make close acquaintance with walk-in campsites #39, 40, 41.

Keep straight (access trail to walk-in campsites parking lot to left). The next stretch offers two benches with a view across the river of Yamnuska and Goat Mountain. Note burls on the spruce tree next to the second bench.

Whitefish day-use area. Yamnuska beyond the Bow River.

C *Rock jasmine*
(Androsace chamaejasme).

Keep straight (to left is an access trail to the amphitheatre and Moraine Trail). The river bank is very unstable at this point so unless you want an impromptu bath stick to the trail which eventually descends to river level.

Keep straight (access trails to left lead to E Loop). Across the river, Highway 1A is very close to the river which is one reason why it's a popular fishing spot. Farther left you can glimpse the lime quarries at the base of Door Jamb Mountain, so called because it stands at the entrance to the mountains. Leaving behind D Loop's picnic tables, you pass under a powerline and through patch of balsam poplars and willows cut by beavers.

Keep right (trail to left leads to Many Springs Interpretive Trail and Elk Flats day-use area). Arrive at Whitefish day-use area parking lot which offers the best view of the whole trail of Yamnuska and Goat Mountain. In spring, the grassy bank is popular with Canada geese who nest on three islands in the Bow River.

B Where's the ford?

Somewhere near the CPR railway bridge was a ford in general use by Stonies and early white travellers above "a waterfall like a ledge right across the river about 7 feet high". This is one likely spot. On the other hand, downstream of the bridge, on the west bank are three cairns thought to be cache cairns built in 1854 by James Sinclair's party. They were on their way from Morley up the Kananaskis Valley to Oregon, and would likely have built the cairns at the crossing place.

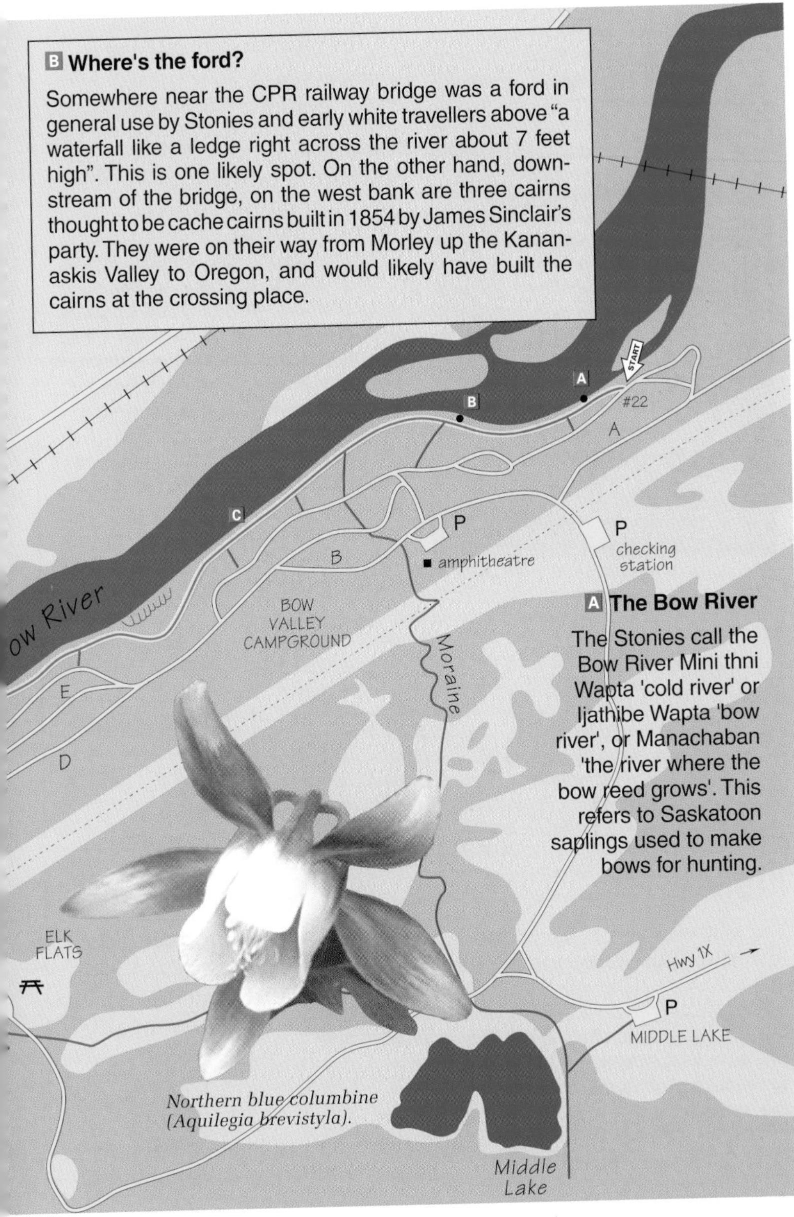

START

#22

A

B

C

P

amphitheatre

P

checking
station

ow River

BOW
VALLEY
CAMPGROUND

Moraine

B

E

D

A The Bow River

The Stonies call the Bow River Mini thni Wapta 'cold river' or Ijathibe Wapta 'bow river', or Manachaban 'the river where the bow reed grows'. This refers to Saskatoon saplings used to make bows for hunting.

ELK
FLATS

Hwy IX

P

MIDDLE LAKE

*Northern blue columbine
(Aquilegia brevistyla).*

Middle
Lake

Yamnuska above the interpretive sign.

E The great McConnell Fault

Dominion geologist R.G. McConnell is commemorated by the greatest of all thrust faults, the McConnell. He first recognised it in 1887. And so can you trace the McConnell Fault all the way down the eastern slopes without too much difficulty. What you're looking for is massive grey limestone cliffs sitting on top of rounded slopes—mostly treed with outcrops of shale and brownish sandstones. In other words, the fault marks the demarcation of foothills and the Front Ranges. What happened is that during the mountain building process older middle Cambrian Eldon limestone was thrust about 32 km to the northeast over the top of younger cretaceous sandstones and mudstones, in this case the Belly River Formation which makes up the foothills.

From guidebook of the 24th International Geological Congress, 1972.

The fault plane is nearly horizontal and with binoculars you can see the actual fault line quite well at the base of the cliff on Yamnuska. After looking at the big limestone cliff (a climbers paradise), lower the binoculars to practise outcrops further down in the trees which are sandstone. If driving to Canmore you cross another three major faults.

F The Mountain with three names

Everybody calls this mountain Yamnuska or Yam for short. The Stoney name is Iyamnathka 'flat-faced mountain.' The official name is Mt. John Laurie "a good friend to the Indians who taught them to preserve their culture and their treaty rights, and helped the nine tribes of our province into the Indian Association of Alberta."

SIDE TRIP TO SAND FOREST

Start from the final bend of the park road as it descends to Whitefish day-use area. A narrow trail pushes through the bushes to the top of the sand slope from where it's an easy surf to the Bow River with many interesting plants to look at on the way down. While this area is accessible from Whitefish day-use area along the bank, it's not recommended you go this way because of crumbling banks.

G The sand forest

Eolian means formed by wind-blown particles. Lacustrine means pertaining to lakes. So what happened here was that a lot of glacial sand was deposited in Lac Des Arcs during the retreat of the last glacier and can be seen in bluffs bordering the lake and in a sand spit exposed in late fall when the already low water levels drop even farther. High winds blow sand particles eastwards and deposit them on both sides of the Bow River which is what you're looking at here.

A showy member of the Cruciferae family.

Many Springs
1.6 km loop

*late Spring
summer
fall*

An easy walk through montane forest and meadows to springs in a calcareous basin where you'll see plants which eat meat!

Start: Highway 1X at Bow Valley Provincial Park. Follow the park road to Middle Lake. Turn left and park at Many Springs parking lot on the left. Note: the park road beyond Middle Lake is open from mid May to mid October.

Walk down the wide track to a junction.

Turn right. A narrower trail leads to a power line right-of-way.

Turn left. Follow the right-of-way downhill to a bridge over Many Springs Creek. En route, look for yellow lady's slipper orchids. Shortly you arrive at a viewpoint overlooking an island in the Bow River.

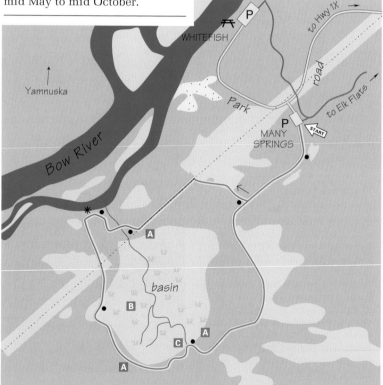

◨ *Gorgeous testicles — Beautiful orchids*

The name 'orchis' means testicles, referring to the shape of the tuberous roots and was proposed by the Greek philosopher Theophrastus, a pupil of Aristotle. 300 years later in the 1st century A.D., a Greek physician called Dioscorides was spreading the rumour that orchids were synonymous with virility and fertility. Two of the more common orchids found here are the round-leaved orchid and the gorgeous yellow lady's slipper.

A good word for mosquitos

Orchids rely on insects for pollination, some only by one particular species. Blunt-leaved orchids, for instance, need mosquitoes for pollination.

Yellow lady's slipper grows in damp woods like here, in gravelly places and along powerline right-of-ways near Canmore. Often seen growing in large clumps.

Don't pick the orchids

Here's why. Many orchids depend on food stored in underground roots for next season's growth. Because flowers often cannot be picked without including one or two leaves, the plant's ability to make food is destroyed and the plant dies. Although orchids produce as many as a million seeds at a time, the seeds have no food reserves and must rely on aids like fungi to break down organic matter into simple nutrients that can be used by the seed. Conditions like moisture, temperature, soil and shelter must also be spot on if the seedlings are to survive.

The gorgeous yellow lady's slipper (Cypripedium calceolus).

Oddities of the Springs

Elephanthead (Pedicularis groenlandica) bears an uncanny resemblance to an elephant's head.

False asphodel (Tofieldia glutinosa).

C The Death Flower

Our very own meat-eating plant is called the butterwort and a very attractive plant it is too. Many people think it's a violet! In Scandinavia the leaves have been used as a rennet to curdle milk, hence the common name butterwort.

Its scientific name *Pinguicula vulgaris* means ' fat' and refers to the glandular hairs on the leaves' upper surface which secrete a greasy sticky fluid. Any insect venturing onto the leaves gets mired in the mucilage. This is one efficient killing machine. The insect's struggles to break free merely stimulate the plant to make more mucilage which probably suffocates the victim. At the same time, struggling also results in the margins of the leaf curling over and secreting a digestive acid. This curling makes the shallow dish deeper and therefore increases its holding capacity of digestive fluids. All this gruesome work takes one to three days depending on the size of the victim. When the leaves at last roll back, usually in about one week , all that's left of the unfortunate insect is a hard black granule of its chitinous parts. Those are the black specks you can see on the leaf surface. Interestingly, unsuitable insects stimulate fluids which have no digestive properties, while too large a prey will cause the death of a leaf by the ingestion of too much fat.

Butterworts (Pinguicula vulgaris).

The springs from the interpretive sign. In the background is Yamnuska.

Ⓒ Tiny Blind Creatures

Under rocks in the springs live aquatic Isopods called *Salmasellus steganothrix*. Not exactly common, these particular isopods have been found in only a few other places in western Canada. Tiny blind creatures, they live out their lives in complete darkness, scavenging on plant debris and are completely oblivious to the world above water, protected as they are from the vagaries of climate by the constant flow of the springs. You may be more familiar with a land dwelling isopod called a sowbug (or pillbug), a fatter version of *S. steganothrix* with 14 very short legs, which lives in the dark under rocks and peeling bark.

The trail turns left, crosses the right-of-way and skirts the basin in the trees (more orchids). In fall, this is one of the best places to spot some unusual migrating warblers. Arrive at a platform overlooking the springs and the interesting vegetation of the calcareous flat. From here, the trail climbs back into forest and meadow country.

Keep right. Return along the old road to the parking lot.

An aquatic isopod.

Horseshoe Falls Dam
4.8 km loop

Early Spring
summer
late fall

A walk along the south bank of the Bow River to Horseshoe Falls Dam. Learn about ???

Start: Highway 1X. Take the turning to Seebe (gas, groceries). From 1X drive 2.3 km through the hamlet and up a hill to a parking area on the left just past the texas gate. Occasionally the gate at the bottom of the hill is closed.

From the parking area follow the trail downhill through meadows to a junction under a powerline.

Go straight, then turn left. Go straight. Arrive on the bank of the Bow River, a local beauty spot where the river is lined by crags and picturesque Douglas firs growing out of niches in the rock.

The Bow River at

B Cardium sandstones

Cardium sandstones are often conglomeratic: i.e. embedded with pebbles of chert and quartzite, and very hard weathering. Wherever the Bow River passes across cardium sandstones there are falls. Or were! The rock is used to anchor dams at 'Kananaskis Falls' and 'Horseshoe Falls.'

Turn right. A trail follows the river down-stream then zigs right under a line of sandstone crags.

Keep straight, then turn left. Turn right. Arrive back at the powerline junction.

Turn left. Pass a boulder on the right and enter open forest with glades.

Keep right. Pass under a powerline. Cross an intersecting trail. (Trail to left offers access to the Bow River for anglers.)

Keep left. Walk out on meadow to a viewpoint for the forebay and Horsehoe Falls Dam.

Return to the last junction and turn left. The trail follows the meadow edge, then climbs to a junction.

Go left. Climb some more to intersect the plant access road.

Turn left downhill. A flat area to left was the site of the staff house built for Calgary Power employees. Later, the company hamlet called Seebe was built upstream between the two dams. Pass the road down to the forbay and an interpretive sign showing how electricity is made and giving you the statistics .

Continuing downhill, keep left at a bend. Keep right (visitor parking to left). The brick building ahead is the original pow-erhouse built in 1911.

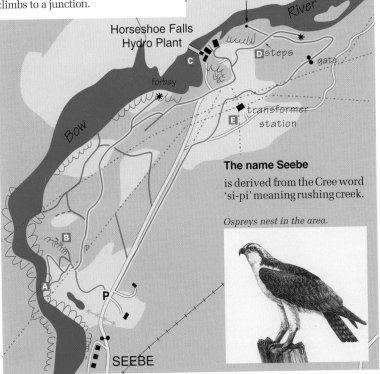

river flow indicator, movie site

Horseshoe Falls Hydro Plant

C

D steps

gate

forbay

E transformer station

Bow

The name Seebe

is derived from the Cree word 'si-pi' meaning rushing creek.

Ospreys nest in the area.

B

A

P

SEEBE

C Horseshoe Falls Hydro Plant

Begun in 1909, Horseshoe Falls was the very first power plant to be built on the Bow River. Calgary Power's (now TransAlta) first president was W. Max Aitkin, Lord Beaverbrook. Another of the founding board of directors was R. B. Bennett, later Canada's future Prime Minister.

The powerhouse, made of 'steel, concrete and brick' still houses the turbines and generators today. The taller transformer station next to it caught fire in September of 1940 and was eventually demolished. As you can see, the four penstocks were once covered over as protection against severe weather. Note the wing wall that protects from floods.

Centre right: the original brick powerhouse in 2003.

Lower right: What you are missing. Beautiful Horseshoe Falls prior to the dam. (PA-2514-11 Glenbow Archives).

D *Steps down to the Bow River.*

through Seebe and tossed a rose to resident Pierette Strappazzon.

• In 1954, Seebe residents watched Marilyn Monroe with delight as she filmed the movie "River of No Return" near the Horseshoe Dam.

Sign at Seebe picnic area.

At road's end go straight. Follow a raised walkway that crosses the penstocks for a view looking up at the dam. Below you is a popular but dangerous fishing spot.

Return past the visitor parking to the next junction. Turn left onto a minor road. Keep straight under a powerline, keep straight. Where the minor road bends to the left head across meadow. Look for steps descending the steep bank. There are two sets dropping a total of 30 vertical m to river level.

On reaching a gravel road go left. It leads to a recorder of water levels. Here and downstream the Indian attack scene was filmed for the movie "The River of No Return" starring Marilyn Monroe.

Return to the last junction. Go left. A trail leads out through meadows to a viewpoint downstream of an island.

Return to last junction and turn left. Follow the road up the hill, winding right through a gate into a large meadow crisscrossed by transmission lines radiating out from the transformer station. The road crosses under a powerline twice, then runs along the side of the transformer station. Cross under three more powerlines en route to a junction.

Turn right onto the transformer access road. Just before reaching the plant access road, turn left under a powerline. While you have the option of walking the plant road back to the parking lot, it's more pleasant to follow the powerline right-of-way that ends at the parking lot.

E Transformer Station

From the generator in the powerhouse electricity travels to the transformer station where the voltage is stepped up—listen to that buzzing! Power lines then transmit the electricity often great distances to substations where the voltage is reduced before being distributed to homes, office buildings etc.

Widowmaker
4.2 km return

spring
summer
fall

An easy walk along the east bank of the Kananaskis River. Be there on race days when contestants run the rapids of the slalom course. Better yet, why not combine this walk with a rafting trip?

Start: Kananaskis Trail (Hwy. 40) at Canoe Meadows day-use area. You can also access the trail from Barrier Lake Interpretive Centre and from Widow Maker parking lot.

From the near end of the parking lot follow a trail a few metres to a fence. Turn left. The trail follows the edge of a steep bank falling to the Kananaskis River. Two viewpoints give views of the slalom course in Shaugnessy Canyon.

Keep right twice. Cross an intersecting trail . To right is another viewpoint, to left the group camping area.

Keep right and slightly downhill. The trail turns left.

At a 4-way close to a meadow turn right. The trail gently descends the bank to the river and follows it along to a bend at a rapid—an excellent place from where to watch kayackers wave surfing in close-up.

Turn left up a gravel track. At a T-junction turn right. Ahead is an Atco trailer used on race days.

Before the uphill turn right. A trail runs alongside the fence above a steep bank overlooking a stretch of river with chutes.

At a T-junction with signpost keep right. Note a put-in trail descending the steep shale bank. The trail now moves inland a bit, with stretches of boardwalk as you walk through damp

A Not a Natural River

At the instigation of kayakers Dave Reid and Bob Smith, the Kananaskis River through Shaugnessy Canyon has been totally re-fashioned for paddlers through the dumping of rocks to create waves, drops and eddies. The work started in a small way in 1983, the bulk of the work being done in 1986 with refinements in 1991, 1997 and 2003. Upto2003 there is 1 km of grade 3 rapids and 53 eddies. The rate of flow is controlled upstream at Barrier Dam by TransAlta Utilities. For the water flow schedule contact their website at www.transalta.com.

Above and lower right:
Views seen from the trail.

Shaugnessy Canyon

Canoe Meadows Day Use

P A

River

B

Kananaskis

C

Barrier Lake Visitor Centre

Tim Horton Children's Ranch

40

Widow Maker

Lusk Creek

P

Widow Maker Day Use

68

Kananaskis Whitewater Festival is held annually on the last weekend in May. Competitions for all levels of expertise include hole riding, wave surfing, obstacle course, ball race, down-river race etc. On land the fun continues with a barbecue and party. For more info contact your local paddling store.

Wolf willow alley. Mt. Baldy behind.

C Wolf Willow
(Elaeagnus commutata)

Wolf willow (Two photos to the left) is common and unmistakable. Look for bushes with pale green leaves covered in silvery scales and berries to match. In spring you are drawn to the plant by the sweet cloying smell of pale yellow flowers. Despite the name it's not a willow at all though it grows in similar locations. It's actually a member of the oleaster family and sometimes called, more accurately perhaps, silverberry. Before plastic, wolf willow berries were used by the Indians to make beads.

To make beads First scrape away the outer shell to reveal the kernel which is striped and oval-shaped. Boil to soften somewhat, then make a hole with a needle and thread beads together. Paint with shellac.

pine forest with deadfall. Look for baneberry, twisted stalk, mares tails.

At a junction keep right. The trail to left leads to Barrier Lake Interpretive Centre parking lot. The centre's attractions include displays, books for sale, washrooms and picnic tables.

After a boggy stretch with two-plank bridges, the trail descends, crosses a small creek and enters wolf willow alley, a long flat section alongside the river. A side trail to right leads to a picnic table.

Keep left. The trail makes a semi-circle to cross Lusk Creek at a bridge.

Keep left. Climb to get above a steep rocky bank. This section gives beautiful views down to the river. Descend to a signboard.

Keep left. (Trail to right descends the bank to picnic tables and the put-in point for rafters.) Enter Widow Maker parking lot.

The trail at **B**

To go rafting contact:
Mirage Adventure Tours at Delta Lodge, Kananaskis Village: 403-678-4949, 1-800-312-7238.
Kananaskis River Adventures at Delta Lodge, Kananaskis Village: 403-591-7773, 1-800-312-7238.
Rainbow Riders: 403-678-7238, 1-877-717-7238
Inside Out Experience: 403-949-3305, 1-877-999-7238

The Kananaskis River at Widow Maker.

Barrier Lake Forestry Trails
2.5 km

spring
summer
fall

After visiting the Colonel's Cabin which tells the story of this former POW camp, take the self-guiding loop through the forest. An ideal trail for people who want to learn more about forest management.

Start: Kananaskis Trail (Hwy. 40) at Colonel's Cabin parking lot.

At the parking area, in front of two flagstaffs, is a boulder with a plaque dedicated to the "Veteran Guards of Canada."

A trail leaves the parking lot. Turn right twice. Arrive at the Colonel's Cabin visitor centre, an Alberta Historical Site. Leaf through photo albums of Prisoner of War Camp #130. Next door is the Alberta Forest Service exhibit and a Guard Tower.

Retrace your steps to the last junction. Keep right twice. At the information board pick up a trail brochure. The ongoing trail crosses Barrier Creek (note the gauge measuring stream flow), then divides.

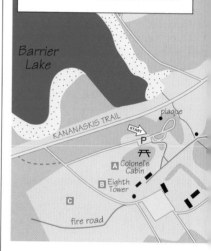

A The Colonel's Cabin
During World War 2 this cabin housed the Camp Commander for Prisoner of War Camp #130, Hugh de Norban Watson (1886-1952). The ornate ironwork of the door handle, the brass ashtray and the chair were all made by POW's. After a stint as a forestry office it's now the visitor centre for the trail.

B The Eighth Tower
Some of you may remember the white fire lookout on McConnell Ridge opposite—a well-known landmark for over 24 years. When Pigeon Lookout (named for stool pigeons) was superseded by Barrier Lake lookout on the summit in 1984, it was taken back down to the Kananaskis Field Station and painted grey, a colour in keeping with its original

The Colonel's Cabin.

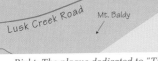

Right: The plaque dedicated to "The Veteran Guards of Canada."

function as a guard tower in POW Camp #130. In 1939 the camp had seven guard towers and two auxiliary towers, supplemented by a low voltage wire warning fence and two high barb-wire fences. Much later an eighth tower with a powerful searchlight—this one—was located outside the compound, about 100 m southwest of where you are now.

◧ Tales from Camp #130

During World War II, the Dominion's Forest Experiment Station was used as a prisoner of war camp for alien internees, Canadian conscientious objectors and prisoners of war. As camps go, this one was more like a holiday camp. Prisoners took educational classes provided by the YMCA, attended church services and painted mountain scenery. A movie theatre, soccer field and skating rink was provided. Some POW's joined woodcutting crews and did the clearing for Barrier Lake Reservoir, while others, as a special privilege for good behaviour, were allowed to climb Mt. Baldy after signing a statement to the effect that they would stay on the trail, return before dark, and not try to escape. I believe the record climb was 90 minutes. Of course, the odd few did try to escape. But where could they go? On September 24 1940, for instance, district ranger Joe Kovach ran into a couple of POW's walking south along the road towards Kananaskis Lakes. By all accounts they were glad to get a square meal and a roof over their heads.

August, 1942, was the year of the great escape attempt. During the evacuation of 500 POW's to a new camp at Lethbridge, seven POW's were missing from the headcount. Two searches failed to show up anything. But then, at a point not too far from the laundry building, a guard kicked an empty coffee can lying upside down on the ground. It had six holes bored into the bottom. Under the can was a gopher hole which on closer examination turned out to be an air hole lined with small cans. On removing the sinks in the laundry, a tunnel was discovered, extending some 20 metres out from the building, and in the tunnel were the seven missing men plus escape equipment including snow shoes. Since extending the tunnel to outside the perimeter fence would have been a five-year job, the idea was that the escapees would remain underground until the camp was evacuated, then return to the washroom and make a break for it.

The barracks were sited in the big meadow beyond the Eighth Tower. You might recognize them as youth hostel buildings along the Icefields Highway. 1942 photo (NA 4823-3 Glenbow Archives).

Turn left, then keep *right.* The trail winds through mostly lodgepole pine forest with the odd white spruce. wintergreens, orchids, twinflowers, fairy bells and blue clematis grow in the shade. Common junipers appear as you near a junction.

Turn right. A viewing platform with interpretive signs gives good views of Mt. Baldy and the Lusk Pass area.

Retrace your steps. Turn right. This is a good stretch to find mushrooms.

Keep left. Cross old road. The trail continues past a soil profile pit, a blueberry patch, and examples of witches broom and pine thinning. Next on the left is a research plot of Norway spruce. The far end of the loop is marked by a shelter. Continue past rows of mugho and Scots pines.

Cross old road. Walk through plantations of Colorado blue spruce, jack pine and Douglas fir.

Turn left. A beautiful stretch through Scots pines precedes a blowdown area where aspens have been bent double by wind and snow. Re-enter lodgepole pine forest. Just before the next junction you pass the veteran pine.

Keep left. Rejoin your outgoing trail.

Return the same way you came.

D Mt. Baldy Viewing platform
Mt. Baldy was named by the POW's who were allowed to climb the mountain without guards in tow. The route headed up trees to just left of the summit. Sometimes a climber got hung up on the cliffs when trying to descend to camp and had to be rescued.

J Veteran lodgepole pine
This 200 year-old tree is a survivor. Now sporting just a few needles, it has survived mistletoe and witches broom infestations and the fires of 1870, 1916 and 1936 when the outer bark was burnt away.

Right: Blue clematis (Clematis columbiana) is a vine which drapes itself over shrubs and young trees. The blue 'petals' are actually sepals.

About Trees

Male cones are much smaller than the female cones.

Straws 30 metres high!

Being rooted to the ground and not able to march off to the nearest river for a drink, trees are dependent on what's happening at root level. In a tree, water molecules are linked in a continuous column, so that when a leaf transpires (gives off water to the air) the water column merely moves up into the root system. Water travels in water-conducting tissue called xylem (sapwood). On hot days, thirsty trees suck up as much as 450 litres!

How Trees work Less than 5% of water absorbed by the tree is actually used. Sunlight energizes chlorophyll in the leaf or needle causing water to split into oxygen and hydrogen. Hydrogen combines with carbon dioxide in the air to manufacture food carbohydrates. So when water is returned to the atmosphere, some of the unneeded oxygen goes too, which is why it's healthy to have plants in your house. The carbohydrates are converted into a tree's basic components, cellulose fibre and lignin, which are delivered to different parts of the tree through a network of cells called phloem (inner bark). Both phloem and xylem are located between the bark and the heartwood in the soft green cambium layer.

Blazes It's amazing the number of people who think blazes move up the trunk of a tree as it grows higher. A tree actually grows from the crown by sending up a new leader which has a whorl of branches. The trunk lower down merely grows fatter with age while branches below the new growth grow both fatter and longer.

Rings Trees grow from the inside out. Each year a new band of phloem and xylem is created. When last year's phloem dies it becomes part of the outer bark, the xylem another ring in the heartwood.

The Plantations

E Norway spruce, planted 1946. As you can see this tree has not done half as well as the indigenous trees. Note the lighter green needles and bigger cones.

F Nursery planted in the 1940s in rows. Norway spruce again, plus Scots pine, caragana and mugho pine.

G Plantation planted in the early 1940s of Douglas fir, jack pine and Colorado blue spruce which grows very well in Calgary gardens. Look for the blue needles of Colorado blue spruce further along the trail.

H Scots pine planted in the early 1940s after POW's cut down lodgepole pine infested with mistletoe. As you can see by the photo opposite, a Scots pine is easily recognisable by the reddish-orange bark which tends to peel off in great strips from the upper part of the tree.

Barrier Lake Trail
1.2 km return

spring
summer
fall

A moderately easy uphill walk to a rocky hilltop with a grand view of the Kananaskis Valley. There is the option afterwards of descending a trail to Barrier Lake picnic sites overlooking the beach.

Start: Kananaskis Trail (Hwy. 40). Turn west onto Barrier Lake access road. Keep left at the junction and drive up the hill to a parking lot. (The right-hand road leads to the boat launch and picnic sites at the lake).

From the parking lot walk to the end of the loop road. Climb steps to a viewpoint with interpretive sign. The grassy strip marks the site of the old road which wound around the *outside* of the hill you are going to climb. From here the trail climbs in easy switchbacks, initially through stunted aspens, then up open slopes carpeted with kinnikinnick and juniper. Wind flowers add colour in late spring.

Turn right on the ridge. A flat stretch between forest and open slopes leads to a rocky summit with interpretive signs. Mackenzie's hedysarum grows between the rocks. On your right the slope falls away in crags towards Barrier Lake. In front is a close-up view of Mt. Baldy and, low down, Barrier Bluffs, a rock climbers' crag.

Return the same way.

Barrier Lake from the summit.

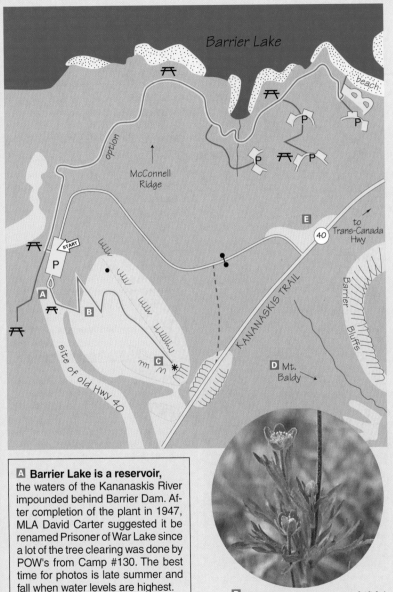

Barrier Lake

beach

option

McConnell Ridge

START

P

A

B

C

site of old Hwy 40

E

40

to Trans-Canada Hwy

KANANASKIS TRAIL

Barrier Bluffs

D Mt. Baldy

A Barrier Lake is a reservoir, the waters of the Kananaskis River impounded behind Barrier Dam. After completion of the plant in 1947, MLA David Carter suggested it be renamed Prisoner of War Lake since a lot of the tree clearing was done by POW's from Camp #130. The best time for photos is late summer and fall when water levels are highest.

B Wind flower (Anemone multifida).

C Wind Effects

Though it may be a lovely calm day for your walk, there are several clues telling you that a lot of the time this ridge gets the brunt of winds blowing down valley. Look at the aspens on the switchbacks. They remain small, stunted and bent. Some pines on the rocky south slope have broken branches, while others have been trained by the wind to lean north. On the summit the spruce (photo to left) wear root-length 'skirts', a luxurious growth of branches around the base which develop below the level of snowpack where it's warmer and more sheltered from the wind.

Mt. Baldy from the ridge. The usual ascent route follows the right-hand skyline.

D A bald mountain?

Although the POW's at Camp #130 have been credited with naming the peak during World War II, they may not have been the first. In 1883 Isaac Kendall Kerr, of Wisconsin's Eau Claire Logging Company undertook a journey with his associates up the Kananaskis Valley to look at timber and it was 3 miles up from the confluence of the Kananaskis with the Bow that they first spotted this 'Bald mountain'. After the late 1940s the name 'Barrier' came into favour because the mountain overlooked Barrier Lake. Finally, in 1984 the name 'Baldy' was reinstated officially. The Stoneys call it something else of course—Sleeping Buffalo Mountain because of its striking resemblance to the animal when viewed from the north. As you drive down Highway 40 from the Trans-Canada Highway you can imagine the rump to the left, and to the right the shoulders and the massive craggy head which is the summit block.

E You are standing on the McConnell Thrust Fault!

The rocky ridge across the lake is named after Dominion geologist R.G. McConnell who in the 1890s discovered one of the great faults of the Canadian Rockies. From the south end of this ridge, the great fault doesn't carry on down the west side of the Kananaskis Valley as you might suppose (these cliffs result from a smaller parallel fault), but resurfaces on this side of the lake, crossing Highway 40 just slightly north of the summit. It's responsible for the eastern escarpment of Mt. Baldy and the entire Fisher Range down to Nihahi Ridge and south towards the Crowsnest.

Barrier Lake beach. Across the water is the south end of McConnell Ridge.

OPTION THE BEACH (1.2 km)

The trail leaves the west side of the parking lot at the biffy.

Straightway turn right at a junction (left-hand trail leads to picnic tables and another viewpoint). A flat stretch, then the trail starts its winding descent to the lake through a mix of pines and aspen forest. Picnic tables appear as you approach the lake.

Keep left. The trail undulates around a deep indent of the lake.

Keep left. Now close to the lake shore you pass more picnic tables on the left. Around here, the beavers have been trimming the young aspens. Turn a corner and arrive at the boat launch parking lot.

Turn left into the parking lot (trail ahead ends shortly at another parking lot near a biffy). Walk down the boat launch, then head left along a beach of pale yellow sand for a spot of paddling and sunbathing.

Troll Falls
3.2 km loop

spring
summer
fall

An easy loop following signed ski trails through pine and aspen forest, meadows, and finally the river bank of the Kananaskis River. The pièce de résistance is Troll Falls which is particularly impressive during runoff.

Start: Kananaskis Trail (Hwy. 40). Turn off onto the Nakiska Ski Area access road. Keep right. Just before the powerline, turn right onto an access road for Stony equestrian trail parking lot. Park at the trailhead.

Follow the road along the powerline right-of-way through a gate.

Turn left onto Hay Meadow ski trail. Turn right. You're now on Troll Falls ski trail.

Keep left. Turn right. The wide undulating trail winds through aspen forest with a grassy understory and a wide variety of flowers.

Cross the 4-way intersection (Hay Meadow trail to right, Ruthie's to left). A narrower trail carries on to Troll Falls, where Marmot Creek plunges over a ledge of hard bedrock. If it appeals, clamber up one of two rough muddy trails forking off to the left from the splash pool. This brings photography buffs to a greasy ledge behind the fall itself.

False Solomon's seal (*Smilacina racemosa*)   Solomon's seal (*Smilacina stellata*)

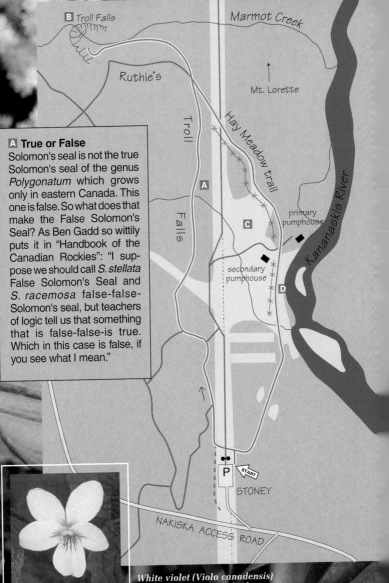

B Troll Falls

Marmot Creek

Ruthie's

Mt. Lorette

Troll

Hay Meadow trail

Kananaskis River

A True or False

Solomon's seal is not the true Solomon's seal of the genus *Polygonatum* which grows only in eastern Canada. This one is false. So what does that make the False Solomon's Seal? As Ben Gadd so wittily puts it in "Handbook of the Canadian Rockies": "I suppose we should call *S. stellata* False Solomon's Seal and *S. racemosa* false-false-Solomon's seal, but teachers of logic tell us that something that is false-false-is true. Which in this case is false, if you see what I mean."

Falls

A

C

primary pumphouse

secondary pumphouse

D

P

START

STONEY

NAKISKA ACCESS ROAD

White violet (Viola canadensis) with purple runways for bees.

Backtrack to the 4-way junction. Turn left. Now on Hay Meadow ski trail you follow a soft-on-the-feet grassy track to the primary pumphouse.

Cross the access road between pump-houses. The trail soon reaches grassy banks overlooking the Kananaskis River. Hay Meadow is on your right. If eagle watching, this is the place to train your telescope on Mount Lorette. The trail continues, back into the trees for the last straight leg to the powerline and access road.

Turn left. Arrive back at the parking lot.

B *Above: Troll Falls.*
Right: Golden eagle.
Right above: an immature.
Photos H. Barry Giles.

C Hay Meadow
Before Ribbon Creek coal mine became fully mechanized it operated on horse power. Ponies were sent to graze this large meadow, hence the name.

View from Hay Meadow of Skogan Pass, Mt. Lorette and the two pumphouses.

D The Way of the Eagle

Exciting news! Thanks largely to Peter Sherrington and Wayne Smith, the concept of golden eagle migration is changing. Ongoing observations show thousands of golden eagles make their way each spring up from the sun-baked south to their breeding grounds in Canada's north via Alberta's front ranges. Travelling 600 km per day in optimum conditions, it takes them less than a half hour to get from Highwood Junction to Mount Lorette. Using thermals, they soar to as much as 300 m above a peak top from where they're in a good position to down-glide to the next peak top. And so on, and all this travelling without even one flap or a meal. At dark they roost on the ridgetops, waiting for the sun to rise and speed them on their way.

When to come: March/April. Optimum time is near the end of March with over 1,000 sightings recorded in a single day. September/October, first half of November. Optimum time is the beginning of October.

Best time: early afternoon to 5 pm.

Best weather: sunny and warm with light to moderate winds.

Where to look: Catch them when they're crossing the Kananaskis Valley at its narrowest points i.e. Fisher Range to Mt. Lorette. On spring mornings, it's been observed that more birds use the Limestone Mountain to Mt. Kidd crossing. You might see 50 or more birds in a thermal at one time. The larger stronger females can often be seen waiting for their mates to play catch-up.

Kovach Pond
0.5 km

spring
summer
fall

Wheelchair accessible

An easy stroll around a beautiful pond which looks so natural it's hard to believe it used to be a gravel pit.

Start: Kananaskis Trail (Hwy. 40). Turn west onto the Nakiska Ski Area access road. After crossing Kananaskis River, turn left onto the access road to Kananaskis Village. At the 4-way junction turn left onto a narrower road which leads to Kovach Pond parking lot.

Take the trail that leads between the biffy and the wood pile to the lakeshore.

Turn left. The trail wanders past picnic tables to a bridge over a small creek feeding the pond. From the interpretive sign look west to Mt. Allan where the site of the coal mine is marked by a patch of bright green grass. Continue around the north shore which has a sandy beach at this point. Not far from the lake you'll find concrete foundations of Norman Holt's truckers' camp. Cross another bridge over the outlet.

Any left turn will return you to the parking lot.

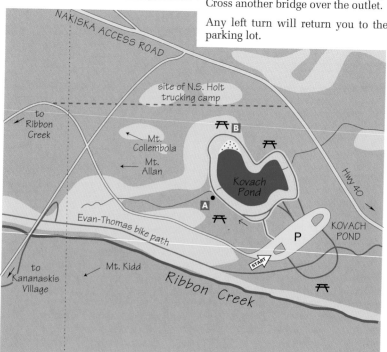

B Kovach who?

Joe Kovach was the Canmore District Forest Ranger and game warden between 1940 and 1953. He had to be versatile. In those days the district ranger fixed telephone lines between ranger stations, built cabins, supervised road construction and clearing for Hydro-electric schemes, kept trails open, captured escaped POW's, checked on logging operations in Ribbon Creek and at Kananaskis Lakes, kept predators, including eagles, to a low level (regrettably, it was the policy of the day), and counted wildlife. Incredibly, on May 21, 1947 he saw 4 black bears, 3 grizzlies, 29 sheep, 11 goats, 9 deer, 128 elk and one moose while driving between Kananaskis Lakes and Ribbon Creek. When elk and sheep overpopulated the valley he trucked them out to other areas. His great interest was his fish hatchery in Canmore which supplied trout to many a mountain stream and lake.

Photo: Joe Kovach collection.
Courtesy Kananaskis Country.

Mt. Kidd reflected in the pond.

How the Kootenay Group Formations ended up in this order on Mt. Allan

150 million years ago, you wouldn't have recognised this place, even had you evolved yet. In the late Jurassic and early Cretaceous periods, streams meandered freely through flood plains and swamps to the Fernie Sea, an epicontinental sea rather like today's Mediterranean. Waves beating for eon after eon against shorelines deposited sediment on the beaches, continually moving it up and down the coastline and mixing it up with mud brought down by the rivers which is why sandstone and mudstone of the same age are found in the same Morrissey Formation. Inland from the beaches, swamps were gradually filling in with sediment, the vegetation turning to peat and ultimately coal with a less than 1% sulphur concentration value indicating these were freshwater swamps cut off from the sea by dunes. Woody casts found in coal higher up the Mist Mountain Formation tell you that trees and bushes grew in the swamp's upper limits. What we now call the Elk Formation ranged from the upper limit of the swamps (hence some coal) to the upper limit of the alluvial plain where meandering rivers deposited silt, mud, shale and fine-grained sand. Braided streams with lots of gravel hardened into conglomerate peppered with chart and limestone fragments carried down from the mountains to the west. The Rock Garden high on Centennial Ridge used to be one of these rivers.

The interior ranges of British Columbia were already more or less there as a result of thrust faults coming from the west. On the plains to the east, the layers of sediment were turning into rock by compression. Meanwhile, the thrust sheets were moving eastward and by compression were piling up the Rocky Mountains over a period of a 150 million years. A few centimetres per year, the plain was being tipped on end, squeezed, folded over, broken by faults, and finally eroded into the shapes you are now looking at.

mine scar

Olympic summit

①*Elk Formation (shales, interbedded siltstones, mudstones, resistant sandstones and cliff-forming chert-pebble conglomerates). From the rockband below Olympic summit to the summit of Mt. Allan.*

②*Mist Mountain Formation (siltstones, mudstones, shales, non-marine sandstones and coal seams). The Ladies Downhill at Nakiska starts from the top of this Formation while the top of the Mens Downhill literally breaks through the Elk-Mist Mountain contact between cliff bands.*

③*Morrissey Formation (gray marine sandstones weathering to brown). These rocks making up the base are mostly tree-covered except for exposures in Marmot Creek.*

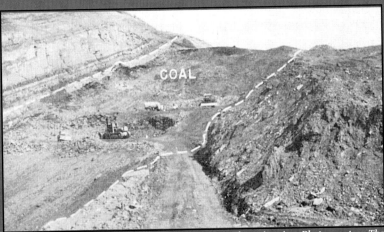

The strip mine. Photo courtesy The Research Council of Alberta.

A The Coal Mine at Mt. Allan

Martin Nordegg, after whom the town of Nordegg is named, started the prospecting craze in Ribbon Creek when he and Bogart Dowling of the Geological Survey made an exploratory dig into the side of Mt. Allan in 1907. Dowling reported 23 coal seams, 16 of which he deemed workable. Getting the coal to the CPR line was the main stumbling block for Nordegg and other individuals who had claims in the valley; no one could afford to finance a spur line, although Lionel Charlesworth went so far as to run a survey. World War I put paid to everyone's plans including Nordegg's. Come 1947, with a serviceable road running down the Kananaskis Valley, the transportation problems were solved and after another geological survey by M.B.B. Crockford and assistant Gordon Scruggs the Kananaskis Exploration and Development Company, a subsidiary of Brazeau Collieries, moved in. For one year they strip mined, then went underground following a rich seam of semi-anthra-

cite coal $34\frac{1}{2}$ feet thick in places. Ribbon Creek was a noisy place during these years, with trucks rumbling up and down the mine access roads and along Highway 40 for Ozada on the CPR line where briquettes were made at the tipples. After 5 years of frenzied activity the mine closed due mostly to increasing freight rates and slackening interest in the briquettes.

The adit has been filled in and the strip mine re-contoured, topsoiled and seeded.

Ribbon Creek Loop
6 km loop

late spring
summer
fall

A walk up scenic Ribbon Creek to the third bridge where you return along forest trails (more often used as cross country ski trails) to your starting point. Generally considered a fairly easy loop with one long steady uphill and corresponding downhill.

Start: Kananaskis Trail (Hwy. 40). Turn west onto Nakiska Ski Area access road. Turn left towards Kananaskis Village. Turn right at the 4-way junction before the bridge. Drive past Ribbon Creek Youth Hostel to Ribbon Creek parking lot at the end of the road.

Start from the coal carts and interpretive sign at the end of the parking lot.

Ribbon Creek trail heads into a meadow below the old quarry which is largely reclaimed. Note bridge remains on the creek bank dating back to logging days. Rocky outcrops mark the entrance to a deep valley where the trail winds below small cliffs, the boisterous river on your left enclosed by willow bushes. Ribbon Creek (Withkathka Waptan) means 'clear rapidly flowing creek, where light reflects on the rapids.'

Cross two bridges separated by a long stretch on the south bank.

A Walking through Time

The old quarry is an outcrop of Lower Triassic Spray River Formation, made up of darkish shales and thin beds of attractive brown siltstone used for facing fireplaces. From the quarry you walk another 400 metres and 50 million years forward into the Jurassic Period, the age of the dinosaurs. The rock belongs to the Fernie Formation, of which the Rock member, less than a metre thick, has yielded 38 species of molluscs. The ammonite *Yakounites (Seymourites) Mcevoyi* was collected here as far back as 1908 by James McEvoy. This same Rock member has yielded even greater treasures in Pigeon Creek to the north which has an abundance of the rare *Stemmatocerus Mclearni*.

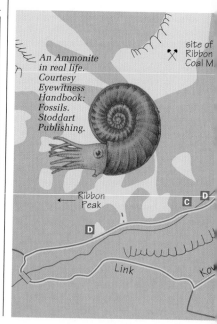

site of Ribbon Coal M.

An Ammonite in real life. Courtesy Eyewitness Handbook: Fossils. Stoddart Publishing.

← Ribbon Peak

C D

D

Link

Ko

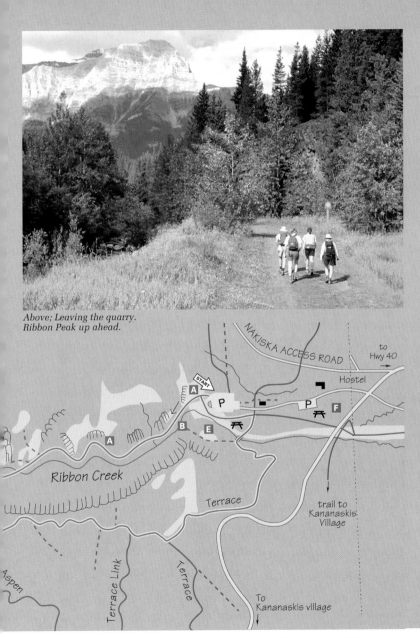

*Above; Leaving the quarry.
Ribbon Peak up ahead.*

B Logging

Logging has been going on at Ribbon Creek on a small scale since the late nineteen hundreds. By the 1930s and early 1940s the American based Eau Claire Lumber Company was firmly established in the Kananaskis Valley with one camp at Evan-Thomas Creek and two in Ribbon Creek. Most of this trail is theirs, the road continuing to the forks higher up the creek where the main camp consisted of two bunkhouses, office and maintenance shed. An interpretive sign and historic trash marks the spot. From here logging roads ran north up North Ribbon Creek as far as the canyon, and south up Ribbon Creek to Dipper Canyon where two more cabins, reduced to four logs high, now serve as a hiker's lunch spot.

D Yellow rattle
(Rhinanthus crista-galli)
In small clearings you'll find yellow rattles, a mint-like plant with yellow flowers. It's parasitic, which means it extracts ready-made food from the roots of other plants which explains the poor growth of surrounding grass and plants. Consequently, this plant is not transferable (along with the paintbrushes) into your garden unless you're willing to dig up an area 3 metres square. (I should tell you now before you even think of it that picking flowers, let alone digging them up is frowned upon in Kananaskis Country.) Seeds rattling around the capsule in a wind give the flower its name.

Left: the second bridge crossing. The mountain through the V is Ribbon Peak and not Mt. Bogart despite what the topo map prints. Mt. Bogart is the much higher peak behind which, in turn, is often mistaken for Mt. Assiniboine. You're in good company. Thomas Blakiston, en route through the foothills to the Kootenay Passes in 1858 made the same error. C

Back on the north bank, the trail enters Engelmann spruce forest with a new understory of horsetails, baneberry, and cow parsnip. Above the trees on the right are the grassy slopes of Mt. Allan.

Turn left onto Link ski trail. Descend and cross Ribbon Creek. A long steady climb through mossy spruce forest festooned with hair lichens brings you to a junction on the bank top.

Keep left. Now Kovach ski trail, the route is generally downhill. Buffaloberry bushes line the trail. Watch for the remains of a cabin.

Keep left. Pass Aspen and Aspen Link trails and some others which are overgrown.

Turn left. Now on Terrace Trail, you start a leisurely winding descent to Ribbon Creek. Before the bridge, explore the flat to the left which was once occupied by a line of shacks. Cross the bridge.

Turn left. A trail leads beside picnic tables to the parking lot.

OPTION

The last junction is the jumping off place for further exploration of the village of Kovach described on the next page. All this area, the parking lots, picnic areas, the hostel, Kovach Pond, was once the site of a coal mining community.

The three-seater biffy.

The Moley block.

E Who was Moley?

A few shacks lined the south bank of Ribbon Creek across from the present parking lot. Used by Calgary Power workers clearing the powerline right-of-way between Ribbon Creek and Kananaskis Lakes, they outlasted the village of Kovach by several years. Half hidden in trees is all kinds of interesting junk left lying around: piles of coal, indecipherable pieces of rusted metal, mounds of overlapping asphalt tiles which look like they might turn into rock formations within the next few million years, the usual can of Roger's golden syrup, pieces of shoes, recognizable remains of a shack painted red and a three-seater biffy in the woods. In front of a foundation hole filled with pieces of motor car is a badly cracked block of cement carved with the enigmatic words 'Moley Manor 1900 Aug'. Predating Calgary Power workers by several decades, who or what Mr. Moley was remains a mystery.

F A Town like Canmore?

The mining village of Kovach, known as 'Ribbon Crick' by locals, sprang up in 1948 and was supposedly a temporary arrangement until a permanent town could be built. As it happened the coal mine closed down in 1952. Which is why there isn't a town like Canmore with tourist facilities called 'Sparrowhawk Inn' or 'Ribbon Crick Trading Post' tastefully

Kovach, showing cottages for the truck drivers of N. S. Holt Trucking. Mechanic Art Rock is shown with his wife, child and parents. Photo Norman Holt, courtesy Kananaskis Country.

scattered through the trees between the highway and the parking lot. Some say the major log buildings — the bunkhouse, cookhouse, and office — were brought downstream from the lumber camp at the forks and re-sited where the far end parking lot and meadow is now. Further east in the area of the lower parking lot, picnic area and hostel, were neat rows of tar-paper shacks housing married workers. You could well be picnicking in someone's former dining room. Further east still, beyond the powerline, the truckers set up camp in the vicinity of the road junctions near to Kovach Pond. All the buildings disappeared by 1969. But you can still have fun delving in the bushes looking for concrete foundations and Rundle stone steps.

Kovach's one room schoolhouse, built in 1950, was ultimately taken over by the Youth Hostel Association who converted the rectangular building into an A frame. The current hostel was built just east of the spot.

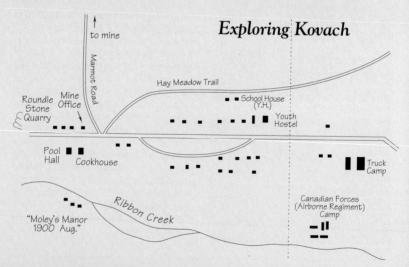

Exploring Kovach

to mine

Marmot Road

Hay Meadow Trail

Roundle Stone Quarry

Mine Office

School House (Y.H.)

Youth Hostel

Pool Hall

Cookhouse

Truck Camp

Ribbon Creek

Canadian Forces (Airborne Regiment) Camp

"Moley's Manor 1900 Aug."

Aspen Loop
5.8 km loop

late spring
summer
fall

A pleasant walk following XC ski trails through the varied forest near Kananaskis Village. Occasional damp meadows harbour some unusual plants and give wide-ranging views of the village and the Kananaskis Valley.

Start: Kananaskis Trail (Hwy. 40). Turn west onto the Nakiska Ski Area access road which crosses the Kananaskis River. Turn first left. Keep straight and cross the bridge over Ribbon Creek. The road winds uphill to Kananaskis Village. Turn second right and drive to road's end at the parking lot adjacent to Kananaskis Mountain Lodge.

Terrace Trail leaves from the west end of the parking lot.

At the 4-way junction go straight. Follow Terrace Trail north, within sound of traffic on the village access road.

Keep left (minor trail to right). Keep left (road to right leads to the staff residences). Turn left at the signpost. Terrace Link is an undulating trail which crosses several damp meadows growing willows, Dwarf birch and sundry orchids like hooded ladies tresses. Ahead is a grand view of Mt. Allan. A descent into spruce forest precedes the next junction.

Aspen trail looking towards the Olympic Summit of Mt. Allan.

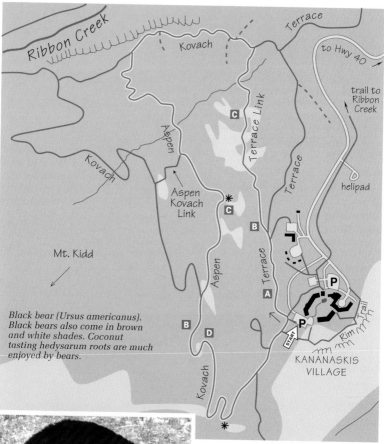

Black bear (Ursus americanus). Black bears also come in brown and white shades. Coconut tasting hedysarum roots are much enjoyed by bears.

▲ What is that black thing coming towards you?

Likely a Lab or Newfoundland dog. But you never know. Black bear warnings are occasionally posted for this loop. A bear doesn't see well so when it stands up on its hind legs it's just trying to figure out your smell. Generally, they run off when they discover you're a human. If not, back off slowly and don't on any account get between a sow and her cubs.

Late yellow locoweed
(*Oxytropis campestris*).

Yellow hedysarum
(*Hedysarum sulphurescens*).

B How to tell them apart

Trying to distinguish between yellow hedysarum and late yellow locoweed has many people confused. Hedysarum always looks droopy and has seeds looking like a string of one cent pieces, whereas the seeds of the locoweed look like small green beans.

C Hooded ladies tresses (right)

This is one of the best trails I know of to find *Spiranthes romanzoffiana* which flowers in late July/August in damp meadows. The slightly twisted spiral arrangement of flowers on the spike looks like braided hair, hence the name. The perfume is vanilla.

D Fringed grass of Parnassus
(Parnassia fimbriata)

At the tale end of the summer, both the regular and the more beautiful fringed grass of Parnassus are found growing near springs or on wet ground in the forest. Both can be identified by a single incredibly small leaf clasping the stem at the halfway point. Whereas *P. Palustris* has oval leaves, *P. Fimbriata* can be distinguished by kidney-shaped leaves and fringed petals. The 16th century name 'Gramen Parnassi' refers to Mt. Parnassus in Greece where the muses of mythology lived.

Turn left. Follow Kovach Trail uphill.

Keep right. Pass overgrown trails to left. Aspens are replaced by pines and buffaloberry bushes. Here and there are clumps of Twinflower.

Turn left at the signpost. Aspen Trail heads uphill.

Turn left (Aspen Link straight on). A lovely downhill stretch through aspens brings you to a flower meadow with bench and a view of Kananaskis Village—a good place for hooded ladies tresses and northern gentians. A little farther on two more meadows gives fine views of The Wedge. The damp meadow at the next junction has elephant heads, yellow rattles and a bench.

Turn left. Now on Kovach Trail (again), you switchback downhill across many meadows running with water where you'll find hundreds of fringed grass of Parnassus. At the third bend is a view of the valley.

Turn left onto Terrace Trail south. Keep straight (road to left leads to reservoir). Keep straight (trail to right is Rim trail). Pass the soccer field, picnic tables and a biffy.

Turn right at the 4-way junction. This leads you back to the parking lot.

Visit Woody's Pub for some Kanachos.

Terrace Rim Trail
4.5 km return

spring
summer
fall

This moderately hilly trail follows a terrace above the Kananaskis River. Although you can walk all the way to Galatea Creek, turn back around the 2 km point where there is a view of Kananaskis Country Golf Course and surrounding mountains.

Start: Kananaskis Trail (Hwy. 40). Turn west onto the Nakiska Ski Area access road. Turn first left. Keep straight and cross the bridge over Ribbon Creek. Wind uphill to Kananaskis Village. Turn second right and drive to road's end at the parking lot adjacent to Kananaskis Mountain Lodge.

Terrace Trail leaves from the west end of the parking lot.

At the 4-way junction turn left. The trail passes a picnic area, a biffy and the soccer field.

Keep right (Rim trail to left). Keep left (access road to reservoir to right). Go left at the signpost (Kovach Trail to right). The trail descends through woods of aspen and pine and is lined with flowers of the mixed forest: in mid summer—asters, harebells, golden rod, bedstraw, wild vetch, scarlet paintbrush, creamy hedysarum, late yellow locoweeds which are white, spirea and puccoon.

Kananaskis Village below Mt. Kidd.

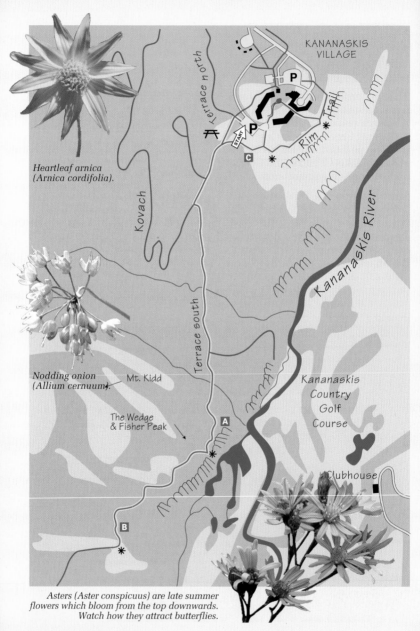

*Heartleaf arnica
(Arnica cordifolia).*

KANANASKIS
VILLAGE

Terrace north

Kovach

Terrace south

Mt. Kidd

*Nodding onion
(Allium cernuum).*

The Wedge
& Fisher Peak

Rim Trail

Kananaskis River

Kananaskis
Country
Golf
Course

Clubhouse

A

B

C

START

P

P

*Asters (Aster conspicuus) are late summer
flowers which bloom from the top downwards.
Watch how they attract butterflies.*

A The Terrace

Kananaskis Village is sited on a terrace for the view. Terrace hiking trail follows terraces all the way between Ribbon Creek and Galatea Creek. A terrace looks rather like the flat tread of a step above a steep riser and like stairs there can be more than one. Terraces can be formed in a variety of ways. In this case it started during the last Ice Age when ice blocked the valley's north end and backed up the Kananaskis River which was a lake at this spot. When the dam melted and normal flow resumed, the river was forced to cut a trench through thick deposits of accumulated gravel which filled the valley to the level of the terrace top, hence the steep face of the riser.

From the terrace a view over the largest beaver pond to the golf course and The Wedge.

Keep straight at the hiking sign (trail to left leads to Kananaskis Country Golf Course at the 15th hole, Mount Lorette course). At the low point in the aspens, you cross a bridge over a small creek, then climb to the edge of the terrace above a short steep drop to a string of beaver ponds. For the next few minutes there are several viewpoints for the golf course designed by Robert Trent Jones who called the location the finest he had ever had to work with. On the right are clumps of Late yellow locoweed which are blue!

Moving away from the edge, the trail undulates, finally settling into a long winding uphill. Just past a woody draw filed with Bracted lousewort you come to a meadow extending far above and below the trail—a good place to finish the walk. Look across the links to The Wedge and Fisher Peak at the head of Evan-Thomas Creek.

B *Bracted lousewort (Pedicularis bracteosa) with fern-like leaves.*

Wild blue flax
(Linum Lewisii).

The Herball or General
Historie of Plants 1597.

◧ This flower blooms just one day
The botanical name for wild blue flax *Linum Lewisii* comes from either the Greek word 'linon' or the celtic 'lin' meaning thread. Fibre spun from stalks is called linen which must be the oldest cloth on record, with fibres found among the remains of a prehistoric camp in Switzerland dating back some 10,000 years! In more recent times, linen clothed the pharaohs of ancient Egypt and was wrapped around the mummies. The seeds are rich in oil used in liniments and cough syrups, in making oilcloth and linoleum and as a drying agent for paints and varnishes.

Return the same way to the junction with Rim Trail.

Turn right onto Rim Trail. Keep right three times. The trail is lined with wild blue flax which was planted, although it does grow naturally here. Follow Rim Trail as it winds above grassy slopes with flowers met with previously plus gaillardia and small-flowered everlastings. A bench looks out across Boundary Flats.

Turn left off Rim Trail (trail straight on leads to the back of the main parking lot). Emerge between lodges into the village square giving access to the hotels, their shops and restaurants, and the Village Centre.

From the ornamental fountain, gain the trail on the left side of the pond which follows an artificial stream back to the parking lot.

Rim Trail below the hotels is
sown with the wild blue flax.

Picnic Island
1.3 km round trip

An easy stroll to an island in the Kananaskis River — a good place for a picnic. Sudden fluctuating water levels are a hazard.

Start: Kananaskis Trail (Hwy. 40) at Mount Kidd RV Park. Drive to the parking lot in front of the Campers Centre. As you can see from the map, the trail can be accessed from all the campground loops.

From the parking lot follow the left-hand trail starting between posts towards the Campers Centre. Almost immediately turn left. Walk across the lawn in front to the building to Loop D campground road.

Turn right. Follow the road.

Keep straight (trail to right leads to the pool). Turn next right onto a trail. Turn left at a 4-way junction. The trail threads between camp sites to a road.

Cross the road to Loop E. Cross two loop roads of area F. The trail continues, starting between sites #6 and #10 at an interpretive sign. Signed 'Mount Kidd Trail,' it descends the bank into spruce forest. A dark stretch precedes the bridge over an abandoned river channel. A short stretch between willows, then you cross another bridge onto treed Picnic Island.

A Alluvial fan

The high ground on the opposite bank is the end of an alluvial fan. The fan is built up of gravels, pebbles and rocks conveyed by the stream running off Mt. Kidd and has spread out from the mouth of the canyon in a fan shape. Here, the Kananaskis River has cut down through the fan exposing the deposition (see photo below).

Mt. Kidd and the alluvial fan from the north end of Picnic Island.

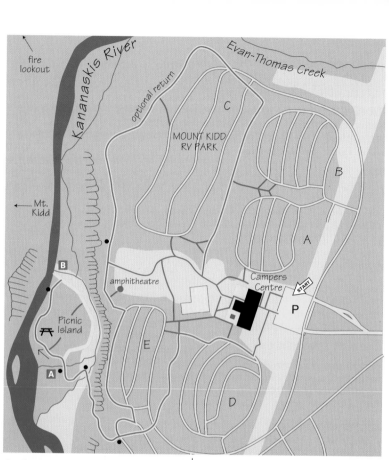

At the junction go left. Keep left (on right is cutoff trail to return loop). Walk past picnic tables overlooking the Kananaskis River.

Turn left. Arrive at a sand bar and a view of Mt. Lorette down river. Sudden fluctuating water levels dictated by dams make paddling dangerous.

Retrace your steps to the junction. Keep left. Complete the loop by walking alongside the abandoned channel. Forays onto the calcareous flat are worthwhile to search for bog orchids.

Turn left and return to Loop F road between campsites #8 and #10. Turn left. Walk around the road to the second bend.

Turn left onto a trail. Turn left onto a road. Between sites #31 and #29 turn left onto a trail. Keep left. Turn right (option is straight ahead). Walk up the long meadow past the amphitheatre.

Keep left. Keep right. Keep right near the tennis courts and horseshoe pits. Turn right. Turn left up the bank. Turn left. Enter the Campers Centre by the

The channel with Picnic Island to the right. Looking towards The Wedge.

door in the corner. You can easily spend another hour in the store, the snack bar and the whirlpools.

Leave by the front door. Jog right. Keep left and return to the parking lot.

OPTION At amphitheatre meadow keep straight past the interpretive sign (view of Mt. Kidd lookout) and follow the forest trail around C Loop and back between C and B/A Loops to the horseshoe pits. Add on 1.1 km.

B Caddis fly larva

You might not recognise the caddis fly larva. In the year before they metamorphose into flying insects, the larva protect themselves from predators by fitting themselves out with portable body cases. Using a glue-like substance secreted from salivary glands, they make cases from anything at hand: twigs, sand grains, small pebbles and, my favourite, pine needles which make the larva look like mini-porcupines. Each species makes a characteristic type of case and North America has 975 species. After pupating inside the case, the pupa crawls out of the water and undergoes a final moult to an adult. For one summer month before they die the moth-like insects enjoy a giddy night life, mating and laying eggs.

Kananaskis Valley – 119

Wedge Pond Loop
1 km loop

late spring
early summer
fall

An easy stroll around a fishing lake, reading interpretive signs.

Start: Kananaskis Trail (Hwy. 40) at Wedge Pond day-use area. For the purpose of this walk, the loop is accessed by a trail starting from the end of the parking lot near the second biffy.

A trail leaves the right-hand parking lot and arrives at a T junction.

Go left. Descend between picnic tables and past interpretive signs to the lake shore where you can make notes on mouth-watering fish recipes. At this point there's a grand view across the lake to the two summits of Mt. Kidd.

Opposite: Mt. Kidd from the east shore. Inset: Stuart Kidd (NA 2451-7 Glenbow Archives).

◪ Mt. Kidd
Stuart Kidd was storekeeper for the Leeson and Scott trading post at Morley 1907-11. He traded furs with the Stoneys and sold everyday supplies which the Stoneys often paid for in ponies which were promptly shipped off to Leeson and Scott's ranch in the Jumpingpound. During the four years he learned to speak Stoney fluently and in 1927 while working as a purchasing agent for Martin Nordegg in Nordegg was made honorary chief, Chief Tah-Osa meaning 'Moose Killer.'

◪ This pond is stocked
To spawn and lay eggs, trout need suitable spawning grounds like gravelly stream beds. And as you can see this lake doesn't have that. So every so often rainbow trout fingerlings are dumped into the water from specially designed tanks mounted on trucks. Their parents are brood stock, raised solely for egg production in brood stations. Eggs are collected, fertilized and sent to Calgary's Sam Livingstone Fish Hatchery to be incubated, hatched as 'sac fry' and reared on a commercial trout food.

▲ The pond

There was always a small pond here, a small turquoise jewel fed by springs and intermittent streams running off the slopes of The Wedge. Unsuitable for fish, it was nevertheless a haven for myriad water insects and amphibians and an important animal watering hole. Stoney Indians call it Chapta Mne 'Pine Lake' because it was` ringed by pine trees. And also Chase Tida Mne 'Burnt Timber Flats Lake' and Ta Mne Na Zen 'Moose Lake.' Contrary to what some people think the Stoneys have never known the lake to dry up. Nowadays, it's larger by almost a hectare, 12 metres deep in the middle and has an unappealing shoreline compared to the sedges and rushes of yesteryear. What happened is that 200,000 cubic metres of mud mixed with dead insects were removed in 33,000 dump truck loads to soil the neighbouring Kananaskis Country Golf Course. Its new depth makes it fish friendly.

Cross the boat launch road. Continue along the southeast shore in close knit pine forest. Pass a cutline to left before reaching the far end of the lake.

Keep right (old road to left). The trail climbs somewhat and traverses a grassy bank offering fine view of The Wedge across the lake. Re-enter pines with an understory of picnic tables where gourmet picnickers can try out the recipe opposite.

Keep left. Arrive back at the parking lot.

Trout Amandine

Sprinkle trout with salt, coarse ground pepper and thyme. Dip in milk, then flour. Place the trout in peanut oil which has been heating up in a frying pan. Fry to a golden brown on both sides. Drain the oil. Add 1/4 cup of butter and 1/2 cup of slivered almonds. Cook until almonds are brown. Remove trout to a platter, top with more almonds and sprinkle with chopped parsley.

*Recipe courtesy of
Kananaskis Country.*

Eau Claire
1.5 km loop

late Spring
summer
fall

An easy interpretive walk through the forest with one glorious view of Mt. Kidd and its unique geology. Learn about the Eau Claire logging company which had a camp in the vicinity around the 1880s.

Start: Kananaskis Trail (Hwy. 40) at Eau Claire Campground.

A Problem solving birds

No, it was not a bear that just went through your campsite while you went to the biffy but the Eau Claire ravens who are avid collectors of anything small, shiny and colourful left on the picnic table like Olympic pins. Experiments whereby lumps of meat were dangled off a string from a platform show their intelligence. Their cousins the crows failed miserably to get at the meat, but many ravens solved the problem by pulling up the string one bit at a time and anchoring it with their feet until the meat reached the platform.

B Istimabi Iyarhe

The south peak of Mt. Kidd is where the north end of the celebrated Lewis Thrust Fault (the crumpled zone) dies out into series of minor crenellations. The Stoney name, meaning 'where one slept mountain' describes a goat hunter who got stuck on the crenellations and benighted. His companions rescued him the next morning.

Istimabi Iyarhe: Mt. Kidd's south summit.

START

A

EAU CLAIRE CAMPGROUND

KANANASKIS TRAIL

Mt. Kidd

B 1

C

2

3

4

D

5

6

7

E

E

F

8

G

9

10

11

old river channel

Kananaskis River

40

C Pale sweetvetch (*Headysarum alpinum*).

G Old river channel filled with willow.

The Kanaskis River showing trees collapsing into the river from crumbling banks. In the distance is Mt. Kidd.

The trail leaves the campground road between campsites #48 and #49. Keep right. Straightaway there is an excellent view of Mt. Kidd's south summit. Willows and sedges tell you you're crossing the old river channel. Look for Douglas maples on the left.

From the first interpretive sign the trail follows the bank of the Kanaskis River past 2, 3 and 4 to a bench. Crumbling banks indicate the river is moving back east across the valley.

At 5 you leave the river and wind through pine forest cluttered with deadfall and burnt lumber. Tall purple larkspur grows in lighter areas. Pass interpretive signs 6, 7, 8 and 9.

At 10 is a view of the old river channel filled with willow bushes.

Keep right and arrive back at the trailhead.

◨ The name Eau Claire

In the 1880s Ottawa lawyer Kristoff McFee went to Eau Claire, Wisconsin, and interested the president of Eau Claire Logging in coming, Isaac Kerr, to look at the Kanaskis Valley. So started the Eau Claire and Bow River Lumber Company in 1884. The main Calgary mill was managed by Peter Prince on his island in the Bow River. The company office is today's 1886 Buffalo Cafe in the Eau Claire Market area.

One of the logging camps was located just downstream of this spot. As nowadays, loggers worked in winter, using horses to skid the logs onto the frozen river. In May at the start of the Spring runoff, the log drivers moved in and so began the two-month long log drive to the mill at two to five kilometres per day.

F Fire

The valley forest hasn't, until now, had a chance to mature for maybe hundreds of years. Fires have been the norm here, on average one every 21 years. That's why travel in the early days was such a chore. In fact the golf course flats are known to the Stoney Indians as Chase tida 'Burnt Timber Flats'. A tall story by Paul Amos blames it all on a Brave named Coyote. A group of Stonies was travelling up the valley en route to B.C. At the bottom of the pass, Coyote told everyone to go ahead; he would catch up with them after working some more on the trail. What he meant by this was evident on their return when they found the whole valley burnt to a cinder. Seriously, the last fire was the 1936 inferno, so the latest pines are around 60 years old. Tidbit: In the 1910s and 20s, fire notices were printed in English, German, Icelandic, Galician, Cree, Chipewyan, Norwegian, Russian, Hungarian, Hindu, Japanese and Chinese.

Tall larkspur/
(Delphinium glaucum)

George Pocaterra and Stoneys on the trail in 1910. (NA 695-20 Glenbow Archives).

E Tall larkspur

When A. O. Wheeler was surveying the Foothills in 1894-7, he noticed that settlers were very troubled over the high mortality rate of cattle. Professor Macoun was summoned and quickly traced the poisonings to this beautiful plant which contains several toxic alkaloids including delphinine.

The Rockwall Trail
0.5 km return

late spring
summer
fall

An easy loop trail leads to a viewpoint above a rock band overlooking Rockwall Lake and the Opal Range. Bring binoculars.

Start: Kananaskis Lakes Trail. Park at the Visitor Centre.

The trail leaves the Visitor Centre parking lot near the telephone and descends past the front porch of the Visitor Centre. It continues by the side of the road, then turns right and winds downhill around a fence to a junction.

Go right on the paved trail. To your right is a big meadow which after snow melt in Spring is a lake. Amazingly enough, the logs and branches at the side of the meadow are driftwood! A short walk through pines brings you round to a viewpoint with bench and interpretive signs. From the top of the rockwall, look down on Rockwall Lake and across to the Opal Range, specifically Mt. Wintour, Elpoca Mountain (an amalgamation of Elbow and Pocaterra) and Gap Mountain. Continue along the trail and descend a short hill.

Keep left where the ski trail comes in.

Turn right and return the same way. En route back to the parking lot visit the Visitor Centre which offers you touch button displays, slides and movies. A comfortable lounge looks out over the big meadow.

Looking across Rockwall Lake to Elpoca Mountain and Gap Mountain,

A Flatirons

The west flank of Mt. Wintour is a pattern of triangular-shaped ridges called flatirons which is another word for the household iron. What happened here is that the harder rock of the spurs were left behind after softer rocks between were eroded away.

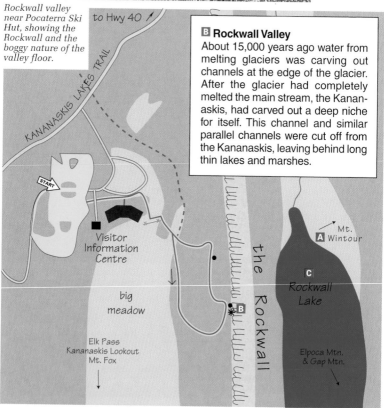

Credits opposite: Sora rail, belted kingfisher and Richardson's vole from "Birds and Animals in The Rockies", Kerry Wood.

Long-toed salamander courtesy "Amphibians and Reptiles of Alberta", University of Calgary Press.

Rockwall valley near Pocaterra Ski Hut, showing the Rockwall and the boggy nature of the valley floor.

to Hwy 40

KANANASKIS LAKES TRAIL

START

Visitor Information Centre

big meadow

Elk Pass
Kananaskis Lookout
Mt. Fox

the Rockwall

Mt. Wintour **A**

C
Rockwall Lake

Elpoca Mtn. & Gap Mtn.

B **Rockwall Valley**

About 15,000 years ago water from melting glaciers was carving out channels at the edge of the glacier. After the glacier had completely melted the main stream, the Kananaskis, had carved out a deep niche for itself. This channel and similar parallel channels were cut off from the Kananaskis, leaving behind long thin lakes and marshes.

◧ Some Valley Inhabitants

Although you're high above the lake, take it from me, having paddled in from Pocaterra Trail, that all along this sinuous boggy valley is a wealth of interesting fauna as noted by park naturalists:

Sora rails *(Porzana carolina)* nest and feed in the area. A Spring migrant, it is rarely seen though you may hear its loud distinctive voice "ah-WIP, ah-WIP, ah-WIP" followed by a high pitched laugh which trails off. It nests in bulrushes and walks along mud flats looking for snails, aquatic insects and seeds.

Belted kingfishers *(Ceryle alcyon)* can often be spotted on dead trees in standing water, ready to dive headfirst into the water after fish. The parents teach the young to hunt by dropping a fish into the water for them. The scientific name refers to Queen Alcyone in Greek mythology who jumped into the sea after learning of her husband's death in a shipwreck. The Gods took pity and turned them both into kingfishers, as a bonus stilling the winds for 2 weeks so they could build a floating nest of fish bones. Ever since a spell of fine calm weather is known as (h)alcyon days.

Long-toed salamanders *(Ambystoma macrodactylum)* are a smart black colour with a gold stripe down the back. You can only see them at night with the aid of a flashlight. Any salamander lucky enough to survive a year from predators overwinters by burrowing into the mud.

Richardson's (water) voles *(Arvicola richardsoni)* reach an incredible length of about 80 cm including the tail! They spend time swimming in the pond or stream, eating wild flowers and digging tunnels called runs. The ridge of soil over the top of their runs is a dead giveaway for inquiring humans and their predators which include coyotes.

Kananaskis River Canyon
1.2 km loop

late spring
summer
fall

A moderately easy loop with lots of steps to witness a sad travesty of the Kananaskis River.

Start: Kananaskis Lakes Trail. Turn right onto the access road leading to Canyon Dam and Canyon Campground. Turn first right into the campground. Pass Loop A on the right. Pass Loop B on the left, then immediately park on the right side near the registration box.

Walk further to the obvious trailhead on the left side of the road before the bend. Come to a junction.

Turn right. Walk through pine forest (One-flowered wintergreens between interpretive signs 2 and 3), then descend the bank to the 'Kananaskis River' at number 4 interpretive sign. A bench overlooks a pool below the falls.

Cross the river by a bridge, the second one. After climbing to the bank top, you hug the canyon rim which is safety-fenced. On your right a dripping pipe, looking like a giant worm from the planet Dune, carries the Kananaskis River to Pocaterra Power Plant.

🅱 Pronounced KAN-AN-ASK-IS

The river in the pipe was named in 1858 by explorer John Palliser after an Indian "of whom there is a legend, giving an account of his most wonderful recovery from the blow of an axe which had stunned but had failed to kill him." This event is supposed to have taken place on the flats where the Kananaskis Country Golf Course is now but nobody knows for sure. Possibly, the Indian in question was the great Cree Koominakoos who lost an eye and part of his scalp in a battle with the Blackfoot in the Willow Creek area but made a miraculous recovery and showed up at Fort Edmonton some weeks later "ready to take to the warpath again." Palliser would almost certainly have heard of his legendary exploits. Whatever, his name was unpronounceable to other tongues and over time the English derivation has been spelt Kannenaskis, Kananaski, Kanasaki, Kananaski's, Kananaskasis, Kannanaskis and Kinnonaskis. Kananaskis Village Chronicles suggests Can-uN-Ask-Us, while a wag at POW Camp #130 called it Kan-a-Nazi. The Indians knew it as 'Lake River,' 'Spirit River,' 'Life-giving waters,' 'tributary of the Cold Water River,' 'Y-shaped fork lake river,' the Y referring to the shape between the Kananaskis River and the Bow River at their confluence.

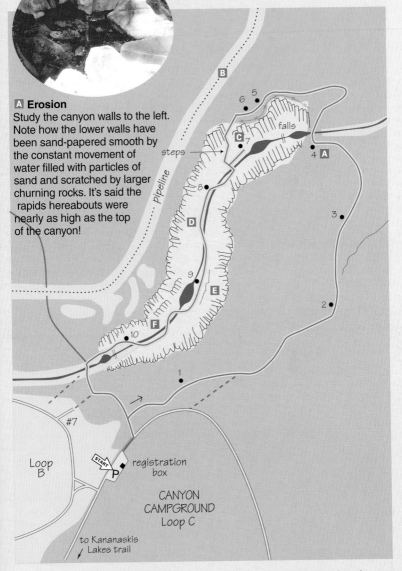

The eroded former bed of the Kananaskis River.

A Erosion

Study the canyon walls to the left. Note how the lower walls have been sand-papered smooth by the constant movement of water filled with particles of sand and scratched by larger churning rocks. It's said the rapids hereabouts were nearly as high as the top of the canyon!

steps

pipeline

falls

Loop B

START

P

registration box

CANYON CAMPGROUND Loop C

to Kananaskis Lakes trail

#7

The steps into the canyon and the second bridge.

D Wild gooseberry *(Ribes oxya-canthoides)* and red-stemmed wild raspberry *(Rubus idaeus* below) are similar to garden varieties.

C *Bladder fern (Cystopteris fragilis).*

Just past interpretive sign 6, the trail makes a spectacular descent down steps into the floor of the canyon. Ferns, saxifrage, ragworts and gooseberries growing in crevices can be examined in close-up. At the bottom, an offshoot to left leads to interpretive sign 7 overlooking the dark sunless pool above the falls.

Cross the creek six more times to the end of the canyon. En route watch for berry bushes on the right slope. At interpretive sign 9 is a bench overlooking Dipper Pool where you're almost sure to see a pair of American dippers flying between the pool and a small waterfall near the end of the canyon.

At the 3-way junction by the 8th bridge turn left. Your trail crosses the river.

Keep left twice (unofficial trails to right are campers' short-cut to Loop B). Climb uphill to a junction.

Keep right. In a few minutes you're back at the trailhead in sight of your car.

F Not skinny Dippers
(Cinclus mexicanus)
Dippers are the plump grey birds with stumpy tails that can't stand still. They're either bobbing up and down on rocks, or flying up and down the creek, or diving and swimming underwater after invertebrates, snails and small fishes. Underwater adaptations: oversized oil glands to keep their feathers waterproof, transparent eyelids to see through under water, flaps to cover their nostrils. Year-round residents, they nest close to water, preferably in the spray of a waterfall.

Chara

E Algae
The creek is merely seepage from Canyon Dam (as you know, the real Kananaskis River is in the pipe). Because the water is so slow moving it deposits fine particles of sand which allow algae to grow, especially in small pools. The slimy looking green strands waving in the current are *Rhizoclonium*, the shorter lime green tufts growing on the bottom are *Chara*.

Marl Lake
3.6 km return

late spring
summer
fall

Easy walking along a paved interpretive trail leads through pine forest and past occasional fens to a pale green lake with a spectacular mountain backdrop. Apart from waterfowl, you may be lucky enough to spot moose and other ungulates. Peruse the notice board at the trailhead to see when Park interpreters are scheduling the next bird viewing walk.

Start: Kananaskis Lakes Trail at Elkwood parking lot.

Also accessible from Elkwood Campground: D Loop between sites #114 and #115, C Loop between sites #78 and #79. The trail also crosses Loop B campground road between sites #52 and #53, and #45 and #46. From A Loop a trail between sites # 14 and #15 leads to the trail.

From the trailhead the trail curves past the amphitheatre on your left.

*Keep straight. Turn left (*trail straight ahead leads to main campground access road).

Turn left (trail to right leads to Loop B). Wind through a mossy forest of fir, spruce and pines.

Cross Loop B campground road. The trail continues to the right of the biffies.

Again cross Loop B campground road. Keep left twice (to right are trails to C and D Loops). Arrive at a trail sign, signalling the proper trailhead to Marl Lake trail beyond all campground accesses. Walk past a fen on the left where the chance of spotting a great blue heron with a Park interpreter is 100%.

A The lovable Whiskey-jack
(Perisoreus canadensis)
As soon as you stop for a bite to eat, a family of whisky-jacks arrives on silent wings to grab a piece of it. Programmed to scavenge on fresh kills from large animals, it now treats us humans as just another large animal with sandwiches. The genus name is Greek for 'to heap up.'. "Its capacity to stow away food is unbelievable" wrote Agamak in the American Field magazine of 1890. To keep it going all winter, balls of chewed food are pasted onto trees with a fluid secreted by specific glands in the mouth.

The popular name of the grey jay comes from the Cree 'wiskatjon'. Its also called Hudson Bay bird, grease bird, moose bird, caribou bird, meat bird, camp robber.

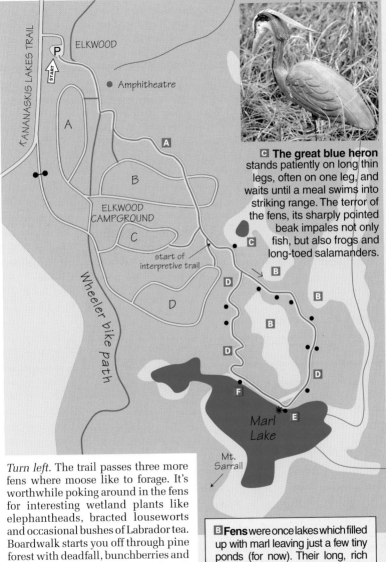

C The great blue heron stands patiently on long thin legs, often on one leg, and waits until a meal swims into striking range. The terror of the fens, its sharply pointed beak impales not only fish, but also frogs and long-toed salamanders.

KANANASKIS LAKES TRAIL

ELKWOOD

P

START

● Amphitheatre

A

B

ELKWOOD CAMPGROUND

C

start of interpretive trail

D

Wheeler bike path

A

B

C

D

D

B

B

B

D

F

E

Marl Lake

Mt. Sarrail

Turn left. The trail passes three more fens where moose like to forage. It's worthwhile poking around in the fens for interesting wetland plants like elephantheads, bracted louseworts and occasional bushes of Labrador tea. Boardwalk starts you off through pine forest with deadfall, bunchberries and a series of interpretive signs. A bench signals your first glimpse of Marl Lake.

B Fens were once lakes which filled up with marl leaving just a few tiny ponds (for now). Their long, rich grasses provide forage for elk, moose and deer all year round.

Marl Lake looking west. Left to right: Mt. Aosta in Elk Lakes Provincial Park, Mt. Fox above Elk Pass, The Turret, Mt. Foch and Mt. Sarrail.

Turn left. Descend to the lakeshore at the platform, a superb viewpoint for mountains and waterfowl. Walk further along the shore fringed with Camas lilies, then at the bench turn back into pine forest.

Keep left. The trail climbs over a pine ridge, then skirts the largest fen.

Turn left onto the two-way trail.

Return the same way you came.

F Marl looks like sand

Streams flowing into the lake dissolve the calcium from limestone in passing and carry it into the lake. Because the lake is shallow and relatively warm it encourages the growth of algae which uses water to produce food. Algae doesn't much like the calcium and releases it back into the water as a greyish coloured powder which settles all over the lake bed. Eventually the whole lake will fill up with marl and become a fen, and finally a meadow.

E Leeches

Each end of these little suckers is a sucker, the posterior one being greater than the anterior one which has a mouth. Food is blood which is stored in digestive pouches in the centre of the body. Leeches attach themselves to their victim by the posterior sucker, then apply the anterior sucker to the skin and make a wound with the aid of little jaws inside the mouth. When it's had its fill, it drops off. While taking the meal, salivary glands manufacture a substance called 'hirudin' which prevents coagulation of blood not only in the victim/patient but also in the leech itself throughout the weeks and months during which the blood is stored and slowly digested. Incredibly, a leech can store up to 10 times its body weight.

D A Bunch of Bunchberries

Cornus canadensis is actually one shrub, the 'individual plants' being branches off a rhizome buried below the ground. Nor are the flowers white, but the incredibly tiny green things clustered in the centre of the white bracts. Normally the flowers remain closed. When an insect or human finger touches the trigger, a tiny spike attached to one of the petals, the flowers spring open, sending a cloud of pollen into the air. The red berries of fall are edible though the hard seed at centre makes them difficult to eat.

Boulton Creek
3 km loop

late spring
summer
fall

A fairly easy forest walk which loops along a scenic bench top and returns alongside Boulton Creek. Numbered posts refer to the interpretive brochure.

Start: Kananaskis Lakes Trail at Boulton Bridge day-use area and parking lot.

From the trail sign, cross the bridge over Boulton Creek and climb the bank to the old cabin.

Turn right at the T-junction. The trail winds and climbs past interpretive sign 1 to the outskirts of Baseball Diamond Meadow where you can often see deer.

B 8,000 years ago
8,000 years ago Baseball Diamond Meadow, and no doubt other open areas above the bank, near #3 interpretive sign for example, was a work area for neolithic Indians of the Mummy Cave Complex who lived and hunted near the lakes as long ago as 5,500 BC. These people produced spear points and tools as evidenced by rock flakes found at this spot.

© Marj Kujat

A Boulton Cabin If this Fish & Wildlife cabin had remained where it was built it would now lie submerged in the waters of Lower Kananaskis Reservoir, somewhere below Lower Lake campground. Its garage was also relocated. You'll pass it on the right if you take the left-hand trail at the T-junction to Boulton Creek Trading Post.

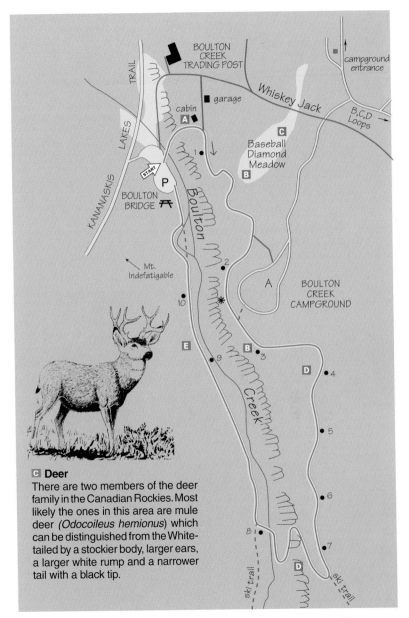

BOULTON
CREEK
TRADING POST

Whiskey Jack

campground
entrance

B.C.D
Loops

TRAIL

LAKES

KANANASKIS

garage

cabin

A

START

P

BOULTON
BRIDGE

1

Baseball
Diamond
Meadow

C

B

Boulton

Mt.
Indefatigable

2

10

*

A

BOULTON
CREEK
CAMPGROUND

E

9

B 3

D 4

Creek

5

6

8

7

D

ski trail

ski trail

C Deer

There are two members of the deer family in the Canadian Rockies. Most likely the ones in this area are mule deer *(Odocoileus hemionus)* which can be distinguished from the White-tailed by a stockier body, larger ears, a larger white rump and a narrower tail with a black tip.

Photo Dave Elphinstone.

In the willows bordering the creek watch for willow flycatchers, thrushes and orange-crowned/wilson's/ yellow-rumped warblers.

E Black-capped chicadee
(Parus atricapillus)

One bird you're almost sure to see and hear is the black-capped chicadee. Listen for 'chicka dee-dee-dee', or the dee dees without the chicka. This small rolly-polly bird with a disproportionately large black head is usually seen upside down picking bugs off the underside of branches. It's quite tolerant to humans who can approach quite closely to get photos. During courtship the male often feeds the female who "shivers her wings like a baby bird". Though appearing a fragile ball of feathers, the chicadee is one tough bird which overwinters in Kananaskis Country, living on a diet of spiders. The also common mountain chickadee has a white eyebrow stripe.

Boulton Creek.

D **What are those large green leaves** on the forest floor? They are not a plant but an algae and a fungus which has gone through the process of lichenization to become a lichen. For growth, the genus *peltigera* depends on rain which is soaked up like a sponge. They don't die during a long dry spell but merely stay dormant until the next soaking. Studded leather lichen *(Peltigera aphthose)*, the top photo below, is a bright green colour, especially when wet and is one reason to hike this trail in the rain. The tiny dark brown 'studs' on the surface are colonies of algae. The greyer lichen is dog-ear lichen *(Peltigera canina)*, named after the dark brown fruiting bodies which look like dogs' ears pricked. In medieval Europe nibbling the lobes was supposed to be a cure for rabies.

Golden-crowned kinglet (Regulus satrapa), a bird of the coniferous forest. Photo Dave Elphinstone.

Keep right (trail to left leads to #3 campsite on A loop of Boulton Creek Campground). Continue climbing past interpretive sign 2 where you're now on the edge of a steep bank above Boulton Creek, looking across at Mt. Indefatigable.

Keep right (Moraine ski trail to left leads to A loop). Past 3, the trail climbs away from the creek, winding and undulating through mixed forest past posts 4, 5, 6, and 7.

Turn right (Moraine ski trail straight on). Switchback down the bank to Boulton Creek and cross.

Turn right at interpretive sign 8 (Boulton Creek ski trail to left). The trail follows the valley of Boulton Creek past signs 9 and 10, coming close to the creek on a couple of occasions. There's a really good patch of One-sided wintergreens halfway between the first river access and interpretive sign 9.

After sign 10, the hiking trail stays left of an oxbow-like lake/beaver pond, probably formed during the glacial retreat. Enter the south end of the parking lot shortly after.

Rawson Lake
7.8 km return

late spring
summer
fall

After a stretch along the south shore of Upper Kananaskis Lake, the trail climbs moderately steeply (height gain 320 m) to a green lake under Mt. Sarrail. Bring your fishing tackle.

Start: Kananaskis Lakes Trail at Upper Lake parking lot. When you turn off Kananaskis Lakes Trail, stay left, keep right, turn right. At the T junction turn left and drive to the far end of the parking lot.

The trailhead is located at the south end of the parking lot. From here Upper Lake Trail sets out along the south shore of Upper Kananaskis Lake, undulating in and out of every little indentation of the shoreline.

At a larger indentation than usual you cross the bridge over Sarrail Creek below the falls.

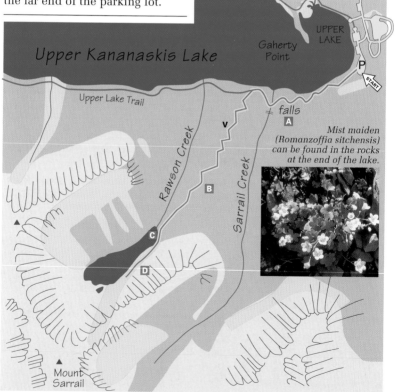

Mist maiden (Romanzoffia sitchensis) can be found in the rocks at the end of the lake.

Around the corner turn left. The Rawson Lake Trail switchbacks through spruce forest, eventually levelling off just before reaching Rawson Creek near the outlet. Continue following the trail to the east shore of the jade green lake where meadows make good lunch spots.

If you come here early in the season just before the grass is greening you'll be in time to see the snow-melt flowers. Blooming in damp ground below melting snow banks and even inside the snowbanks are spring's first flowers of the alpine meadows.

Return the same way.

A *Sarrail Falls.*

C **Rawson Lake is named after** Dr. D.S. Rawson, a world famous limnologist who studied the physical, chemical, meteorological and biological conditions in freshwater lakes, mostly in regard to fish stocking. In 1936 and again in 1947 Rawson had a look at both Kananaskis Lakes at the urging of the Calgary Fish and Game Association. Remarkably, fish stocking in the upper lake goes back to 1914 when Cutthroat were introduced quite successfully into its "deeper, colder, murkier" waters. Possibly this was George Edworthy who carried up thousands of minnows and fingerling trout and dropped them in, never knowing if they survived. Regular Rainbow planting began in 1935. Currently, the lake receives about 20,000. Why stock at all? Ever since it became a reservoir, fluctuating water levels hinder the establishment of aquatic plants which hinder the establishment of aquatic insects which the young fish need to survive.

Mt. Sarrail above Rawson Lake.

B Old Forests

There is no mistaking the old forests. The air feels cool and humid and there's this indefinable aroma of decaying humus. The trees are mainly spruce which have grown up in the shade of aspens and pines when the forest was younger (see photo opposite). And on the forest floor is layer upon layer of rotting plant debris. A peaty mossy layer holding moisture creates a microclimate all of its own, growing thick mats of mosses, lichens, fungi, wintergreens and orchids. If not interfered with, this state of affairs can last for several centuries before the next stage in the life of a forest.

White globeflower (Trollius albiflorus).

Snow buttercup (Ranunculus eschscholtzii).

D *Snow-melt Flowers*

White globeflower This is a handsome plant, easily distinguished from anemones by its lush bright green foliage. Like anemones, the petals are actually 5-8 sepals coloured cream with a distinctive inner fringe of bright yellow stamens. When the flowers are partly closed they look like small round balls. Gardeners know it as trollius.

Alpine or snow buttercup The most beautiful buttercup to my mind. Only a few centimetres tall, the whole plant looks like it's been dipped in lacquer. Shiny bright green leaves are deeply toothed and 5 yellow petals—huge in comparison to the rest of the plant—have this glossy surface which comes from an oily substance in outer epidermal cells. The generic name *Ranunculus* means 'little frog' and reflects the entire family's love for damp habitats.

Upper Kanananaskis Lake
3.6 km one way

late spring
summer
fall

An easy stroll along the east shore of Upper Kananaskis Lake provides superb views of the mountains to the west. Failing a car at each end of the trail, return the same way.

Start: Kananaskis Lakes Trail at Upper Lake parking lot. When you turn off Kananaskis Lakes Trail, keep left, keep right, turn right. At the T-junction turn right and park in the far parking lot.

From the north end of the parking lot a trail crosses a bridge, then heads past interpretive signs to the boat launch road.

Upper Kananaskis Lake showing Upper Lake Dam below Mt. Indefatigable.

Cross the road. At the trail sign, the trail continues, heading out along the top of Upper Lake dam. On your right, where once the boisterous Kananaskis River flowed over Twin Falls is a grassy bank, and a view of White Spruce parking lot, and the channelled seepage between the two lakes.

At the far end of the dam, keep left. The trail winds around a bay, well inland of Gaherty's Point.

Keep right on the main trail.

> OPTION The rough trail to left leads to Gaherty's Point fireplace (a bit of Kananaskis history).

▣ George Pocaterra

Pocaterra was adamantly opposed to the hydroelectric scheme at Kananaskis Lakes but this was in the days before Greenpeace and environmental reports, so he and Patterson had to be content with writing commiserating letters to each other. Pocaterra Creek, Pocaterra Ski Hut/parking lot, and Elpoca Mountain are just some of the places named after him. That a dam and power plant should be included in the long list is ironic.

Pocaterra in 1911.
(NA 695-1 Glenbow Archives).

Son of the Mountains

What a life! Born an Italian count, George Pocaterra came to Canada in 1903 as an upper-class remittance man with $3.75 in his pocket. After working at various ranches he established the Buffalo Head Ranch, one of the first dude ranches in Canada and it was here where he met the Stoneys who were semi-nomadic at that time. He became blood brother to Paul Amos and for over 50 years hunted and travelled with him to places where no white man had ever been before. In 1933 he sold the ranch to author/adventurer R. M. Patterson and returned to Italy on family matters where he met and married Calgary opera singer Norma Piper. The idea was for him to manage her brilliant career in Europe but that dream died with World War II and they escaped back to Canada, first to Patterson's old cabin on the Ghost River, and finally to Calgary where Norma taught singing and George continued his involvement with coal mining schemes.

"Upper Kananaskis Lake"
by George Pocaterra

Carry me back
To Kananaskis shores
Its magic waters
And its changing moods
Majestic Mountains
And foaming waterfalls
Enfolded softly
By mystic woods!

There's where I laid
A-gazing and wondering
My soul deeply stirred
By a longing so great!
It was joy and yet pain
The craving to fathom
The innermost meaning
Of such beauty revealed.

Heart of the wilds
Yet friendly its nature
By its visible glory
So fondly providing
A much needed medium
To all who are striving
To an all-satisfying
Spiritual Beyond!

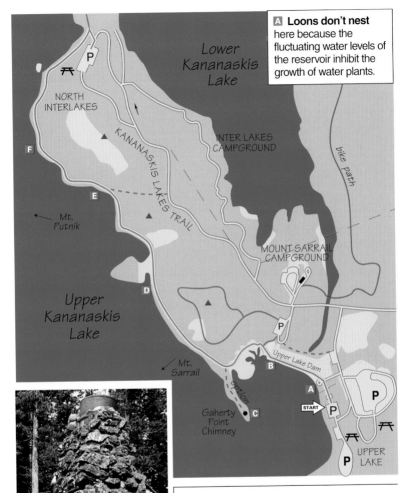

A **Loons don't nest** here because the fluctuating water levels of the reservoir inhibit the growth of water plants.

Lower Kananaskis Lake

NORTH INTERLAKES

P

KANANASKIS LAKES TRAIL

INTER LAKES CAMPGROUND

bike path

← Mt. Putnik

F

E

D

Upper Kananaskis Lake

← Mt. Sarrail

MOUNT SARRAIL CAMPGROUND

P

Upper Lake Dam

B

A

START

P

P

option

Gaherty Point Chimney

C

UPPER LAKE

P

C **Gaherty's Point**

A fireplace is all that's left of a large log cabin built for the president of Calgary Power, Geoffry A. Gaherty, as a honeymoon suite. This was in 1933 before the earth dam raised water levels. Tourists of the time were mainly Calgary Power workers, their friends and relatives who made up fishing parties.

Peter Lougheed Park – 147

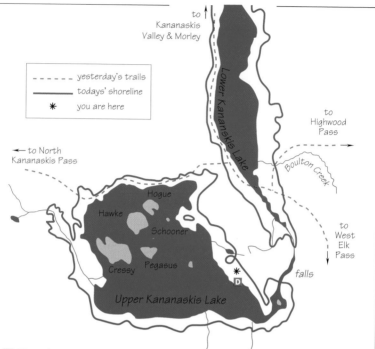

D Changing routes and shorelines

Before dams, the country looked very different. The lakes were smaller by a third, the water divided into bays by peninsulas and islands so thickly forested they resembled black bristle tops. All the islands—Hogue, Cressy, Pegasus, Schooner, and two nameless islets—are under water with the exception of the tip of Hawke which sports a few larches. All the other rocky islets you see are the tips of former peninsulas.

Indian trails took a completely different tack to today's roads. The trail up Kananaskis Valley, for instance, came in along the *west* side of Lower Lake (the east shore was deemed too swampy), then divided near Inter-lakes campground. Here, one trail forded the river close to Lower Lake where it was relatively shallow and passable by horses, then divided on the east bank with one trail heading south over West Elk Pass to Elk Valley (great hunting), and another climbing the line of Packers ski trail to Highwood Pass and Elbow Lake. From the vicinity of Interlakes Power Plant, yet another climbed to the upper lake, then carried on over North Kananaskis Pass into the Palliser River. Until driven back by the Stonies who were relatively new on the scene, the Kootenai came over the two passes to canoe around the islands and hunt elk.

Upper Kananaskis Lake pre dams, showing Schooner Island at centre. Photo: Whyte Museum of the Canadian Rockies.

The main trail follows the east shoreline beneath the Canadian Mount Everest Expedition Interpretive Trail. Below the trail are crags guarding gravel beaches which makes access to the water difficult. Later on, the trail descends to lake level and you pass a peninsula with bays on either side. At high water levels the meadow floods, covering up unsightly stumps and making an island of spruce trees.

Keep left (old road to right leads through to Kananaskis Lakes Trail). The trail runs below another hill. Directly west lay Schooner Island which if it still existed would be right up there with Spirit Island on Maligne Lake as front cover material for calendars. Opposite an islet, the trail turns right into a large bay and ends at a trail sign overlooking Lower Kananaskis Lakes (see contents page).

Turn right. Walk up to North Interlakes parking lot.

E The High Price of Power

Turning Kananaskis Lakes into reservoirs began in 1914 when M.C. Hendry of the Water Power Branch submitted a report assessing their storage possibilities. He had personal reservations about the scheme and hoped the beauty of the (upper) lake would not be lost sight of. Nothing happened until 1930 when Calgary Power began work on a hand-hewn spillway designed to raise water levels in Upper Lake. It was a rather primitive log structure which relied on two logs being pulled out at intervals to control the flow. Two projects, one in 1936 when a channel was cut through the centre of the riverbed between the lakes almost to the top of Twin Falls, and the other in 1942 when the dam was further raised to increase storage to 100,000 acre feet, "sounded the death knell for the islands and the wild-flowing river in between".

E The Legend of Schooner Island

When the wind blows strongly from the west, it's easy to imagine the incoming waves, foaming at the crest, as white horses. Perhaps this is the basis for the following story from the Stoneys:

There was this person named Gapeya who, due to his cowardice, lost many horses which went charging off across the water to the small island with few trees. A man with a vision of horses told the others, "I want one person who is brave, without fear, to accompany me. It has to be this type of person to accompany me in order to capture this many horses." The Kootenays had heard this declaration and were coming from over the mountains from the west, but before they got there the same cowardly Gapeya volunteered, "I'll be the one. I'll be the one." In due course, the horses came charging towards them. "In the lead was a grey. As he galloped closer there flashed a weird light from his eyes and as he whinnied and opened his jaws there burst out flames." As you can guess the sight was too much for Gapeya who fell back to the shore crying "Ki Kiha" "look out Kiha" while an audience watching them from a distance groaned with disappointment for there were many good pintos among the herd. The horses galloped around the man with a vision who was standing chest deep in the water and returned to the island where they kept shaking themselves all over.

Canadian Mt. Everest Expedition Trail
2.3 km loop

late spring
summer
fall

Despite the name, this is a moderate uphill walk past interpretive exhibits to a hilltop with spectacular views over both Kananaskis Lakes.

Start: Kananaskis Lakes Trail at White Spruce parking lot.

Keep right (trail to left leads to the dam and Upper Lake trail). Plunging into spruce forest, the undulating trail winds past three interpretive signs telling you about the laying down of rocks and the mountain building process.

Keep right. The understory is changing to menziesia bushes and feather mosses on damper ground. Look for greenish-flowered wintergreens and common pink wintergreens, particularly around the junction area.

B Why Mount Everest?

In case you're wondering about the strange name, Interlakes Trail was renamed the Canadian Mount Everest Expedition Trail in 1984 to honour the successful Canadian expedition of 1982 led by Bill March which put two men on the summit.

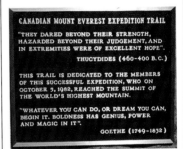

CANADIAN MOUNT EVEREST EXPEDITION TRAIL

"THEY DARED BEYOND THEIR STRENGTH, HAZARDED BEYOND THEIR JUDGEMENT, AND IN EXTREMITIES WERE OF EXCELLENT HOPE".

THUCYDIDES (460-400 B.C.)

THIS TRAIL IS DEDICATED TO THE MEMBERS OF THIS SUCCESSFUL EXPEDITION, WHO ON OCTOBER 5, 1982, REACHED THE SUMMIT OF THE WORLD'S HIGHEST MOUNTAIN.

"WHATEVER YOU CAN DO, OR DREAM YOU CAN, BEGIN IT. BOLDNESS HAS GENIUS, POWER AND MAGIC IN IT".

GOETHE (1749-1832)

A What you're missing

If the lakes had remained unspoiled, tourists would have been flocking to the parking lot, cameras at the ready, to capture on film the beautiful Twin Falls. Captain John Palliser en route to North Kananaskis Pass in 1858 described it thus, "The wild and beautiful Kananaskis River leaps over a ledge of rock in its valley from a height of 20 feet, and rushes on its way through a dense forest of pines". In case you're interested, Calgary Power employee Tom Stanley managed to film it before its demise.

The falls between the lakes. n.d. (Courtesy Forest technology School).

D **Mt. Sarrail,** after General Maurice Sarrail (1856-1929). 'The only Republican general' was a radical and an anti-cleric in a conservative and Catholic French army during World War 1. His rapid promotion as Commander of the Third Army appeared to have been assisted by his political connections. Commander-in-Chief Joffre didn't get on with the man at all and was only too glad to remove him after the Third Army suffered heavy losses during the enemy's surprise offensive in June 1915. Sarrail found an alternative post to command, an army in the east that had not yet been constituted. Between October 1916 and April the following year Allied forces sent to Salonika to aid the Serbs saw little activity, the inaction partly explained by

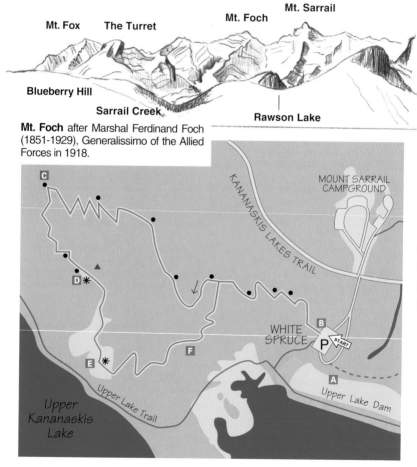

Mt. Foch after Marshal Ferdinand Foch (1851-1929), Generalissimo of the Allied Forces in 1918.

Allied disagreements over strategy and partly by the personality of General Sarrail whose "conduct and reputation for political intrigues failed to command the confidence and co-operation essential if such a mixed force was to pull its weight". After a change in prime minister his wartime career came to an end.

Mt. Lyautey after General Herbert Lyautey, Minister of War for France in 1916.

Mt. Putnik to rhyme with Sputnik, after Field Marshal Radomir Putnik (1847-1917), a popular hero who commanded the Serbian Army during World War 1. After repelling two Austrian invasion attempts, he and his forces met their match on October 1915 when overwhelming numbers of Austrian, German and Bulgarian troops launched a co-ordinated attack. Forced to retreat, Putnik successfully evacuated the Serbian army by escaping over the Albanian mountains to the Adriatic.

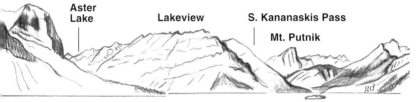

Aster Lake   Lakeview   S. Kananaskis Pass   Mt. Putnik

gd

The view from the south ridge of Upper Kananaskis Lake.

C Walter Wilcox was the first

Between 1914-1916 the Boundary Commission (founded to delimit the boundary between Alberta and British Columbia) were in the area. While it's true that chief surveyor, A.O. Wheeler and other members climbed mountains, the joy of making a first ascent was secondary to placing satisfactory camera stations, so very often they just climbed onto the end of a ridge for the view. One such camera station was located on this hill's twin to the north called Hogsback. Although they did a lot of naming, they were not the first climbers at the lakes by any means. 15 years previously a party led by Walter Wilcox finally reached Upper Lake via a convoluted route to the south, having missed the trail up North Kananaskis Pass from the Palliser River. Two of the things Wilcox did was run up to North Kananaskis Pass and back in a day, then solo Mt. Indefatigable's south peak, an easy climb popular with today's scramblers. The Boundary Commission climbed only three of the summits seen from this viewpoint: Lakeview, Mt. Tyrwhitt and the next peak to the north. It was left to superwoman Katie Gardiner and guide Walter Feuz to polish off Mts. Lyautey, Foch, Sarrail, Warrior Mtn., and a string of others in July of 1930.

E Alberta's oldest lodgepole pine

lives just across the lake. It took seed after the fire of 1546 during the reign of Elizabeth 1st and a year before Mary Queen of Scots was executed. After that fire it took 240 years for the spruce forest you see now to gain prominence. From afar, the tree appears to be dead but low down a few short branches sport clumps of needles.

F *One flowered wintergreen (Moneses uniflora).*

Read about the first peoples in the Kananaskis Valley. After a bench stop at the Stoney Indians interpretive sign, the trail climbs a steeper slope via zigzags and steps onto the north ridge, then continues winding uphill to the summit. There are plenty of benches for rest breaks. At the top are interpretive signs and a view over the lakes.

The trail descends the dry and rocky south ridge where several openings give you the best views from the trail of Upper Kananaskis Lake. On the sunny south-facing slope Kinnikinnick and Juniper replace feather mosses and menziesia.

A last lingering view from a bench, then the trail turns back into spruce forest with One-flowered wintergreens. Look for clumps after the initial winding descent levels out.

Turn right. Return the same way.

Opposite: Upper Kananaskis Lake from the Elekes viewpoint. Indefatigable Trail.

Indefatigable Trail
5 km return

summer
fall

An incredibly scenic trail which overlooks Kananaskis Lakes as it follows the lip of an escarpment to a final viewpoint in the larch zone. Because of its strenuous nature, (height gain 482 m) and loose rocky sections, it's recommended you wear lightweight hiking boots. The upper altitude of 2494 metres may bother some people.

Start: Kananaskis Lakes Trail. Drive to the end of the highway and park at North Interlakes day-use area.

From the parking lot walk down to the signboard on the dam.

Go straight. Follow Three Isle Lake trail out across North Interlakes Dam. It crosses the bridge over the spillway then turns left.

Turn right almost immediately. Initially, Indefatigable Trail gains height rather slowly through spruce forest. After crossing a two-log bridge, it turns left below the bottom of a rocky ridge, then begins a steep, somewhat rocky climb along the east side of this ridge, finally gaining the backbone of the ridge at the Wendy Louise Elekes memorial bench—a stupendous viewpoint for Upper Kananaskis Lake.

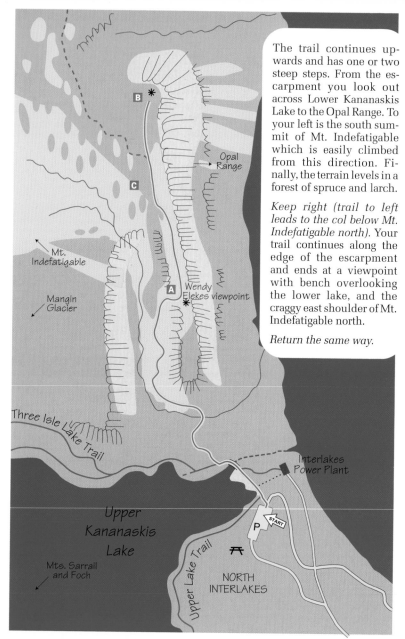

The trail continues upwards and has one or two steep steps. From the escarpment you look out across Lower Kananaskis Lake to the Opal Range. To your left is the south summit of Mt. Indefatigable which is easily climbed from this direction. Finally, the terrain levels in a forest of spruce and larch.

Keep right (trail to left leads to the col below Mt. Indefatigable north). Your trail continues along the edge of the escarpment and ends at a viewpoint with bench overlooking the lower lake, and the craggy east shoulder of Mt. Indefatigable north.

Return the same way.

B Glacier lily (avalanche lily, dogtooth violet, adder's tongue, fawn lily, snow lily, trout lily)

OK! Which name is wrong? This beautiful member of the lily family is found only in meadows and open forest near treeline. Carpets of lilies follow a retreating snow line which in this location is about the end of June. Black bears and grizzlies love the plant too and will tear up large areas to get at delicious fresh bulbs. The corms are also edible by humans but I'm not recommending you do this since harvesting means the death of the whole plant.

Erythronium grandiflorum. Photo Leon Kubbernus.

A Hardly Indefatigable

Indefatigable was yet another World War 1 British battle cruiser. Because of lack of time and money the 'Indefatigables' were as cheaply built and had all the faults of the 'Invincibles' which were the first wave of British battle cruisers: poor armour protection and vulnerability of magazines to the flash of bursting shells. Whoever named them was a optimist. She came to an untimely end at the Battle of Jutland in 1916, finished off early in the battle. "At the end the ship blew up. Sheets of flame were followed by dense smoke which obscured her from view. All sorts of stuff was blown into the air, a 50-foot steamboat to about 200 feet, apparently intact". It's horrifying to realise over 1,000 men perished. Only two survived.

The south summit of Mt. Indefatigable.

Photo Dave Elphinstone.

Blue grouse *(Dendragapus obscurus)*

Unlike the more common ruffed which 'drums' to attract females, the male blue 'hoots', about 5-7 times per call. He does this by inflating and deflating a brightly-coloured pouch located on both sides of the neck. Blue grouse hang around at treeline all year round, growing 'crampons' on their toes in fall to help with winter travel.

Amazing Rufous hummingbirds

If you wear red get ready to be buzzed. The sudden whirring noise is not a swarm of hornets but a gorgeous iridescent hummingbird who thinks you're an indian paintbrush. They love the colour red. The male *Selasphorus rufus* is rusty-red himself.

Amazing facts about this 3-gram wonderbird: the wings beat 40-80 times a second, hearts beat 1,260 times a minute, respiration is 250 breaths a minute. Unique wing movements let birds hover, fly straight up, down and backwards like a helicopter, and also upside down! Unable to soar or glide like eagles to conserve energy, it nevertheless travels about 700 km nonstop in 24 hours on its annual spring migration from Mexico.

Blue grouse. Photo Don Beers.

Elbow Lake
4 km return

summer
fall

A short but fairly strenuous uphill walk to a source of the Elbow River—brightly-coloured Elbow Lake. Bring your fishing tackle.

Start: Kananaskis Trail (Hwy. 40) at Elbow Pass day-use area. This stretch of road is open June 15th to December 1st.

Stay left on the main trail (the trail to right is the old highway which now sports a few picnic tables accessible from the parking lot).

The trail, once an old road which has been narrowed by lining rocks on both sides, starts off with a steep climb below talus slopes. Higher up, where the angle eases, keep your eyes peeled on the dry left-hand bank for such interesting plants as alum root, stonecrop, lilac and yellow beard-tongues, grass of Parnassus and around the crossing streamlet, purple marsh willowherb. A few windings, and the trail levels across the run-out zone of a large avalanche path.

Keep right (the trail to left is now covered in slash). The trail re-enters forest and swings to the left up a hill.

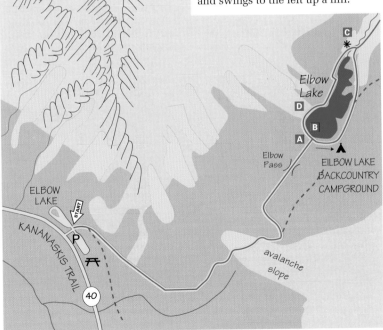

Elbow Lake from the south shore. The mountain to right is part of the Mt. Rae massif. To left is Tombstone Mountain.

(Valeriana sitchensis).

A Bigger Fish

Between 1985 and 1988 Trout Unlimited spread 5 tonnes of grain in the lake annually to encourage the growth of organisms in the food chain. Down the line, this should result in larger fish for the frying pan.

B Wild Valium

After a frosty night, the pinkish-white flowers of valerian give off a sickly sweet scent which can be overpowering (it does, however, attract a large number of insects). The Blackfoot name apoks-ikim means 'smell foot'. An Indian delicacy at one time, the cooked roots are a black gooey mess smelling and tasting of tobacco. The dried root was, in fact, sometimes used in tobacco mixture and was smoked for its calming effect. In case you haven't guessed, valerian is the forerunner of valium.

Go right (again, the trail to left has been covered with slash). Gentler inclines bring you to Elbow Pass. A short descent and you're at the lakeshore T-junction.

LAKE CIRCUIT (1 km)

Turn right. A narrower trail leads in a few minutes to the backcountry campground with picnic tables.

Stay left (biffy trail to right). Follow the heavily-forested east shore through more camping spots into more open country of meadows and willows.

Keep left (the sketchy trail to right leads to Rae Glacier). Your trail soon rejoins the old road at a creek crossing.

Turn left. The road crosses the infant Elbow River. No bridge, but a couple of logs are adequate. Look back for a wonderful view of Mt. Rae, the highest peak east of Highway 40.

Continuing, you will want to stop often on the trail which follows every indentation of the west shore. In particular, top-to-bottom talus slopes allow spectacular views of surrounding mountains and also harbour some unexpected edible treats like blackcurrants.

At the junction, turn right and return the way you came to the parking lot.

Lake circuit. Crossing the infant Elbow below Mt. Rae. The Rae Glacier is just out of sight to the right.

The red snows of the Rae Glacier, the easternmost glacier in the Canadian Rockies.

⊂ The Red Snows

Joining the infant Elbow just below the lake is another far more boisterous creek which arises in twin cirques below Mt. Rae, the true source of the river which runs through Calgary. The photo on the left shows the Rae Glacier in summer, the snow streaked with red. Watermelon snow is caused by the alga *Chlamydomonas nivalis* which has a single red spot and for photosynthesizing relies on minerals from rock dust blown onto the snow. Summer skiers disturbing the surface have concentrated the organisms.

Alpine rock cress (Arabis lyallii).

D Talus

or scree is rock which has fallen from the cliff face, either piecemeal or in big chunks. Most often it's caused by the freeze-thaw action of water. When water freezes in cracks it exerts a tremendous pressure to the sides of the cracks, causing them to widen and deepen. Over time angular blocks break off. The maximum angle of repose for angular blocks is 30-40 degrees. A talus slope saturated with water moves downhill like a river and is called a rock glacier (there's one higher up the highway). Generally, talus slopes are too unstable for plants except at the sides and bottom where nothing much is moving.

Silky scorpionweed (Phacelia sericea). Nice to touch, this fuzzy purple flower grows among rocks in full sun. Silvery green leaves and a stem covered in soft silvery hairs contrast with a spike of bright purple flowers. Long filaments capped by bright orange anthers make this flower unmistakable.

Highwood Pass Meadows
1 km return

summer
fall

A short stroll through the meadows of Highwood Pass, the highest pass navigable by motor homes in Canada. Interpretive signs lead to a rest stop in the trees.

Start: Kananaskis Trail (Hwy. 40) at Highwood Pass parking lot. This stretch of road is open June 15 to December 1.

Start at the trail sign

The trail crosses Ptarmigan Creek and heads out across a meadow dug up here and there by grizzlies after hibernating ground squirrels.

Go left. Now on boardwalk you head past a slate of interpretive signs informing about nunatuks and seas of ice flowing through the pass.

These meadows are not renowned for their flowers; there's just the odd wind flower, a yellow heather colony, slender beardstongue and valerian. The final section of boardwalk leads past larches to a viewing platform in a clump of alpine fir overlooking a meltwater channel.

Return the same way. Look for Storm Mountain arch.

The meadows, looking northeast.

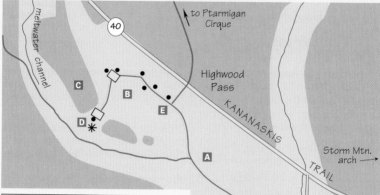

A Columbians wear earrings

The little critters doing sentry duty in front of their burrows are columbian ground squirrels *(Spermophilus columbianus)* which are not to be confused with Richardson's ground squirrels which are found mainly in the foothills. The earrings? It's part of a study by park naturalists.

The colony you see here is subdivided into territories controlled by a dominant male who guards several females, yearlings and juveniles. He's the one doing sentry duty. Each animal has its own summer burrow

Spermophilus columbianus.

which has several bolt holes for emergencies including dead-safe entrances under the boardwalk. Female nesting burrows and winter dens are the deepest at two metres. Interestingly, a sump hole is dug next to the hibernation chamber to drain water percolating down from the surface. Savvy males will also put in a supply of rot-resistant seeds for the wake up breakfast. Columbians live on average three years, sometimes up to six. Of that time, 7 months per year is spent in hibernation which ends in late April for the males, early May for the females. For three frenzied weeks the males fight amongst themselves to impregnate as many females as possible. Gestation takes 24 days, weaning of young a month which brings us to July. No matter how good the weather hibernation begins in mid August, sometimes earlier. Fall, when the vegetation has died down, is the time the shadow of the grizzly falls upon the meadow. Bears do the rounds digging up hibernating columbians, usually the inexperienced yearlings who tend to dig shallow burrows.

◉ Larches

Highwood Pass is perhaps the easiest if not the best place to see the alpine larch *(Larix Lyalli)* in close-up without walking very far. The only cone-bearing coniferous tree to shed its needles, the timberline larch is responsible for the annual fall pilgrimage of larch lovers who wait for exactly the right weekend — there is usually only one — when the needles turn orange. Softness is the byword. Notice how the very short needles grow in feathery clusters from knobs on twigs covered in a soft woolly down. Likewise, walking in a larch forest on an understory of needles and grouseberry (grouseberry and larches go together) is a sensuous experience akin to walking across a very expensive Axminster carpet with several rubber underlays. Because Highwood Pass lies at the lower altitude range for these trees, some larches have reached maximum size with one tree studied measuring 17.2 m in height and 61.6 cm in diameter. One is 350 years old.

◉ Wolves on the comeback trail

Wildlife biologists have been studying a pack which travels back and forth between Highwood Pass and Castle Mountain in Banff Park—a distance of 100 km. The distance is nothing compared to the travels of Pluie. This collared female from the Peter Lougheed Park pack was such a regular visitor to Eureka, Montana and Sandpoint, Idaho "researchers jokingly referred to her as a cross-border shopper."

Canis lupus.

D Rock crawlers—a rare find

Grylloblattodea are actually proto-types of today's crickets and grass-hoppers, and were known only as fossils prior to their discovery near Banff as still living insects. That this discovery occurred as recently as 1914 is hardly surprising. Ento-mologists are not likely to be grub-bing around on a cold winter's night when the little critters are most ac-tive. Rock crawlers love cold, living out their lives under rocks near gla-ciers or snow patches. Conversely, they hate heat and escape summer by burying into the soil to a depth of about half a metre. Should you be lucky enough to see these rarities, don't pick them up. It's said the heat from your hand could kill them. What do they look like? Superfi-cially, they resemble earwigs, but have cockroach-like legs for run-ning around. In this they differ from crickets which hop.

Grylloblattodea

From Ninety-two Gnats, Nits and Nibblers, University of Illinois Press.

E Arches

Rock arches or windows are a more common occurrence in the Cana-dian Rockies than you might think, but it isn't often you get to see two from the same stretch of road. Both occur on extremely thin ridges known as fins. Over time, erosion by snow, ice, rain and wind perforates any weak layer existing in the fin, ultimately causing disintegration and collapse. The hole left behind can get so large only the arch re-mains, as is the case with the Tyrwhitt 'wishbone' arch.

As seen from the boardwalk Storm Mountain arch emerges from the dark mountain background.

Tyrwhitt Arch is visible from north of the pass by looking in a south-westerly direction.

Ptarmigan Cirque
4.5 km return

summer
fall

A short but rather strenuous climb (height gain 230 m) into a cirque above treeline. Alpine flowers, fossils and ptarmigan are just some of the interesting things to be seen. The upper altitude of 2438 metres may bother some people. Expect occasional closures due to grizzly sightings.

Start: Kananaskis Trail (Hwy. 40) at Highwood Pass parking lot. This stretch of road is open between June 15th and December 1st.

At the trail sign follow the trail out into the meadow.

Take the right fork. Cross the highway at the pass and switchback uphill through fir and spruce forest.

Turn left. The trail levels and wanders across alpine meadows back-dropped by the cliffs of Mt. Arethusa.

Keep right (a secondary trail carries on into the head of the cirque below Mt. Rae). The interpretive trail crosses the creek above a small waterfall.

The alpine meadows.

C Dr. John Rae

Mt. Rae (3218 m), the highest peak east of Highway 40 was named after Dr. John Rae, born in the Orkney Islands in 1813 and appointed surgeon in his twentieth year to a Hudson Bay Company's ship in 1833. It was while he was working as a doctor in the Mackenzie River District that he became well-known as an explorer, first from a journey made in 1846 to survey 100 miles of coastline around Committee Bay, and secondly for his four expeditions to find out what had happened to the (last) Franklin Expedition of 1845 which vanished while searching for the North-West Passage in two ships, the HMS Erebus and HMS Terror. Between 1847 and 1878 twenty-five search expeditions were sent out from England and America and it was during the early

(NA 1252-2 Glenbow Archives).

trips that three graves were discovered on Beechey Island, those of crew members William Braine, John Hartnell, and John Torrington, which have since been 'rediscovered' in the mid 1980s. It was left to Dr. John Rae's final expedition of 1853-4 to discover silver plated evidence in the form of cutlery in the hands of the Pelly Bay Eskimos, a find which paved the way for later expeditions who were able to narrow down the search for Franklin's men, after the ships were abandoned, to King William Island and the Adelaide Peninsula and over the years reconstruct the tragedy.

Incidentally, when the bodies of Braine, Hartnell and Torrington were exhumed by scientists from the University of Alberta it hit the television news and the front pages of newspapers all around the world. The major contributing factor of the tragedy was not a hostile climate, starvation or scurvy, because the officers and crew were dropping like flies, Franklin among them, even before it became necessary to abandon ship when there was plenty of food and shelter. Unguessed at by Rae, the exhumation pointed the finger at lead poisoning from incorrectly soldered canned food.

At the creek crossing, the south summit of Mt. Rae comes into view. The normal ascent route starts from the cirque, climbs to the col overlooking the Rae Glacier, then follows the narrow south ridge. The south summit is actually a pinnacle which turned back many an aspiring first ascent party.

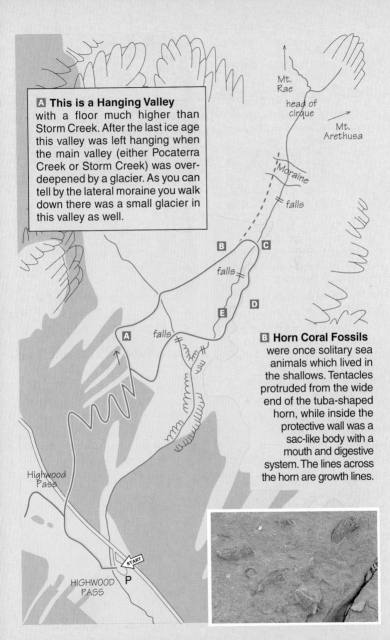

A This is a Hanging Valley
with a floor much higher than Storm Creek. After the last ice age this valley was left hanging when the main valley (either Pocaterra Creek or Storm Creek) was over-deepened by a glacier. As you can tell by the lateral moraine you walk down there was a small glacier in this valley as well.

Mt. Rae

head of cirque

Mt. Arethusa

Moraine

falls

B

C

falls

E

D

A falls

Highwood Pass

HIGHWOOD PASS

P

START

B Horn Coral Fossils
were once solitary sea animals which lived in the shallows. Tentacles protruded from the wide end of the tuba-shaped horn, while inside the protective wall was a sac-like body with a mouth and digestive system. The lines across the horn are growth lines.

D White-tailed ptarmigan

It's easy to walk right past ptarmigan whose summer plumage blends with the rocks. Very tolerant of humans with a camera, they don't seem to mind you following as they move about pecking on green shoots and catching bugs. Count the number of birds. Sure you've got them all? In the summer you're most likely to see the mother hen and between four to eight young who stay together until fall when they move down to their wintering grounds below treeline.

In winter, turning white is not so much a camouflage job as a means of increasing insulation, because without the pigment melanin there are more air spaces within the feathers. At this time the birds of the cirque tend to flock together as they subsist on seeds and the twigs of alder and willow bushes. During bad storms or extreme cold they bury themselves under the snow in protected tunnels.

Alpine spring beauty (Claytonia megarhiza).

Purple saxifrage (Saxifraga oppositifolia).

The trail turns down creek, winding through rocks and small patches of meadow.

Eventually the trail re-crosses the creek above a waterfall and arrives at a junction in first trees.

Turn left and return the way you came.

Below: White-tailed ptarmigan (Lagopus leucurus).

Moss campion (Silene acaulis).

E Flowers of the Boulder Field

You'll find two basic types: cushion plants and succulents. Both share a long taproot, sometimes more than one, which is both an anchor and a probe searching for moisture deep within the rock piles.

Cushion Plants Wherever you find moss campion you'll find wind, lots of it. The plant is supremely adapted to cold fast-moving air. First of all it prostrates itself to the ground to take advantage of higher protuberances like rocks which slow the wind's velocity. Secondly, its densely interwoven branches of uniform height cushion the wind's drying effect and allow the inside of the plant to retain moisture. The plant also retains moisture by catching blowing leaves and soil in its cushion and filtering them down to ground level where they eventually form a mound of moisturizing soil. The height of these mounds give you some idea of the plant's age. Another indicator of age is the flowers which only come into profuse bloom after about 20 years of slow growing.

Succulents Succulents like the alpine spring beauty, roseroot and purple saxifrage found in the area, have a great deal in common with cactus: they deal with the desiccating effect of wind by coating their leaves with wax. Notice how the leaves of the spring beauty are shaped into a rosette and how alpines are generally spread out. With no other plants close by for competition, the plant is able to receive nutrients, light and moisture from all directions.

Karst Spring
9 km return

*late spring
summer
fall*

For the most part an easy walk along a disused logging road which winds through the heart of the Mount Shark Ski Trails. From Watridge Lake a narrow forest trail climbs more steeply to a spring which is possibly the largest of its type in North America. Bring fishing tackle for Watridge Lake.

Start: From Smith-Dorrien/Spray Trail (Hwy. 742) turn west onto the Watridge Logging Road signed Mount Shark Ski Trails. Follow it for 5.3 km to its terminus at Mount Shark parking lot.

The trail, signed 'Watridge Lake', starts from the information board at the entrance to the parking lot. Follow the narrow trail out to the closed portion of the Watridge Logging Road beyond the gate.

Turn left. Keep straight, then right at junctions 3 and 22. The logging road dips to cross Marushka Creek, then climbs a hill to junction 21.

Keep left. Keep straight at junctions 20 and 19. Throughout this section, the road is obvious as it passes junctions 16, 15 and 13. Behind your back views are opening up of the Kananaskis Range (Windtower, Mts. Lougheed, Sparrowhawk, Buller and Engadine). To your right is Mt. Nestor and spectacular Cone Mountain. On the left is Tent Ridge and Mt. Shark. You can even glimpse Spray Lakes Reservoir.

Keep right. The road descends towards Watridge Creek.

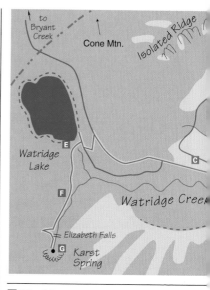

A 'Shark,' a name worth commemorating

We're back to 1916, the last days of the Battle of Jutland. What happened was this. The German High Seas Fleet were running tail between legs to a safe port 'chased' by the British Fleet which in reality hadn't much clue as to where the enemy was in the days before radar. So it was quite a surprise to the Third BCS led by Commander Loftus Jones in the Destroyer Shark, when three enemy battle cruisers appeared out of the mist and his division came under a deluge of shells. One struck the Shark's wheel, another disabled the main engines. At great risk, another ship came between the enemy and the Shark, volunteering assistance, but Loftus Jones, though badly wounded in the thigh and face replied, "No, tell him

B Another Story

When Calgary was bidding for the 15th Olympic Winter Games, Tent Ridge and Mt. Sparrowhawk between them were touted for alpine skiing events. The runs were ready-made courtesy of Spray Lakes Sawmills. After the bid was won, this area was suddenly discarded in favour of Nakiska at Mt. Allan.

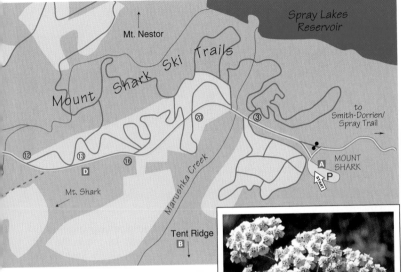

to look after himself." Though reduced to two men, the gun crew maintained fire with the midship gun and when one dropped from lack of blood, the commander took his place. A shell took off his right leg. "As his strength ebbed, Commander Loftus Jones feared lest his ship should fall to the enemy. When he asked what had happened to the flag, a man tending him replied that it had been shot away. In great distress he ordered another to be hoisted". And so the Shark sank with all colours flying. Jones floated clear, supported by a lifebelt, while about 12 other survivors swam to life rafts. Seeing battle cruisers sweeping past, Jones asked if they were British and on being told that they were uttered his last words, "That's Good!".

Yarrow can also be pink.

C Yarrow for Toothache

Yarrow lines the roads in snowy profusion. Never mind the flowers. It's the leaves which count. A friend swears this works. For toothache due to a lost filling or a chipped tooth, simply stuff a few fresh leaves in the cavity and the pain disappears. You can also steep the leaves in hot water to make a soothing tea tasting of sage.

Watridge Lake and Cone Mountain.

Keep straight at junction 12. The road crosses rushing Watridge Creek.

Keep left on the better road at junction 11. The road bends left up a hill into a cutblock near junction 10, then at the trail sign enters spruce forest and becomes a two-lane ski trail built in 1988/9.

Keep straight on the wider trail. (The narrow trail to the left diving into the trees is the original trail to Watridge Lake). Your trail undulates to an important junction with signpost.

Turn left downhill. At the bottom of the hill turn right. In a few metres keep right. In less than a minute you reach the east shore of Watridge Lake, a beautiful green lake surrounded by Mts. Shark and Turner and Cone Mountain. The shore is circumvented by a water-logged angler's trail. It's from the north shore that you hear Karst Spring roaring away in the forest.

D The Watridge Logging Road
This area was logged in the early 1970s by Spray Lakes Sawmills who had taken over the lease from Eau Claire Logging Company in the 1950s. Logged hillsides and roads like this one provided the basis for the Mount Shark cross-country and biathlon racing trails, and for 'Assiniboia Ski Resort' which never came to fruition but helped win Calgary the bid for the 15th Olympic Winter Games.

Backtrack a few metres to the last junction. Turn right. The signed trail to Karst Spring crosses the lake's tiny outlet stream on boardwalk. A calcareous flat around the outlet is one of best places I know of for tall white bog orchids. Also look for white paintbrush on drier ground, elephant-heads, butterworts and the delicious berry of the dwarf raspberry.

▣ *Bog Flowers*

Labrador Tea
(Ledum groenlandicum)
Is also called swamp tea, bog tea and Hudson Bay tea because it was used by lower class employees of the company. Look at the underside of the leaves. Not only are they rusty-coloured, but also woolly which protects the pores from becoming clogged by moisture rising from wet ground. Because this plant absorbs so much moisture via the roots, it's dependent on the leaves to throw off the excess via perspiration.

Dwarf raspberry *(Rubus arcticus)*
Unlike the more common wild raspberry, this one likes water and trails all over the ground.

To make tea: Place a handful of fresh leaves in boiling water and allow to simmer for about 5 mins. If using dried leaves, about 1 tsp. per cup should be sufficient. The fragrance and yellowy-green colour is very much like jasmine tea. Caution: the leaves contain an oil called hedum which can affect the heart if taken in large doses. So keep the tea weak. Other than that it's supposed to be good for colds, sore throats and headaches.

Tall white bog orchid
(Habenaria dilatata)
The dazzling white flowers give off a scent worth getting wet for.

◪ Feathery Feather Mosses

tend to cover the forest floor in a soft spongy carpet. The four commonest are, *Rhytidiadelphus triquetrus* (goose-neck/frightened cat-tail) *Hylocomnium splendens* (stairstep), *Pleurozium schreberi* (big red stem) and *Ptilium crista-castrensis* (knight's plume). The other common 'mosses' of the forest floor are the clubmosses which—surprise—are not moss family members at all despite the name. On rocks in the creek and lining the banks in the splash zone are another set of mosses belonging to the *Bryum, Pohlia* and *Cratoneuron* genera.

Lycopodium annotinum (stiff clubmoss) grows near the trail.

Mosses have no roots and only a poorly developed plumbing system, so to photosynthesize, every part of the plant has to hold onto moisture as long as it can which is why mosses grow on moist ground in shady places. While excellent at retaining water, mosses can also hack drought by a process called poikilohydry, whereby plants dry up and become temporarily dormant.

Above: a feather moss.

The trail wanders through an interesting forest, approaching Watridge Creek a couple of times then steepens for the final zigzag to an overlook. Karst Spring is an amazing sight. Gliding smoothly from under a cliff in a dark grotto, the water thunders down a rocky creekbed between boulders covered in bright green mosses.

Return the same way.

'Elizabeth Falls just below the grotto. Sunlight hardly ever penetrates to the spring. To minimize disappointing photos due to lack of light, I recommend you carry in a tripod.

G The Great Mystery

On all maps the stream issuing from Watridge Lake is shown as the source of Watridge Creek. The greater mystery to me is why it took people so long to realize that the insignificant trickle running under the boardwalk could not possibly be the fast-running river you crossed earlier between 12 and 11. There has to be another source and there is. Discovered by Dean Marshall, then foreman with Spray Lakes Sawmills, Karst Spring is possibly the largest spring of its kind in North America. Where does the water come from? The most likely theory is the lower lake in the basin west of Smuts Pass, the water sinking underground and following a subterranean stream, coursing through labyrinths or held up in a underground reservoir perhaps (the rate of flow varies little between summer and winter), changing valley and slope and passing under Mt. Shark before rising again at Karst Spring.

Chester Lake
9 km return

summer
fall

A moderately strenuous walk, first up logging roads, then through forest and meadows to a mountain lake in the larches.

Start: Smith-Dorrien/Spray Trail (Hwy. 742) at Chester Lake parking lot.

Leave the parking lot at the trail sign behind the upper biffy.

Keep left (Blue trail to right). The logging road crosses Chester Creek and winds uphill to a junction.

Turn right. Keep left. Keep straight three times. Turn left. Turn right. Turn left. Easy stretches alternate with steep climbs. Fireweed, rhododendron, menziesia, grass of Parnassus and pearly everlasting grow by the road side.

Go straight then keep right. The road bends back left and you come to the five-way junction.

Turn first right. Keep left uphill. Bend right The road levels and to your right are views of the highest peak between Mt. Joffre and Mt. Assiniboine, Mt. Sir Douglas.

Turn left at the trail sign. A narrow twisty trail heads uphill through fir forest. It levels and crosses a small meadow which like all the other meadows you will cross is not of the flowery kind but supports low growing willow like *Salix arctica.* Pass the first larch. Another forest climb

Mt. Robertson and Sir Douglas from the end of the logging roads.

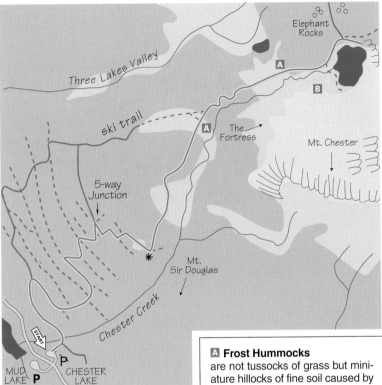

brings you to a second meadow, bumpy with frost hummocks. Another stint through forest brings you to the third and largest meadow with clear views ahead of Fortress Mountain, Mt. Chester and Mt. Galatea. On your right the creek is meandering alongside the trail. Chester Lake is reached in another 5 minutes.

Take time to explore the area. The trail to right crossing Chester Creek ends at a boulder field in the larches. The trail to left leads to camping spots and ongoing options.

Return the way you came.

A Frost Hummocks

are not tussocks of grass but miniature hillocks of fine soil caused by alternate freezing and thawing of the ground. Soil which freezes expands and puts pressure on unfrozen areas which are pushed onto mounds. The same principle applies to frost heaves in pavement.

Chester Lake.

Photo Don Beers.

B Pikas

Boulder fields at the edge of the meadows are home to a colony of pikas, small lovable animals with fur on the soles of their feet not yet discovered by Stephen Spielberg. They're a lagomorph and so related to guinea pigs and rabbits. Generally, you hear them before you see them. A loud "eek" out of all proportion to their size warns other pikas of approaching humans and predators like weasels, lynx, wolverines and eagles. Actually the little critters are amazingly tolerant of humans and make use of you to their own advantage, dashing about the meadows snipping off flowers from under your feet in total disregard

B Blue-blooded Wolf spiders

Related to true tarantulas, these dwellers of rocks and scree are not at all shy of people and love nothing better than to share a warm tent. They have six large forward pointing eyes and another two on top of the head, all the better to spot their prey which can be seen from about 6 cm away. Unlike other spiders with sheet webs or orb webs, they run down their prey, leaping on the victim and piercing it with the fang. Movement triggers pursuit.

Spiders with pale blue abdomens are not a different species, but the females who are carrying around an egg sac attached to spinnerets. These spherical balls made of woven silk enclose genetic material. Females spend an awful lot of time sunbathing and congregating with other females. Some say the warmth speeds up development of the eggs. At the appropriate time, she pierces the outer covering of the egg sac, releasing as many as 40 babies which cling to her abdomen or back for dear life. It doesn't matter if they fall off; they simply follow the silken life line and climb back up her legs.

Spiders moult as a means of increasing size. They shred their hard exoskeleton at intervals and produce a new one. The bigger the spider, the more the moults. At second moult the young leave their mothers.

Left: A full-sized wolf spider (Pardosa).

of eagles circling overhead. Pikas expend a lot of energy in late summer and early fall harvesting grasses and flowers which are dried on flat rocks before being stowed away for winter use in their runs among the rocks. Because they are unable to develop enough fat deposits, pikas can't hibernate during the winter. So not only do they fill their dens to bursting point with hay but also cache a large amount at a nearby convenience rock as well. Although the pika develops a thicker winter coat, there aren't many calories in grass to keep him warm so this always-on-the-go animal must eat hourly and supplement his diet by re-ingesting fecal pellets of partly digested food which is high in protein.

The store.

Warspite Lake
4.5 km return

summer
fall

A fairly hilly forest walk on interpretive trails to a pond which is unusual in many respects. It's a good place to spot birds and exercise your talent for identifying berries.

Start: Smith-Dorrien/Spray Trail (Hwy. 742) at Black Prince day-use area.

From the garbage disposal unit, the trail heads right.

Cross the old logging road (don't go down to Smith-Dorrien Creek). The trail crosses Smith-Dorrien Creek further upstream via a log bridge, then backtracks to the logging road on the west bank. Pass two interpretive signs.

Turn right Follow the logging road up a long hill past interpretive sign 3 into the cutblocks.

Turn right onto a narrow trail. A bench offers a good view back towards Kent Ridge. Then the trail descends into Warspite Creek past interpretive signs 4 and 5. Look for White rhododendrons among the menziezia bushes.

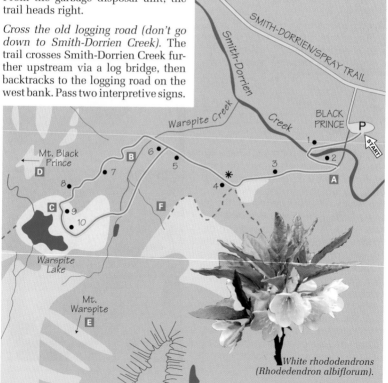

White rhododendrons
(*Rhododendron albiflorum*).

A Sign-eaters

It's fun to watch the gradual demise of wooden trail signs down the Smith-Dorrien valley. The fastest demise I've ever seen was the original signage along the Mount Shark ski trails which completely disappeared in only one summer. A few paint flakes on the ground told the story. The culprit? Porcupines, who not only love munching plywood but also varnish, glue and lead paint of any colour. Their taste in food also extends to anything salty from sweaty runners to wooden biffy seats. Additionally, they have developed a passion for rubber, as in car tires. Before civilization invaded the forest their normal summer fare was grass.

The hard-to-read sign at **A**.

Porcupine (Erethizon dorsatum).
Photo Don Beers.

B Loco berries

The bracted honeysuckle berry *(Lonicera involucrata)* is on some poison lists. On the other hand, some herbalists reckon it's edible if you can hack the horrible taste (better after a few frosts, apparently). The Indians claimed eating enough of these berries would send you loco, hence the Latin name. Juicy black berries have distinctive gaudy crimson bracts to remind you of its hallucinogenic property.

Warspite Lake from the northeast shore.

Keep right (no sign) Read interpretive sign 6, then cross Warspite Creek. The trail continues, winding past lots of Bracted honeysuckles into a chaotic landscape of boulders. With the change of scenery comes a new lot of flowers: Prickly/Common/Spotted saxifrages, purple penstemons, yellow columbines, felworts, and gooseberry and blackcurrant bushes growing between the rocks.

After passing interpretive signs 7 and 8 you arrive at the rocky shores of Warspite Lake which is completely enclosed by rocks and has an underground outlet. Ahead is Mt. Black Prince. To its left Warspite Cascade tumbles from a higher cirque holding Black Prince Tarns below Mt. Warspite. This is the place to leave the trail and explore the lake shore. In damp ground beside the main inlet stream you'll find red-stemmed saxifrage, alpine willowherb, one-flowered wintergreens and snow buttercups. To the right, a trail leads through a band of spruce to a meadow under the cliffs where you get a better view of the cascades.

Birds to watch for include Townsend's warbler, Wilson's warbler, northern waterthrush, common yellowthroat, and Lincoln's sparrows in early spring.

⊂ Birds that nest on the ground
The vulnerability of the eggs and the young accounts for the behaviour of these two birds.

Killdeer. Photo Dave Elphinstone.

Looking west from Warspite Lake towards the Spray Mountains.

Killdeer *(Charadrius vocferus)* is a noisy bird with two distinctive black bands across the upper chest. Nests are out in the open. Should the female think you're getting too near to the nest, she will run some distance away and feign injury by dragging her tail, holding up one wing and uttering loud cries of distress. When you're sufficiently far away from the nest, she flies off, miraculously cured.

Spotted sandpiper *(Actitus macularia)* is easily recognised when standing or walking by its distinctive teetering action caused by constant flexing of its legs. When spooked, it takes to the air, fluttering around with wings sharply down-curved. The black spots on the underside appear during breeding season and are completely lacking in the fall just before migration. In this bird, the stereotyped male/female images are reversed. The larger more aggressive females woo the males who do most of the incubating and looking after the young. The females, meanwhile, are out playing the field. Likely this promiscuity has the purpose of producing multiple clutches to offset the large number of eggs lost to predators.

Spotted sandpiper chick, just hatched. Photo Don Beers.

Battleships

The Kananaskis Range was once called the Ship Mountains because so many peaks were named after British ships sunk in the Battle of Jutland during World War 1 by the German High Fleet. The names spilled over to this range.

The Battle of Jutland was played out in the days when wireless telegraphy was in its infancy and radar unheard of, when neither side knew where the other was or even where their own ships were half the time. This battle, of course, was the inspiration behind the popular game of Battleships.

HMS Warspite grounded in Prussia Cove, Cornwall.

D Mt. Black Prince The British armoured cruiser HMS Black Prince came to a fearful end at midnight on May 31st 1916. After being seriously damaged by a heavy shell she had withdrawn from action but not from the battle area. Because she could still steam she followed in the wake of the 'Iron Duke', an unfortunate decision by Captain T.P. Bonham for which he was to pay dearly. Remember, nobody knew where the enemy was at any given time, so call it fate when she ran smack into Scheer's Second SG a second time. Under concentrated fire from no less than five German battleships, she blew up and sank with the loss of all her crew.

E Warspite Lake, Creek, Cascades, Mt. The odd ship out, HMS Warspite didn't suffer the fate of the Black Prince, though she had a darn good try, serving in both World wars with distinction and becoming known in her old age as 'the old lady'. On May 16 1916, for instance, she inadvertently saved HMS Warrior from sinking — for the time being anyway. With her steering gear damaged, Warspite could only make a large circle which brought her between Warrior and the enemy, thus drawing unwanted fire upon herself. Then, the stand-by steering engine was accidentally connected with 10 degrees of helm, so round she went again, making a second circle, coming within range of Scheer's Second SG and suffering 13 hits before the trouble was recognised.

She was a not a ship that died easily. When the time came to tow her to the breaker's yard in the Clyde in 1947, she took destiny into her own hands. Slipping the tow during a storm, she first stranded herself on an underwater ledge, then ran aground in Prussia Cove, and was finally beached near Marazion where she was broken up over a period of 5 years. If you ever holiday in England you can still pick up pieces of HMS Warspite from the beach at St. Michel's Mount in Cornwall and view the Warspite bollard on the cliffs above Prussia Cove.

The long ridge of Mt. Kent rises above the boulder field.

🄵 Yellow columbine

(Aquilegia flavescens)

Red versions *(A. formosa)* grow on the western slope of the Canadian Rockies. Blue ones (*A brevistyla*) grow further north. This version, sometimes tinged with purple or pink, is a plant of the eastern slopes and is very common in Kananaskis Country, being seen alongside woodland trails, in alpine meadows and in all rocky areas above and below treeline. The generic name comes from 'aquila', an eagle, because the spurs of the petals resemble talons. These are the nectaries where nectar collects. The shape is such that the flower can only be pollinated by long-tongued insects and by hummingbirds. Leaves can be easily confused with those of meadow rue, but fortunately, both are edible though not particularly appealing to the taste buds. Various sources say that steamed leaves taste like snow peas.

The trail continues past interpretive signs 9 and 10, then turns away from the lake and wends its way across the boulder field which extends all the way to Warspite Creek. Cross. A short stretch through forest leads to a T-junction.

Turn right. Return the way you came.

Peninsula
1 km return

spring
summer
fall

A very short easy stroll to the end of a peninsula jutting into Lower Kananaskis Lake. The ideal walk for anglers.

Start: Smith-Dorrien-Spray Trail (Hwy. 742) at Peninsula parking lot.

The trail starts from the far end parking lot at the trail sign to the left of the old road.

Keep right (to left a trail leads to picnic tables). Turn left. Meadows hereabouts harbour Yellow beardstongues, Northern Gentians and assorted ragworts. The trail makes an almost straight line down the backbone of the peninsula between little bays on the left with overgrown access trails and the northwest bay where Smith-Dorrien Creek flows into Lower Kananaskis Lake. It's a grand stretch of trail for wintergreens of all kinds, but particularly large clumps of the Greenish-flowered version.

Go right A few minutes walk leads to a cairn at peninsula's end and a view down lake of the Elk Mountains.

Turn right. Return the way you came.

Lower Kananaskis Lake from the end of the peninsula.

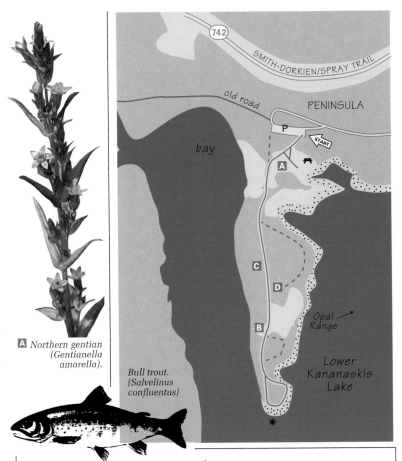

742

SMITH-DORRIEN/SPRAY TRAIL

old road

PENINSULA

P

START

bay

A

C

D

Opal
Range

B

Lower
Kananaskis
Lake

*

A *Northern gentian
(Gentianella
amarella).*

*Bull trout.
(Salvelinus
confluentus)*

B Bull Trout, Alberta's official fish
The fighting Bull trout has become a
casualty to overfishing. Lower Kananaskis Lake used to be one of the top
bull trout fisheries in Alberta, but now
this bay and adjoining Smith-Dorrien
Creek which is the trout's fall spawning grounds are closed for fishing in-
definitely. And elsewhere a bait ban is
in effect plus catch and release.

Bull trout can live up to 20 years and
feeds largely on other fish, thereby
keeping the lake's sucker population
in check. This fish was once known as
Dolly Varden, a character in a Charles
Dickens novel who wore pink speck-
led calico. In the 1980s the separation
of Dolly Varden into separate species
occurred and what is now known as
Dolly Varden (*S. malma*) is found
mainly on the west coast.

C The Ornamental Buffaloberry

By far the most dominant bush on the peninsula, it is easily recognised by its red or orange juicy-looking berries and by its leaves which have soft silvery undersides covered in rusty dots. Though popular with bears, and rich in beta carotene and iron, the berries are scarcely palatable for human taste, being extremely bitter. Nevertheless, in the old days the Indians, perhaps recognising their nutritional value, mixed the berries with buffalo meat to make pemmican.

While concentrations of the foaming agent saponin are not high enough to make eating berries dangerous (saponin is also the foaming agent in detergents), don't eat too many. It isn't at all likely, given the other common name of buffaloberry is soapberry. Incidentally, saponin is also present in beets, soybean seeds, alfalfa seeds and green tea.

Recipe for Indian Ice cream

In a bowl beat a few buffaloberries into a pink froth. Add lots of sugar. Water is optional. Tip: the berries taste better the next spring when the sugar content is increased threefold.

D *Greenish-flowered wintergreen (Pyrola chlorantha).*

Pyrola is a diminutive of pyrus, meaning pear and refers to the pear-shaped leaves.

Cat Creek Waterfall
4 km return

This interpretive trail guides you past the site of Ford Mines main camp with its relics of the coal mining era to a picturesque canyon with waterfall. The first half of the walk has some steep hills where the trail climbs over a ridge.

Start: Kananaskis Trail (Hwy. 40) at Cat Creek day-use area. Use the far end parking lot beyond the picnic shelter. This stretch of highway is open between June 15th and December 1st.

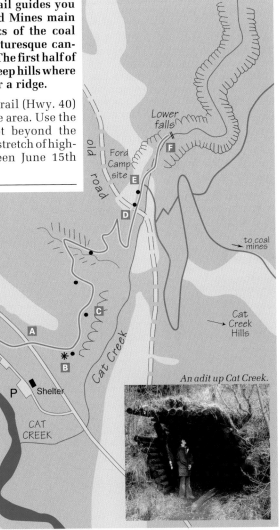

An adit up Cat Creek.

① **Mt. Bishop** William Avery Bishop, 1894-1956, was Canada's outstanding and controversial fighter pilot of the First World War, known for his aggressive, almost reckless tactics. Billy Bishop went to war all right. Posted to No. 60 Squadron March 1917, only a few months after qualifying as a pilot, he single-handedly attacked a German Airfield on June 2, 1917, destroying three Albatros III's that came up to intercept him and evading at least five other German pursuers. By August his score had risen to 47 and he returned to Canada with the rank of Major and the Victoria Cross. During command of No. 85 Squadron in March 1918 he added another 25 victories in France for which he received the Distinguished Flying Cross.

② **Horned Mountain** was named both for its shape and for Horn coral found on its slopes.

Cervus elaphus. Photo Don Beers.

③ **Mt. McPhail** honours N.R. McPhail of the Surveyor General's staff who was killed on November 1917 during the First World War. It's old name was Pyramid.

④ **Mt. Muir** is named after Alexander Muir (1830-1906) who wrote "The Maple Leaf" in 1867.

B *The High Rock Range from the first interpretive sign on the trail.*

A Elk and Road Closures

Highway 40 is closed December to mid June partly to protect from poaching the large 200+ elk herd which overwinters on the low hills east and west of the highway, living off twigs, aspen bark, pine needles and frozen grass. During the 1988 Winter Olympics, when the highway remained open "to expedite members of the Olympic family to and from Nakiska", elk feeding stations were set up in an effort to reduce elk/vehicle collisions. Less salt was used during sanding operations and snow berms on the shoulder were kept low for easy escape from approaching cars.

D Old Roads and River Channels

The previous highway followed a former tributary of Cat Creek dating back to the last Ice Age. Incidentally, at the point where this old road joins the present highway and north to Lineham Creek you are driving along the old drainage channel of the Highwood River itself. That's the longitudinal slightly undulating meadow where the cattle like to congregate. Undulating because of small alluvial fans deposited by small streams falling from the steep slopes to the east.

Here, you are standing on layers of gravel brought down by Cat Creek which has changed its course innumerable times across this flat. About half a kilometre to the southeast you can trace another old river channel, more sinuous and narrow—that of ancient Cat Creek. The upper end nearest to Cat Creek is blind; that is, blocked by gravel and presently covered by trees.

C *The Cat Creek Hills and terraces.*

From the trail sign the trail climbs the bank to Highway 40.

Cross the highway. The trail climbs to a bench at a viewpoint for the Highwood valley backdropped by the Great Divide. The Elk Range lies to the right of Weary Creek Gap, the High Rock Range to the left.

The trail levels along the top of a steep bank with views across Cat Creek to the grassy Cat Creek Hills where the elk like to overwinter. A short uphill, then it's all switchbacks down the far side of the forested ridge to the valley bottom.

Cross the previous highway. The trail continues past a bench and the remnants of Ford's camp. At Cat Creek nearby is the ruins of an old bridge and the access road leading to the coal mines up Cat Creek.

Your trail, colour-coded black with coal dust, heads across to Cat Creek upstream of the old bridge and at the entrance to the canyon crosses to the east bank. On the right wall note the coal seams. Recross the creek and arrive at Lower Cat Creek Falls.

Lower Cat Creek Falls at the end of the trail in the canyon.

🟥 The Canyon

During the waning of the last ice age the Highwood River valley bottom was at a much higher elevation, likely on a level with the top of the gorge. Geologists reckon a lake filled the Highwood valley at this point and that gravel carried down by Cat Creek was deposited as a delta at the meeting of creek and lake. When the lake drained, Cat Creek started eroding downwards, first through the gravels, then through a bedrock of sandstone and conglomerate to create the gorge you see today.

🟥 Ford Mines

This clearing was the site of Ford Highwood Collieries Cat Creek camp. A good many years had passed after George Dawson had first reported coal in the area during the geological survey when Henry Ford, a real estate salesman turned prospector from Nova Scotia, leased 11,637 acres of government land in the Highwood at 1.00 per acre. Fourteen seams, ranging from two metres to six metres in thickness were worked in upper Cat Creek and above Stoney Creek just east of Highwood Junction. Though you won't see any workings on this trail, anyone going higher up the valley and into side valleys will walk right past a few of the old entrances.

Although the anthracite was of very high quality, this venture was doomed to go the way of all ventures in what is now Kananaskis Country. Transportation costs to civilisation were simply too high and in winter it was a continual struggle to keep the coal wagons moving along the Lineham Company Road which is today's Kananaskis Trail and Highwood Trail combined. As usual, plans to build a railroad came to nought.

Grass Pass
6.5 km return

spring
summer
fall

A moderately strenuous uphill walk up Pack Trail Coulee to a grassy pass between the Bull Creek Hills and Holy Cross Mountain. There is the option of ending the trip at scenic Fir Creek Point under the Boundary Pine described by R.M. Patterson in his book "The Buffalo Head." Although the trails are not official, signposted or maintained in any way, they are well-used by hikers.

Start: Highwood Trail (Hwy. 541) at Sentinel day-use area. After the gate turn left into the equestrian parking lot.

Return to the highway and turn right. Pass the sign "Sentinel day-use area".

Immediately, turn left up a good trail. The trail circles to the right and after an uphill joins an old 4-WD road heading up Pack Trail Coulee.

Turn left. The trail continues uphill then levels off. All along this stretch on both sides of the trail are Douglas firs mixed in with balsam poplar, spruce and lodgepole pine.

An avenue between twisted aspens shaped by wind leads to the creek crossing. The main valley creek is quite tiny and easily jumped. This signals the return to more climbing, this time through extensive meadows of bunch grass to Grass Pass where four trails meet. Look back down Pack Trail Coulee for a view of Mt. Burke and Zephyr Creek, named for the prevailing west winds.

A **Douglas Fir**
(Pseudotsuga menziesii glauca)
The tree is named after Scottish botanist David Douglas who, after his last trip to North America in 1827, fell down a pit in the Sandwich Islands and was trampled to death by a wild bull. The next thing you should know is that Douglas firs are not firs at all, hence the Greek word *pseudos* in the botanical name meaning false. It's actually a member of the pine family. To confuse matters further, other common names include Oregon spruce. Old giants have a massive trunk with fire resistant deeply furrowed bark of a reddish brown colour which is unmistakable.

B What is Bunch Grass?

In fall the grass dries out and turns golden brown. Come spring, new green shoots grow up around the outside, enclosing the bunch of old grass in the middle which remains edible for many many years. Take it from me, well-developed bunch grass tussocks are to walkers what moguls are to beginner skiers. Count yourself lucky you don't hike in Peru where two-metre high monsters are best negotiated by swimming techniques.

Late fall in Pack Trail Coulee. The trail to Fir Creek Point crosses the grass slope near the skyline.

OPTION FIR CREEK POINT (1.6 km return)

Turn right uphill, then immediately right again. Follow the long-established cattle trail which traverses the meadows to Fir Creek Point, located on a ridge descending from the Bull Creek Hills. En route, you pass two springs which are the source of the main valley creek.

Out on the point there's a magnificent view to the west of the High Rock Range, Mount Head and Grass Pass. Besides the celebrated Boundary Pine, there's lots of other shapely limber pines in the area for photo buffs.

Return the same way.

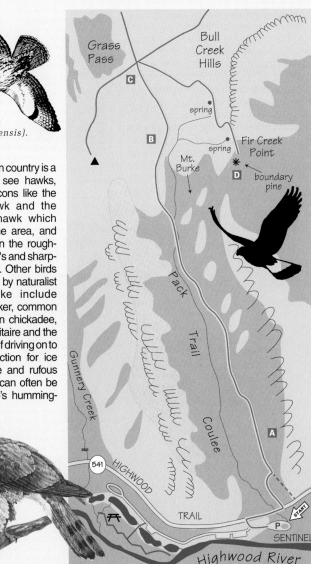

Red-tailed hawk (Buteo jamaicensis). Voice: keeer-r-r.

C This fine open country is a good place to see hawks, eagles and falcons like the red-tailed hawk and the northern goshawk which both nest in the area, and during migration the rough-legged, Cooper's and sharp-shinned hawks. Other birds recorded so far by naturalist Richard Clarke include Clark's nutcracker, common raven, mountain chickadee, Townsend's solitaire and the American pipit. If driving on to Highwood Junction for ice cream, calliope and rufous hummingbirds can often be seen at Laurie's hummingbird feeders.

The northern goshawk (Accipiter gentilis) is the largest, the swiftest and most frightening of all hawks. Its prey includes grouse, owls, ground squirrels, hares, ducks, small birds and other hawks. It resents you getting too close to a nest, so be warned. Voice: kak kak kak.

D Limber Pines *(Pinus Flexilis)*

There's only one photogenic tree in the Canadian Rockies and that's the limber pine whose long graceful branches deformed by wind into grotesque shapes is beloved by the Ansel Adams school of photography. Don't bother looking near the Great Divide where the rainfall is heaviest. They prefer the dry, well-drained rocky soils of the eastern slopes. That they grow on exposed rocky hillsides at all appears to be a result of an amazing dependency between the tree and Clark's nutcrackers. The birds' staple food is limber pine seeds which they store for winter use on rocky ridges where the wind tends to blow the snow away.

Another Limber pine lower down the same ridge.

Patterson's Boundary Pine at Fir Creek Point.

Bear Lake
2 km return

spring
summer
fall

A short uphill walk through flower meadows and open forest leads to a fishing lake stocked with grayling. Catch and Release is in effect.

Start: Johnson Creek Trail (Hwy. 532). 5.6 km west of Indian Graves Campground, turn right into a parking lot.

From the parking lot the trail heads uphill through flower meadows.

Keep straight where a grassed over road comes in from the left. Continue uphill, climbing between aspens on the right and open pine forest on the left. Pass a small brown pond at a junction.

Keep to the right. Walk along the dam above Bear Lake. A convenient dead tree sticking out of the water is posted with the current fishing regulations.

The small brown pond and Windy Peak Hills.

Gaillardia (Gaillardia aristata).

Silky lupin (Lupinus sericeus).

◩ *Meadow Flowers*

Lupines

Introduced into England's gardens by botanist David Douglas, the lupine is normally blue but here you'll find some that are white. The generic name *Lupinus* comes from the Latin "lupus," meaning wolf. It was thought that lupines robbed the soil of nourishment when actually the reverse is true. Nitrogen stabilizing bacteria in tiny nodules on the roots enrich the soil. Joan Ward-Harris in her book "More than Meets the Eye" describes how in 1954 a mining engineer in the Yukon digging through frozen silt came upon some ancient lemming burrows with a horde of seeds. Carbon-dated, they proved to be between 10,000 and 15,000 years old, 8,000 years older than the oldest known seed of the time which was that of the lotus flower. When placed on damp filter paper, six seeds germinated within two days, and a year later one plant produced mature flowers. It was the beautiful blue lupine.

Sticky geranium (Geranium viscosissimum).

Bear Lake from the dam.

LAKESHORE TRAIL

Follow the trail along the east shore.

Keep right (trail to left leads to the lakeshore). This trail takes you into a small circular clearing.

Keep left (the right-hand trail is an alternative route to Big Iron Pond. The steep twisty descent into the north fork of Johnson Creek makes this route less attractive than the north fork route described on page 202, particularly on the return.)

Keep right. The trail now follows the west shore with many access trails leading to the water. Pass the little brown pond.

Turn right at the small brown pond. Return the way you came.

B Arctic grayling

Normally a cold water fish of the northern forests, the arctic grayling has been introduced into suitable lakes south of the Peace River area. Bear Lake was stocked in 1985 and again in 1987. A member of the salmon family, it is easily distinguished from trout by its very large colourful dorsal fin, Along the east bank, Westwind Flyfishers (financed by Buck for Wildlife) have laid down a whole pile of gravel which they hope will encourage the fish to spawn.

Big Iron Pond
7 km return

spring
summer
fall

A fairly strenuous walk, initially through pine forest and flower-filled meadows below the eastern escarpment of Hailstone Butte and finally over a ridge to a fishing lake stocked with arctic grayling (catch & release). The route is entirely unofficial and therefore not signposted or marked in any way. Expect some steep hills, minor creek crossings which can be jumped and an indistinct section across meadow marked by cairns. For the more adventurous.

Start: Johnson Creek Trail (Hwy. 532). 7.8 km west of K-Country boundary turn south into an unofficial camping/parking area by the side of Johnson Creek. Park nearest the road.

The trail starts from the north side of the road opposite, to the right of the sign, "No motorized vehicles beyond this point". The old logging road, initially grassed, follows the north fork of Johnson Creek past the two-log ruins of a cabin to a flower meadow.

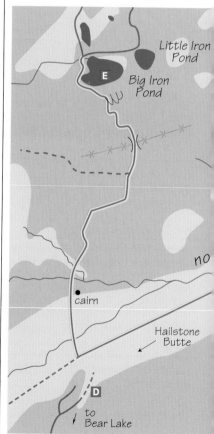

Little Iron Pond

Big Iron Pond

cairn

no

Hailstone Butte

to Bear Lake

C Derocherville
This valley was logged in the first decade of the 20th century. It all started in 1903 when Frank Derocher, out looking for the Lost Lemon Mine, found coal in Johnson Creek and in neighbouring valleys. For several years he operated a very successful coal mine and sawmill. Up sprang the company town of Derocherville (Indian Graves campground) which consisted mainly of his 8-roomed house and its outbuildings. Later the sawmill was bought by Ed Mason who moved it up the valley to opposite the north fork.

B Dung Party

The photo shows common alpines (the dark ones) and field crescent (or crescentspot) butterflies getting their salts and minerals. They also like mud, fermenting sap, occasionally carrion, but above all, flowers. Commonly, the upper wings and under wings of butterflies have a different pattern and colour. This is especially noticeable in the field crescents which have a very light beige underside while the upper wings exhibit a gorgeous chequerboard of orange, black and white spots, blotches, borders and arches. The dark patches near the base of the wings absorb infrared radiation which warms the body. Some butterflies, particularly the whites and sulphurs, also have ultraviolet reflection patterns which are quite invisible to us but which help them recognise another of their species at mating time.

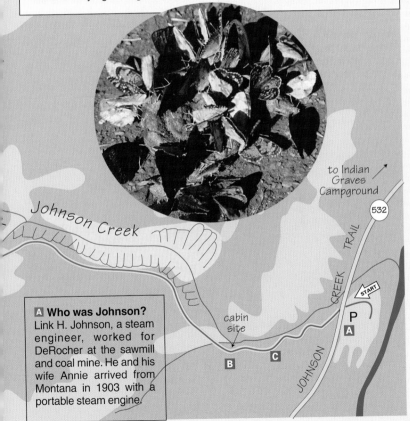

A Who was Johnson?

Link H. Johnson, a steam engineer, worked for DeRocher at the sawmill and coal mine. He and his wife Annie arrived from Montana in 1903 with a portable steam engine.

The big meadow below Hailstone Butte.

Follow the narrow cow trail down the centre of the meadow. Watch for where the forest edge on the left comes close to the trail (blue salt lick in trees).

Turn right. A faintly-defined trail in the grass crosses the meadow to the creek. Jump across and aim for a cairn at the meadow's edge. Cross the tributary, then on what is now a very well-defined trail climb into the pines. A flat stretch heading right precedes the final climb to a low point in a ridge. A short, steep winding descent brings you to Big Iron Pond, the colour of Big Rock Traditional Ale.

Step across the tributary and follow the trail as it climbs fairly steeply onto a bench above the creek, now incised in a mini-gorge to your right. The road turns west and ends between willow trees, portals to a magnificent longitudinal meadow below the eastern escarpment of Hailstone Butte.

The good trail heads left around the west shore to the north shore where there's a strip of meadow, not grass but flower leaves. Flowers include yellow columbine, goldenrods, lupines, camas lilies, beardtongues, pussy toes, vetches, paintbrushes and blue-eyed grass. The trail carries on to Little Iron Pond a short distance away, then cuts across country to Iron Creek.

Big Iron Pond. View from the south shore of Sentinel Mountain.

D *Bronze bells grow from a bulb. Each flower is a perfect diminutive lily, quite fragrant.*

E The Summer of the Dragonfly

At the bottom of the dark pond, overwintering larvae survive by eating overwintering mosquito larvae. Come spring, they undergo an incomplete metamorphosis, meaning that in immature stages the body resembles that of the adult but has modifications which allows it to live in a different habitat. Mature larvae crawl up plants out of the water, the cuticle splits down the head and thorax and out climb this season's new adults with wings.

The summer is the rest of their life. And a hectic time it is too with aggressive males engaging in frequent dog-fights over the water while defending territory and their mates. Often the male will remain attached to the philandering female until she has lain her eggs. She does this by simply dropping the eggs into the lake. They sink to the bottom and hatch into larvae which overwinter at the bottom of the dark frozen pond.

Dragonflies eat unpopular insects like mosquitoes and horse flies.

Plateau Mountain
9 km return

An easy walk up a gas well access road to the summit of Plateau Mountain, an ecological reserve. This is a wonderful walk on alpine tundra with sweeping views in every direction and many interesting things to look at both underfoot and in the air. Because you are above treeline all the way, dress for strong winds which are the norm in this part of the Canadian Rockies. The altitude of 2524 m may affect people not used to it.

Four-parted gentian (Gentianella propinqua).

Start: Forestry Trunk Road (Hwy. 940) at Wilkinson Summit. The highway is closed December 1st to April 30th between Cataract Creek and the pass. Drive north up the Plateau Mountain Road for 3.7 km to a parking lot on the big bend. A locked gate a little further on precludes public vehicles.

Jacob's ladder (Polemonium pulcherrimum).

Walk up the road past treeline. The road bends left and arrives at a col. All along this stretch browse for alpine flowers both up hill and down the slope. Two members of the gentian family to look for are moss gentian *(Gentian prostrata)* and four-parted gentian *(Gentiana propinqua)*. Bighorn sheep are seen occasionally. From the col, the road winds easily up the western escarpment at a break in the cliffs onto the plateau proper where you'll find your first evidence of patterned ground.

Turn right (the road to left leads to the north end and the ice cave, too long a walk for the purpose of this book.)

A Jacob's Ladder

P. pulcherrimum meaning 'very handsome', grows profusely on the bank below the road. The common name describes the fern-like leaves which look like miniature ladders. If you crush them between your fingers they smell awful, rather like skunk. Blue forget-me-not-like flowers are beautiful and fragrant, though not as beautiful as the alpine species *Poleminium viscosum* which grows in windy places at the southern range of Kananaskis Country.

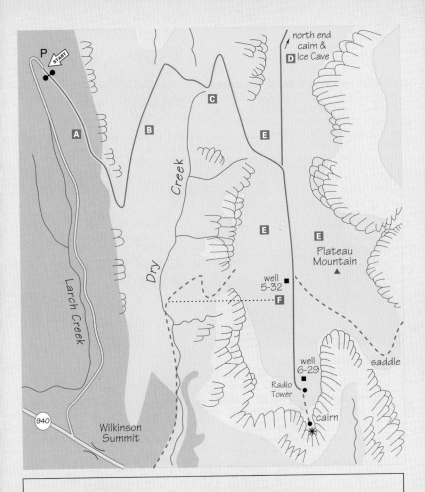

B This is a nunatak

During the last ice age the glaciers flowed around Plateau Mountain to a height of about 2380 m, just a little higher than the col where you are now standing. From this location, the eye can follow a definite series of parallel lines around the steep sides which are called trimlines. The country must have looked rather like the interior of Greenland looks today with flat islands of rock barely protruding out of the ice. Over the ages, the bedrock on the summit has been shattered into small pieces by frost action into what is called a fell field or felsenmeer (meaning rock-sea in German). To see what strange things happened to the rocks, read on.

Careful you don't step on that caterpillar crossing the road. Caterpillars have one or possibly two host plants to feed on and though butterflies are a little less choosy (if they eat at all), it helps to know the most likely places to find a certain kind of butterfly because butterflies tend to like the same environment they grew up on when they were caterpillars.

Riding's satyr *(Neominois ridingsii)* feeds on grass and acts rather like a grasshopper.

Labrador sulphur (*Colias Nastes*) feed on alpine milk vetch and other alpine legumes.

◻ Tundra is tundra

So you always thought tundra was just grass. Here on the summit of Plateau Mountain there are four main kinds:

Shrub tundra occurs on well-drained areas, often stony and sloping. White mountain avens predominate plus locoweeds, creamy hedysarums, silver rock cress, arnicas, blue beardtongues, black-tipped ragwort, yarrow, yellow paintbrush, western bistort and forgetmenots.

Small areas of **heath tundra** are found mostly upslope of the damp sedge tundra. It's characterized by yellow heather as you might expect plus woolly everlasting, wandering daisy and alpine goldenrod.

Sedge tundra A bog on flat ground is not formed in the normal way of water running downhill into a depression. What has happened here is that just a few feet below the surface, the ground is still permafrozen and rain water has nowhere to go except hang around the surface and provide moisture for sedges, Moss gentians, smooth-leaved cinquefoils, field chickweed, elephantheads, wild onions and tufted hair grass.

Alberta fritillary (*Clossiana Alberta*) feed and lays eggs on white mountain avens. Can be distinguished from the C. astarte by its smaller size and slow relaxed flying just above ground.

Astarte fritillary (*Clossiana astarte*) feed on spotted saxifrage. Wary of people's approach and a fast flier.

Magdalena alpine (*Erebia magdalena*) feeds on campions. I've seen these black beauties on black lichen (*Umbilicaria krascheninnikovii*) growing on rocks in patterned ground areas. Apparently females lay their eggs on the rocks.

Lichen-sedge tundra We're into patterned ground now where the ground is very dry. Look for fragrant sedge, various lichens (*Omphalodiscus, Cornicularia aculeata, Peltigera canina, Krascheninnikovii, Umbilicaria hyperborea, Centraria cucullata*), spotted saxifrage, mountain chickweed with saxifrage -like leaves, bladder campion, roseroot, pygmy bitter-root and more buttercups.

Plants on the rare list
Two alpine fireweeds (*Epilobium saximontanum, E. platyphyllum*), alpine everlasting (*Antennaria alpine var. media*), pygmy bitter-root (*Lewisia pygmaea*), mountain parsnip (*Angelica Dawsonii*), showy sandwort (*Arenaria rossii*), yellow fleabane (*Erigeron ochroleucus*), the flame-coloured lousewort (*Pedicularis flammea*), a ragwort (*Senecio conterminus*) and a primrose (*Primula egaliksensis*).

Patterned ground on the summit. In this view we're looking west to the mountains of the Great Divide.

Ice cave entrance.

D Ice Cave

Clusters of hexagonal, plate-like ice crystals and extruded fingers of ice. Rare and delicate ice flowers and corkscrew stalactites. Located at Plateau's north end and accessed by a bit of a scramble is the celebrated Plateau Mountain Ice Cave. I'm afraid, you're 30 years too late to see any of its beauty. There's a gate across the entrance, put there in 1972 by the Alberta Forest Service. Too many visitors over 40 years had resulted in smashed ceiling pendants. Additionally, a rising inside temperature was melting the ice plates which were developing small icicles at their lowest points. I'm happy to report that since closure, fresh platelets are beginning to form.

E Patterned Ground

is a relic of the time when the climate was much colder and wetter. How have the frost-shattered rocks, called felsenmeer, arranged themselves into a pattern of polygons? First, the fissures are a result of surface contractions resulting from seasonal low temperatures and intermittent drying out of the soil. On a smaller scale, wet mud contracts into polygonal shapes when dry. Frost sorting caused by continual freezing and thawing forced the larger rocks upwards and outwards. Once the rocks were at the surface, seasonal heaving by ice in soil slid these larger blocks towards and into the fissures, leaving islands of finer material in the centre.

On steep ground at the edge of the plateau the stones are aligned in stripes down the slope. Take a look on the return journey.

Your road makes a straight line towards the south end. The cross wind can be fierce on the summit plateau; I hope you have a windproof. The highest point of the plateau lies to your left and is marked by a cairn hard to distinguish in the jumble of patterned ground.

Return the same way.

OPTION (add on 5 km return)

Keep right (reclaimed road to left leads to a well site). Pass gas well 5-32 on your right. In another 2 km, Well 6-29, an RCMP radio tower and a Canadian & Western Natural Gas weather station mark the end of the road. From the radio tower carry on across grass to the large cairn on the southern edge which overlooks the flat top of the Savanna Creek anticline on the far side of Highway 940. Much further away you'll see some spectacularly-shaped peaks, amongst them Crowsnest Mountain, Beehive Mountain, and the two Elevators as people from Nanton call them. One is still unclimbed. Below you, unseen, is January Cave which harbours animal bones, including those of brown and collared lemmings, dating back 33,500 years!

Footnote
Thanks in large measure to Husky Oil, 5570 hectares of the mountain is now an ecological reserve. No more wells will be drilled in the reserve. In exchange, Husky has the rights to directional drilling from outside the area, can continue to operate the two wells within the reserve, and is granted some amount of royalty holiday for these two wells.

F "Old Flattop is the most perfect oil dome I've ever seen".
Plateau Mountain is a classic example of a large-scale anticline. What happened is that the softer stratas of younger ages eroded and left behind this very hard resistant quartz sandstone which overlies a dome of Rundle Group limestones. A closed dome of Rundle Group limestones is where you're likely to find oil and gas retained in 'traps'. The oil rush started in 1937 when Calgary prospector W.D. MacIlvride called in Joe Irwin, head geologist of Anglo-Canadian Oil Company, to make a survey. This resulted in Ozzie Hogg pushing a fledgling Highway 532 over the Hump. Drilling results were disappointing, hence the name Dry Creek. Things didn't really get going until the 1950s. Nowadays, Husky Oil operates two wells on the summit. In the dehydration facilities buildings, water vapour is separated from the gas which is then piped down the west slope. Note wind speed indicators and buildings chained to the ground. Doctor/author Morris Gibson recalls being called out to a rig and finding all the men roped together for safety.

Sandy McNabb
1.8 km loop

early spring
summer
late fall

An easy and pleasant stroll through typical foothills country of pine and aspen forest to a viewpoint overlooking the Sheep River.

Start: Sheep River Trail (Hwy. 546) at Sandy McNabb Recreation Area. Drive down the access road and turn third left into a small parking lot (the second and third side roads are adjacent). Trail brochures can be picked up at the trailhead. Water is available from the tap en route.

From the trailhead a narrow trail heads through a chequerboard of aspens and damp meadows growing Bog birch.

Shortly after crossing a small bridge over a spring and passing a water tap on your left you arrive at a junction.

Turn left. The trail winds through pine and aspen forest, avoiding the muskeg in the centre of the loop which is where the ski trail goes. Ultimately you cross the stream issuing from the bog. This stretch is a good place to find the dark-eyed junco.

Keep right. In Spring there's a particularly large bunch of bluebells (lungwort, *mertensia paniculata*) on the right at the boardwalk section.

Arrived at the edge of a steep bank falling to the Sheep River you'll find a cluster of interpretive signs and benches marking the trail's highlight—a view of the day use area, Mt. McNabb and on the skyline the pointy peaks of the Front Ranges.

The view from 12 of the picnic area down by the Sheep River and Mt. McNabb.

A Sandy McNabb

Who was Sandy McNabb? In 1910 Alexander 'Sandy' came to DeWinton from Glasgow, Scotland with his brothers Andrew and Jimmie and Daniel during the oil boom years of 1913-14 to work for the Royalite Oil Company. Sandy was largely instrumental in founding Turner Valley's Fish and Game association who called his favourite fishing spot Sandy McNabb's (Fishing) Camp. That's the flat down by the Sheep River where the picnic area is now.

B Bluebells

are officially known as mertensia or tall lungwort *(Mertensia paniculata)*. The common name bluebell is not to be confused with harebells which are also called bluebells or with English bluebells which are really hyacinths.

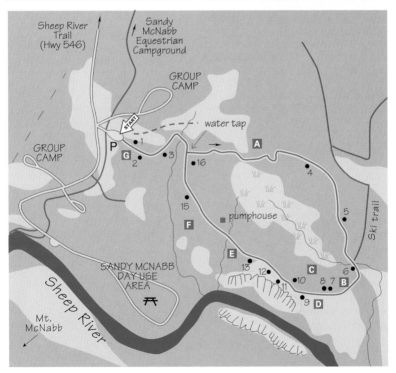

D Blue-eyed Grass, the new wave flower

For a long time Earth had no flowers. They evolved during the Cretaceous Period when the dinosaurs were on the wane. At this time Insect pollination was the up and coming thing and plants responded by evolving into a variety of forms and bright colours all aimed at attracting the insects. Flowers are still evolving today, becoming more efficient and streamlined with some parts fused. But right now the new-fangled monocots are greatly outnumbered by old fashioned flowers called dicots.

New wave flowers can be recognised instantly: petals and sepals number three or multiples of three, while leaves are a simple one-piece with veins running parallel and far less varied in shape with nothing much in the way of toothed edges. Some monocots produce bulbs and rhizomes for reproduction and food storage. For those plants using insects, protruding stamens means pollen is more easily disseminated. Male and females parts are always on the same plant. Compare the blue-eyed grass with the white "dicot" geranium you'll see later on or with meadow rue which has separate male and female plants.

Blue-eyed grass (Sisyrinchium montanum).

C The Mob in the Aspens

In recent years common crows (*corvus brachyrhynchos*) have been nesting in this vicinity, gobbling up grasshoppers from the long grasses. As you approach the alarm system goes into action. You're likely to be greeted with either the 'assembly call' (raucous and intense) or the 'scolding call' (less raucous, more staccato and continuous). All the other birds in the vicinity respond by flying to the rescue (it's called mobbing) and joining in the racket. Amazingly, crows have eight different alarm calls for different circumstances.

E Spotted coral root orchid

Elusive, bizarre, it's said the flowers look like midget acrobatics on a pole. Don't for one minute think you're going to spot this beauty at this same spot every year. No one can predict when or where coral-roots are going to pop up. You see, this totally red orchid lacks chlorophyll and so can't manufacture its own food and is therefore totally dependent for survival on fungi and decaying matter on the forest floor. coral-root? There are no real roots. Part of the stem buries underground where it branches and interweaves in a manner rather like coral.

F Red-naped Sapsuckers (*Sphyrapicus varius*)

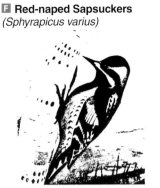

are also called yellow-bellied sapsuckers. They drill orderly rows of small holes horizontally across tree trunks, then by means of a brush at the end of the tongue, lap up the oozing sap together with any small insects stuck in the sap — hence the name sapsucker. What I find intriguing is the claws which resemble those of a parrot with two toes pointing backwards.

The south-facing slopes falling towards the river are home to all kinds of sun-loving flowers like early yellow loco weed, sticky geranium, camas lilies, puccoon, and above all blue-eyed grass which grows in profusion during the latter half of June.

Gradually the trail moves away from the bank and wanders through aspen forest to the junction near the water tap. En route you cross another creek issuing from the bog you have circled around. Note the pumphouse up the hill.

Keep left and return the same way to the parking lot.

G Grasses

In late August the flowers die down and are eclipsed by the splendour of the grasses which have grown as tall as a cow's back. Grass grows from the base upwards like hair so it can be cropped by animals and still grow. Seeds are distributed by wind, feet and droppings. Some with barbs like Porcupine and Needle grass catch on fur or passing socks.

White geranium A perfect example of a Dicot.

Timothy *(Phleum pratense)* is easily recognised by the column. Its value as forage was recognised in 1750 when seed was collected from the wild and sown in cultivated fields in Europe. One of the early producers was Timothy Hansen.

Wheatgrass *(Agropyron intermedium)*. In intermediate wheatgrass which grows round here, the ends of the leaves have short hairs visible under a magnifying glass. When a plant becomes dehydrated, the leaves roll up into tight tubes, thus reducing the available surface to the desiccating effect of wind. Another agropyron is quack grass (*A. reparium*).

Bromegrass *(Bromus)* Here the species is likely meadow bromegrass *(Bromus biebersteinii)*, another import and not terribly attractive to cattle.

Bluegrass *(Poa)* can be distinguished from other grasses by its boat-shaped leaf tips. There are 19 species in the mountains and foothills alone. The Kentucky version is used for lawns and golf courses.

Bighorn Sheep Lookout
0.8 km return

late spring
summer
fall

A ten minute stroll across Nash Meadow brings you to a hide where there's a good chance of spotting bighorn sheep on the meadows below or on the walls of the Sheep River gorge. It's also one of my favourite low altitude viewpoints. Bring binoculars.

Start: Sheep River Trail (Hwy. 546) at Bighorn day-use area. This stretch of road is open between May 15th and December 1st.

Leave the day-use area at the trail sign.

The trail passes through luxurious meadows of long grasses to a hide overlooking Nash Meadow (in Stoney, Anawichadabi) above the Sheep River gorge. At one time these flats were ploughed and seeded with oats, and at other times fenced off for cattle grazing. The buildings, once the Sheep River Ranger Station, are now the Sheep Field Centre.

Return the same way.

A **Sheep River Valley Sanctuary**
To protect flocks which have been here for thousands of years, this sanctuary was established in 1973, thanks largely to the efforts of ranger Joe Macovic. In 2002 it was incorporated into the slightly larger Sheep River Provincial Park.

The view of Nash Meadow (Anawichadabi) under Missinglink Mountain (right). On the skyline are the mountains of the Highwood Range.

B A Sheep Tradition

This river was named 'itou-kai-you' on David Thompson's map of 1814 and 'itukaiup' on the Arrowsmith map of 1859. In 1792, Hudson's Bay Company scout Fidler identified the river in his journal entry as 'eetookiap', while present day Stonies call it 'Kiska Wapta'. All of which translates to Sheep River.

C The weird name Missinglink

The English name has always fascinated me. I imagined the mountain as some inverted Rift Valley littered with the bones of some lost Lucy. Then I discovered that on early maps pre-1907 the valley, after which the hill is named, was written 'Missing Lynx Creek' which presents a totally different picture and a more logical one.

D Bighorn Sheep *(Ovis canadensis)*

Although sheep can easily dig through the bit of snow which falls in this area to get at the grasses underneath, as winter deepens they much prefer to nibble on nutritious twigs like buffaloberry and rose bushes. This is because as grasses cure, they lose protein so that even at winterstart, grass has only half the summer protein content left. Sheep don't like deep snow at all. With their short legs they're easy meat for predators, which is why they hang around the gorge or on the rocky south face of Missinglink Mountain which is periodically swept by Chinook winds. Come spring, sheep flock to mineral licks. A high intake of potassium and water from new foliage leads to excessive sodium loss and a temporary period of negative sodium balance.

If driving further to the flats have the camera ready for sheep close-ups.

ⓔ *Horrors in the Grass*

Because sheep have learned that if they stay in the sanctuary they won't be shot at, they tend to hang around the same lush meadows all year round, thus laying themselves open to all kinds of nasties which are enough to make anyone think twice before wading into the grass.

Lung Worms These are parasites that are ingested and lodge in the membranes of the lungs, causing irritation and the clogging of air passages. Not surprisingly, an infected sheep has difficulty in breathing and has a cough. Some of the worms are coughed up into the grass, starting up the whole cycle again.

> **R. B. Miller Station, est. 1950**
> Located just up the road is one of the two field stations established by the University of Calgary. Since 1981 researchers have been studying the Bighorns and the effect diseases have on "reproductive success."

Ticks — the stuff of Stephen King horror stories. It's better to find one tick on you than two. Did you know that after two ticks mate on the host, the female drops to the ground and lays up to 10,000 eggs? One presumes there is a shortage of suitable hosts for mating or the foothills would be a tide of red between March and June. Each stage in a tick's life needs blood. The eggs hatch into six-legged larvae which attach themselves to little critters like mice. As eight-legged nymphs, they go after slightly bigger game like ground squirrels. When fully formed, ticks wait patiently in the grass for the big league brushing by — particularly sheep, but also deer, coyotes and sweaty humans. In sheep country check yourself not only in spring, but right through to November.

Banding a Peregrine.

F Peregrine Falcons

In the 1960s peregrines were almost wiped out by pesticides. Not directly, but indirectly as the pesticide DDT passed through the food chain. Small birds ate insects sprayed with DDT, then the falcons ate the small birds, and either died themselves or were affected in a much more insidious way. DDE, the main breakdown product of DDT, caused the birds to lay eggs with shells so thin they were prone to breakage during incubation. Or else the eggs were infertile. By 1970 emergency measures were being taken in Alberta by the Wildlife Service Hatching Facility at Wainwright. Young Peregrines were placed in boxes at 28 days of age and taken to suitable cliffs including the ones rimming Missinglink Mountain. Boxes were anchored part-way down a cliff and the birds fed with food dropped to a hack box until they become able to fend for themselves.

Raptor Migration

Be here with telescopes and Peterson's field guide in the last two weeks of September to the first week of October. Overhead, thousands of ospreys, bald and golden eagles, sharp-shinned Hawks, Cooper's hawks, Harlan's hawks, northern goshawks, and, of course, the peregrines are journeying south to Central and South America. Another excellent viewing spot is Windy Point parking lot. Note that during Spring migration (last week of March and first week of April) when the raptors return to their nesting sites, the highway is closed to vehicles.

Left: The hack box.
(Both photos Julie Bauer).

A group of Cree on a horse raiding venture came upon some Stonies camped in this place. The Crees' initial shooting at teepees had wounded the father of two braves. Very angry, Ozija nurhe (Bear's Ear) and his brother between them, though grossly outnumbered, managed to kill and wound the Cree so that only two got away. Meanwhile "this Gapeya (Tall One or Long One) that individual ran away and jumped over the gorge here to save himself from the raiders". Though tall, he was a clumsy. He hid with the women and children and didn't help defend the camp.

Nearby, in 1855 the Blackfoot raided a Stoney camp located on west bank of Dyson Creek just downstream a bit of the flats. All women and children fled into the forest leaving three braves to defend the camp plus an old woman, the sister of Chief David Bearspaw who carried the sack of shot. The three were holding off their attackers, but the shot sack was almost empty, so the old woman picked up an axe and danced, singing a powerful medicine song. At that moment the clouds burst and drenched the Blackfoot, leaving their powder useless. Oddly enough, the rain didn't touch the Stonies and the Blackfoot, not knowing that their enemies were almost out of powder decided to withdraw.

Ⓖ *Anawichadabi 'raided encampment clearing of flats'*

Longer ago, there was a battle between the Stoney and six Blackfoot, part of a small group headed for Edmonton in a roundabout way to trade. Stonies massacred the Blackfoot and took all their belongings: war paints, clothing, tomahawks, bows and arrows, spears, bone knives, necklaces and horses, and left the men lying there on the grass. When the rest of the Blackfoot arrived at this spot they found their comrades all lying dead in the meadow. The dead were laid out on platforms made from aspen trunks tied together with rawhide throngs and raised high above the ground.

Illustrations from 'Canadian Pictures' by the Marquis of Lorne. Sketches by Lorne and Sydney Hall were engraved by Edward Whymper who is best known as the conqueror of the Matterhorn,

Bluerock Creek
2.2 km loop

late spring
summer
fall

A moderately easy circular walk above the gorge of Bluerock Creek to look at 50 year-old logging sites.

Start: 1. Sheep River Trail (Hwy. 546) at Bluerock Creek parking lot on the north side of the road. 2. Sheep River Trail (Hwy. 546) at Bluerock Campground. The trail starts from the turnaround point at the west end of the campground near site #30 (trail sign). This stretch of road is open between May 15th and December 1st.

From the parking area at start 1 walk across to Bluerock Creek where it emerges from the gorge to look at potholes. Return and climb steps to start 2 at the end of the campground road (sign). This was the site of the first highway bridge across Bluerock Creek.

Keep left. Continue climbing to a junction at a viewpoint above the gorge.

Go right. The trail switchbacks uphill then traverses a steep slope of scree, shale and scrub.

View from the traverse of Bluerock Creek and nameless peaks.

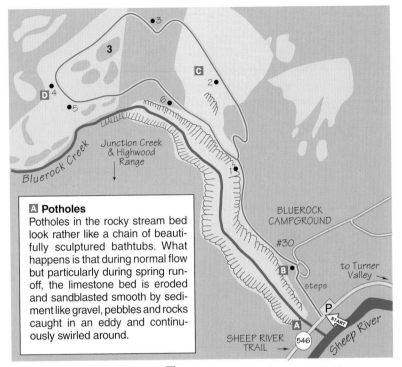

A Potholes

Potholes in the rocky stream bed look rather like a chain of beautifully sculptured bathtubs. What happens is that during normal flow but particularly during spring run-off, the limestone bed is eroded and sandblasted smooth by sediment like gravel, pebbles and rocks caught in an eddy and continuously swirled around.

Junction Creek & Highwood Range

Bluerock Creek

BLUEROCK CAMPGROUND

#30

to Turner Valley

steps

SHEEP RIVER TRAIL →

Sheep River

B The dizzying Bluerock Creek road bridge in 1924.
Photo J.A. Hutchison. Courtesy Forest Technology School.

Blue beardtongue (Penstemon albertinus),

Common stonecrop (Sedum lanceolatum)

Rough-leaved alumroot
(Heuchera cylindrica)

(Photo below). Once seen, the bell-shaped yellow flowers and round leathery leaves with frilly edges are unmistakable. Nowadays, Alum (potassium aluminium sulphate) is used as an emetic, and as a disinfectant and styptic on cuts to stop bleeding. Indians used the raw roots of this plant for all the same purposes. The Blackfoot, for instance, mixed dried root with buffalo fat to rub on saddle sores. Boiled root tea was gargled for sore throats and mouth ulcers.

Silver-leaved scorpionweed
(Phacelia hastata)

(Left). Missing from every popular field guide covering Alberta and the Canadian Rockies except Scotter and Flygare. Like the more familiar Scorpionweed it has a fuzzy appearance caused by bearded filaments protruding out of the flowers which are whiteish in this case. I really like this flower for its red stems and aromatic lance-shaped leaves rimmed with red.

D The Sawmill Site

Trees in the area were first logged by John Lineham's crew at the beginning of the century. The major fire of 1910 put an end to it and it wasn't until the 1940s that loggers returned. Specifically Napp Lafavre who operated a mill here in 1947 for a few short years, not to salvage poles and posts from fire kill but to cut green timber. Trees less than 10 inches in diameter were left to grow into the trees around you.

It's worth wandering down to the flat by the river and poking about in the grass for common 'artifacts' like boards and rusty syrup cans. Across the river is a more interesting dump with cups and saucers. Five men operated the mill for one dollar a day plus keep which was a board and canvas bunkhouse located at the edge of the clearing. Note the traces of a bridge over Bluerock Creek and a road on the far bank. Timber trucked out this route gained the 'highway' sketched out by Lineham's crew via what is now Sheep Horse Trail and the Bluerock Equestrian campground access road. Interestingly, in Lineham's day bunk houses were built of logs but were nevertheless transportable in that the roof poles went with them every time they moved the camp.

A ribbon of spruce forest, then it's all downhill into the logged area, a gentler landscape of meadows and pines overlooking Bluerock Creek. At the bench are views of unnamed mountains above Junction Creek and Bluerock Creek. It's here you leave the trail to wander down the hill to the site of the logging camp.

After crossing a small creek, the trail makes a spectacular return along the top of the gorge.

Keep straight at the viewpoint. Keep right at the end of the campground road. Descend steps to the parking lot.

The lower traverse above the gorge.

Junction Creek Loop
1.2 km loop

late spring
summer
fall

An easy interpretive walk which climbs to a viewpoint in a meadow with exhibits, then finishes with a forest walk above a boisterous section of the Sheep River.

Start: The end of Sheep River Trail (Hwy. 546) at Junction Creek day-use area. Park in one of three lots on the return loop road. This stretch of road is open between May 15th and December 1st.

From the centre parking lot follow the old Junction Creek logging road towards the Sheep River.

Almost immediately turn left. Head through the picnic area, walking parallel to the highway.

Turn left. Cross the downside loop road. Cross the upside loop road. The trail winds uphill through a large meadow to interpretive exhibits and a bench with grand views of Junction Creek and surrounding mountains.

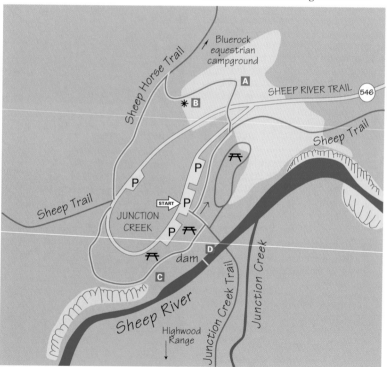

A Chickweed Sandwiches

In this reclaimed meadow you'll find lots of clover, chickweed and strawberry plants. To make chickweed sandwiches chop up stems, leaves (even flowers) and slap between two pieces of whole-wheat bread liberally buttered with mayonnaise. The taste is exactly like cress.

Chopped up leaves of all three are terrific sprinkled in salads, adding zingy wild tastes and extra nutrients like copper and iron. Care is needed with strawberry leaves which must be completely dry, because partially wilted or damp leaves develop a poison during the drying stage. Clover leaves should be small. The Latin name *clava* means club and refers to the resemblance of the trefoil leaf to the three-headed club of Hercules. The club on playing cards imitates the clover leaf.

Top: Wild strawberry (Fragaria virginiana). Bottom: shickweed/ startwort (Stellaria spp.).

Photo below: The interpretive signs, looking up Junction Creek.

*John Lineham
(Glenbow Archives).*

B The Father of Okotoks

John Lineham was one of those people life throws up occasionally who are larger than life. Literally. He reached 6'9" and weighed in at 320 lbs. Lineham was so superstitious, he would never start a job on a Friday and never on any account have shoes removed from a dead horse. Without fail he always carried a big buffalo coat around with him because "You never know about the weather here". True.

Born March 21, 1857, he was just another English immigrant who came west via Montreal, Ontario and Manitoba, arriving in Calgary in 1882 via a Red River cart.

Not just any immigrant. His long list of achievements is astounding. His hugely successful butcher shop in Calgary, 'Dunn & Lineham', was later sold to William Roper Hull who sold out to Pat Burns with far-reaching repercussions. He served in the Northwest Territories Legislative Assembly between 1888-1898, holding the Calgary seat for two terms under Governor Dewdney. During the Riel Rebellion he freighted for the government and it was after this that he turned to a new venture, buying up timber rights in the Sheep and the Highwood River valleys. He single-handedly established the town of Okotoks around a sawmill on the Sheep River built in 1891 and became its first mayor. Hard to realize now, but lumbering was the town's main industry for the next 25 years. If, after this walk, you drive around Okotoks checking out restaurants note the street names like Lineham, Martin, Elizabeth, Elma; all named after family members. Lineham Post Office opened in 1894 across the river from Turner Valley but somehow escaped being the nucleus for a town called Lineham.

With Allan Patrick and Arthur Sifton (later premier of Alberta), he shipped in Alberta's first drilling rig and in 1901 his company struck oil in the future Waterton National Park near Cameron Lake—a short-lived operation.

In 1905 he was instrumental in establishing the boundary between Alberta and Saskatchewan. As a Shriner, he donated land for Lions Park, helped to establish the Masonic Lodge and to develop the Alhazar Temple in Calgary. Four years before his death he established the Lineham Ranch (brand Lazy L) with his brother William.

All these achievements merited not one but three Lineham Creeks in Alberta which somehow has escaped the notice of the Geographic Naming Board. One you passed on your way in. Another lies north of Cat Creek on Highway 40, and the third lies in Waterton Park where there is also a Mt. Lineham and Lineham Lakes.

At the junction in the forest, turn left (the trail to right is a horse trail to Bluerock Equestrian Campground). Descend through forest to the loop road, emerging just right of the biffy.

Turn right onto the road. Stay on the road (the gated road to right is Sheep Trail). Turn right. The trail continues, descending slightly to a fenced-in viewpoint above the Sheep River. Upstream is a bit of whitewater where the river is becoming encased in cliffs. From here the trail heads back to the old Junction Creek logging road. En route look for the remnants of a tumbling dam under water.

Turn left. Keep left. Arrive back at the centre parking lot.

D *Tumbling dams were built by Ernest Dagget. Apart from the remnant seen above, several in a better state of preservation can be seen by hiking up Junction Creek.*

C Lineham Log Drives

During winter cutting, logs were hauled out to points along the river bank where they could be rolled easily into the water during spring runoff. Spring log drives employed 35-40 men who scrambled down banks to get stranded logs moving again. Two boats followed behind, bringing up the rear. It was the usual practise for tent camps along the way to come equipped with Chinese cooks.

A 7 mile log jam, 1911. (NA 695-33 Glenbow Archives).

Whiskey Lake Loop
3.5 km loop

late spring
summer
fall

A longer loop from Junction Creek day-use area. You climb to a scenic pond and return on forest trails to the Sheep River. Finish with a lovely stretch above the gorge.

Start: The end of Sheep River Trail (Hwy. 546) at Junction Creek day-use area. Park in one of three lots on the return loop road. This stretch of road is open between May 15th and December 1st.

From the middle parking lot follow the old Junction Creek logging road towards the Sheep River.

Almost immediately keep right. Turn next right. The trail continues between picnic tables and the river with one or two side trails leading down the bank

to fording spots for those people accessing Junction Creek. After a viewpoint, the trail wanders up the bank to the loop road.

Turn left onto the road, then almost immediately left again through a gate. You are now on the Sheep River fire road, known as Sheep Trail.

You climb a hill to a viewpoint looking straight up Junction Creek to your left and ahead to Gibraltar Mountain.

B Pixie Caps, a fungus
The forest floor has all kinds of interesting stuff to look at. The photo is likely *Cladonia chlorophaea*, which look like golf tees or wine glasses. The greeny grey erect hollow tubes called podetia are fruiting stalks.

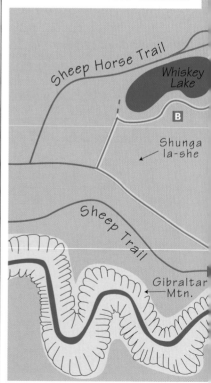

The east face of Gibraltar.

A Gibraltar Mountain

is named after the famous rock at the mouth to the Mediterranean Sea although it doesn't look a bit like it. It used to be called Sheer Cliff in the old days and in 1918 was the scene of a tragic accident when a young worker from Burns Coal Mine slipped and fell over the cliff. His body still lies somewhere on a ledge or in a gully. The overhanging profile on the right, 500 metres high, saw the first extended aid climb in the Canadian Rockies, a nine-day marathon by Billy Davidson and Jim White.

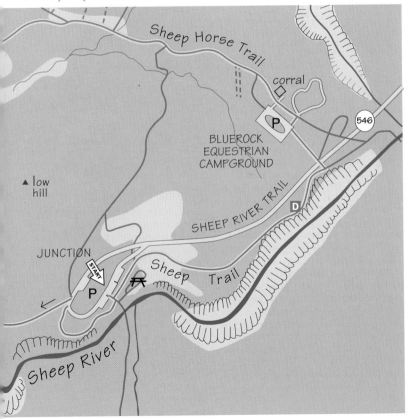

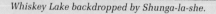

Whiskey Lake backdropped by Shunga-la-she.

⊂ Water Snails

At low water a tide line of snails rim the lake. Water snails *(Lymnaea)* have a protective coiled shell twisting to the right. Squished under the shell is the visceral mass i.e. the digestive system. Now when shells coil it means less room for the internal organs; in the case of water snails, the right excretory organ and the right auricle of the heart are sometimes missing altogether. Coiling plus torsion, a strange process whereby the visceral area plus shell reorientates at 180 degrees to the head and foot means that the digestive system becomes twisted into a figure of 8, resulting in the discharge of excrement onto the top of the head!

If you paddle, the chances of picking up schistosoma are quite good. Don't knock the snails, they're just part of the cycle, simply hosts for yet another parasitic worm at the larval stage. After leaving the snail, the tadpole-like cercaria have 24 hours to find a warm-blooded host like waterfowl or beavers for their next transformation into adults where they go into the reproductive phase. Fortunately, in our part of the World the larva's attempt to bore through human skin to get at a blood vessel offering a through route to the intestines doesn't work but causes intense discomfort before the larva dies.

Turn right (no sign). This is where you leave the old road (and official trail) for a wide track of grass and dirt strewn with pine needles.

Turn right (yellow tape around tree). Be careful this is not the junction with Sheep Horse Trail. This trail is a straight narrow line through the pines.

Turn right at the end of the straight. A very pleasant old trail undulates through open pine forest above the south shore of Whiskey Lake as John Lineham called it. Surely not for the purity of the water but for whiskey breaks during logging days. You emerge in a large meadow at the east end of the lake, a very pleasant spot in the sun, backdropped by Shunga-la-she of the spiral strata rising above the lake to the southwest.

At the far side of the meadow pick up a faint trail in the grass.

Turn right. By following the edge of the meadow you join Sheep Horse Trail in just a few minutes.

Turn right. Sheep Horse Trail is characteristically wide and muddy. Walk between spruce forest and muskeg to a junction with signpost.

Turn right (Bluerock Creek Trail to left). The going is drier on the old logging road.

Keep straight. Two revegetating logging roads on either side of a small creek crossing are easily ignored.

Keep left (the unsigned but well-used trail to right is a short-cut to Junction Creek interpretive trail and the day-use area). A long downhill stretch follows.

Keep left (short-cut trail to parking lot on the right). The trail reaches Bluerock Equestrian Campground between the off-loading ramp and the corral.

Cross the road. The trail continues.

At the campground road turn right. Turn left onto the main access road. Walk down the road to Highway 546. (The alternate equestrian trail shown on the map has two steep hills).

Cross. A few metres in from the highway pick up 'Sheep Trail'.

Turn right. Initially the trail follows the edge of a spectacular gorge of the Sheep River where I've had good luck in spotting sheep, then wanders away from the river a bit, reaching Junction Creek day-use area at a meadow with a mountain view .

Keep left. Now on Junction Creek Interpretive Trail you weave between parking lots and picnic tables.

Turn right. Arrive back at your starting point.

D *The gorge of the Sheep River, looking downstream.*

McLean Pond Trails
1.5 km return

early spring
summer
late fall

A woodland walk with a good chance of spotting moose. Avid birders should extend the walk to McLean Pond.

Start: McLean Creek Trail at McLean Creek recreation area. Turn first right off the access road into the campground entrance. Turn left, then almost immediately right into a parking lot. The trail leaves the far end of the lot at the sign.

B King of the marsh

This is a good trail for spotting moose who like to eat willows, sedges, horsetails and pond weeds. Normally, they are quiet retiring creatures. Be wary during the fall rut, though, when males become unbelievably ornery. With legs one and a half metres long and spreading hoofs, moose find deadfall and deep soft snow no obstacle in a chase.

Start off by following the cutline.

Keep straight three times (second trail to right comes from A and B Loops, the next trail on the left leads to the amphitheatre.). Turn right at the 4-way junction onto a cutline. Turn left. You're now on the gravelled interpretive trail.

Turn left. Two lush meadows on the left of the trail relieve the forest gloom. Cross a small brown creek. Blackened stumps and deadfall hereabouts are evidence of the disastrous 1910 fire which swept the entire eastern slopes from the headwaters of the Sheep and Elbow Rivers to the forest boundary.

Keep left. Return the same way you came.

The big meadow.

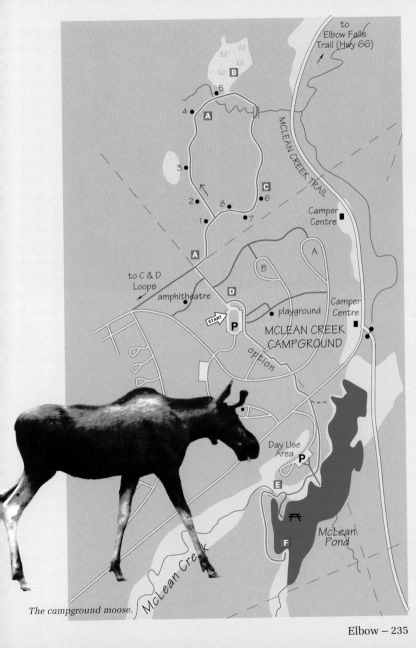

to
Elbow Falls
Trail (Hwy 66)

B

5

4 **A**

MCLEAN CREEK TRAIL

3

C

2 8 6

1 7

Camper
Centre

A

to C & D
Loops

B

A

amphitheatre

D

playground

Camper
Centre

START

P

MCLEAN CREEK
CAMPGROUND

OPTION

Day Use
Area

P

E

McLean
Pond

F

McLean Creek

The campground moose.

C *Burnt-over pine.*

D *The beautiful common pink wintergreen (Pyrola asarifolia).*

The Herball or General Historie of Plants 1597.

A Plants of the Path

This plain-looking plant grows all over trails and gets trampled. Common plantain *(Plantago major)* is also called indian wheat because its seeds can be added to cakes, cookies, bread and breakfast cereals to add valuable vitamins C and K.

TO MCLEAN POND (2 km return)

Just before reaching the parking lot, turn left. Hereabouts, Common pink wintergreens grow in profusion.

Keep right (two trails to left lead to the playground and Loops A and B). Cross Loop B access road. Cross Loop A access road. Cross the main access road. The trail parallels the picnic area access road. McLean Pond is reached at the intersection of a well-worn trail from the picnic area parking lot to a fishing promotory.

The trail (with offshoots to picnic tables on the lakeshore) continues to McLean Creek, enclosed by willows and bulrushes—a good spot for birders. A worsening trail crosses the creek and traverses the steeper south shore to another promotory.

Return the same way to the parking lot.

E Sedges have edges

and rushes are round'. These brown flowering plants are common great bulrushes *(Scirpus validus)*. Despite the name, it belongs to the sedge family and therefore has stems which are triangular in cross-section. The filling is porous and filled with air to keep underwater parts buoyant.

The pond's popular with anglers after rainbow trout.

F *McLean Pond, a dirty orange colour after heavy June rains.*

Fullerton Loop
7 km return

early spring
summer
late fall

Leaving Allen Bill Pond, this moderately strenuous loop takes you alongside the Elbow River, then up a grassy ridge with viewpoints —the real glory of this walk — before returning back down a side valley to the river. A nice walk to combine with a barbecue.

Start: Elbow Falls Trail (Hwy. 66) at Allen Bill Pond day-use area. Follow the road to the left to a parking lot and picnic sites.

> **A Allen Bill Pond** is named after Allen H. Bill who was a former editor and outdoor columnist for the Calgary Herald. Come back in winter when this erstwhile gravel pit becomes a popular skating rink.

The trail leaves the parking lot and heads across to the Elbow River. Duck under the highway bridge. Then cross Ranger Creek and on a cutline access/ logging road walk alongside the Elbow River through flowery meadows. Cross a small creek.

Turn off to the left. A narrower trail passes through a gate in a drift fence.

Wend left. Rejoin the cutline access road which climbs uphill.

Go straight at the bend. Your trail leaves the road and heads into a valley.

Allen Bill Pond with Ranger Ridge in the background. Fullerton Trail follows the ridge-line from right to left.

B *Purple fleabane (Erigeron peregrinus), one of many flowers on Ranger Ridge.*

Keep left (cutline to right). Cross the creek.

Keep straight. Turn left. Shortly you pass through a gate and begin the unremitting climb up Ranger Ridge. On your left the grassy slope is broken up by sandstone outcrops. The climbing ends at a bench, a viewpoint for mountains off to the west.

Follow the ridge-top to the right. Now joined with a cutline access road, you cross a cutline. The left side of the ridge gives intermittent views, this

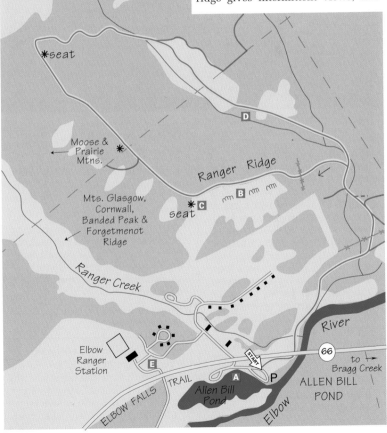

Ranger Ridge, looking back down the trail.

◙ What is aspect?

Lets suppose you're lost in the forest without map and compass and the sky is overcast. Which way is east? All you have to do is look at the vegetation. For instance, compare both sides of this valley or both sides of Ranger Ridge. East and particularly north-facing slopes are often damp gloomy places, perhaps harbouring some snow patches, with dense stands of spruce/pine and an understory of mosses and lichens. Conversely, south and west-facing slopes are sunny dry places with meadows and groves of aspen, pine and Douglas fir. In this neck of the woods, strong westerly winds give ridge-top trees a definite lean to the east, another indicator.

time of Nihahi Ridge, Moose Mountain and Prairie Mountain. At the far viewpoint is a seat.

Turn right. From a notch the road departs the ridge through forest strewn with deadfall to a small valley. Cross the creek.

Turn right. Leave the road for a narrow trail which follows the east bank of the creek, alternating between meadows and aspens groves. Recross the cutline, then a side creek. Cross the main creek.

Keep left. Return the way you came to the parking lot.

AFTER BARBECUE OPTION

Visit the grounds of Elbow Ranger Station to view the totem and the site of the original ranger station. See if you can figure out where the photo on the right was taken from.

D The Boston Tea Party Tea

Tall smooth goldenrod *(Solidago gigantea)* flowers in late summer at the same time and place as purple asters. The leaves make a rather nice mild anise-flavoured tea. The story goes that when American colonists rebelled against British taxes by dumping a cargo of taxable tea into Boston harbour, there was no tea around to drink at the Boston Tea Party so someone made a brew of dried goldenrod leaves and called it Liberty tea. It proved so popular it was later exported to China with great success.

The original ranger station of 1927 and the bridge over Ranger Creek. Photo J.A. Hutchison. (Forest Technology School).

Head represents a hunter holding up a piece of elk hide and giving thanks to the Creator.

Charred pole represents burned-over forest.

Buffalo skull and horns represent the continuous generation of animals.

Base log shows a regenerated forest growing up through burned-over forest.

The circle of rocks represent a medicine wheel.

E Elbow Ranger Station Totem
was designed by Lindsay Dumas and represents forest succession and the interaction of early peoples with the environment.

Diamond T
4 km return loop

early spring
summer
late fall

Mostly a forest walk which includes a rather strenuous climb onto a hill top. You return along valley trails through meadows and pine forest harbouring calypso orchids.

Start: Elbow Falls Trail (Hwy. 66) at Station Flats staging area. Start from the left-hand parking lot. The trail is signposted 'Elbow Valley Trail.'

A short distance from the trailhead is a junction.

Turn left. Initially follow Elbow Valley Trail to a meadow.

Turn right. Coming up is a steep but short climb to an intersecting cutline.

Turn left, then next right. The trail rises gently through pine forest with an understory of alder bushes. Pass through the drift fence.

Turn right at the hitching post. A short climb leads to the trail's high point on a hilltop open towards the west. From the bench the view of forested foot-

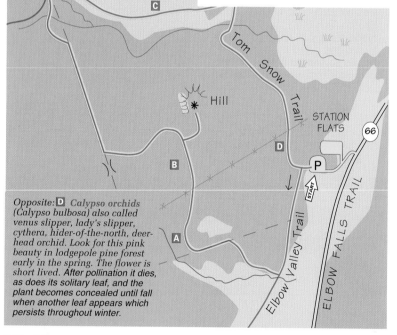

Opposite: **D** *Calypso orchids (Calypso bulbosa) also called venus slipper, lady's slipper, cythera, hider-of-the-north, deerhead orchid. Look for this pink beauty in lodgepole pine forest early in the spring. The flower is short lived. After pollination it dies, as does its solitary leaf, and the plant becomes concealed until fall when another leaf appears which persists throughout winter.*

A Pines in lines

The pines are all the same height because they're all the same age. And that's because the pine forest before this one burnt down. Strangely enough, Lodgepole pines reproduce best through fire. Young trees shed their cones annually, but after about 20 years, mature trees keep their cones which usually remain closed, the scales stuck together with resin. Now when a fire happens along and burns down the forest, the heat softens the resin and allows the cones to open, so releasing winged seeds into the carbon-rich ground for germination. This method is so wildly successful, the new young forest commonly forms a "matchstick 'or' dog-hair forest" which is quite impenetrable. Over time the weaker and slower growing trees die off, opening up the forest.

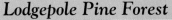

Lodgepole Pine Forest

B Alder understory

Geen alder *(Alnus crispa)* fills in the spaces between the pines. It's instantly recognisable by the shiny green leaves, notched all around the edge, which look like they've been dipped in lacquer. In the spring, male catkins are the usual yellowish pendulous type. Female catkins are woody and look like little dark brown pine cones and are not to be confused with the fruit which looks like a nut.

Male and female alder catkins.

Valley meadows at the sage bank.

hills is not remarkable, though you can pick out people completing the loop in the valley down to the right.

Return to the junction and turn right Descend the hill to a cutline.

Turn right The trail follows an undulating stretch of cutline, crossing three tiny creeks en route.

Turn off left. Parallel the cutline.

At a junction keep right. The trail touches on an old road. Intersect another cutline at right-angles.

Immediately turn off the old road to the right. Cross the main valley creek (salt lick). You are now on the return loop which is a straightforward walk through meadows on the sunny side of the creek. In the valley bottom is the occasional white spruce. Look up to the right at the hill you climbed.

Turn right. Now sharing the trail with Tom Snow Trail, you recross the creek and initially run parallel to it between bogs, beaver ponds and pussy willows on your left and on your right, spruce forest covering the lower slopes of the hill. Around the gate is a good place to find calypso orchids.

Turn left. In a few minutes you regain the parking lot.

G Pasture sage *(Artemisia frigida).*

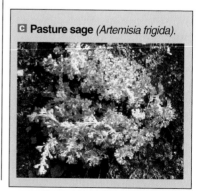

Paddy's Flat
2.2 km

early spring
summer
late fall

An easy trail, ideal for hot summer afternoons when sunbathing, paddling and rescuing capsized canoeists in the Elbow River is the order of the day.

Start: Elbow Falls Trail (Hwy. 66) at Paddy's Flat campground. Non campers start from the far end of B Loop at the trail sign between sites #25 and #26. Campers can pick up the trail as follows: A Loop between sites #12 and #13, C Loop between the registration box and the water pump, D Loop next to the biffy between sites # 56 and #57, E Loop between the garbage disposal unit and site #97. Also accessible from C Loop at the amphitheatre.

At the trail sign on B Loop keep right (left is uphill to A Loop). The trail descends one terrace, coming close to C Loop, then turns away again downhill.

Keep left. On reaching the Elbow River turn right. The main trail turns upstream.

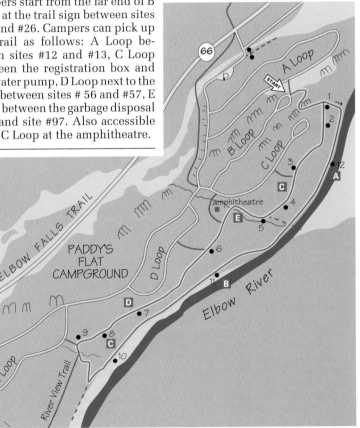

Above: The Elbow River in summer.
Left: The river at spring runoff.

B Sand and Sandstone

Over a hundred million years ago this was a huge swampy plain filling up with sand and mud brought down by nameless rivers from far off nameless mountains. The deeper layers of sand gradually compressed into a rock called sandstone. Here the rock was uncovered by the Elbow River cutting its way down through all the gravel left after the Ice Ages.

A The name Elbow

is just over a century old. Up to 1880 the river was known as Swift Creek. Hokaikshi meaning 'moose' appears on David Thompson's and Arrowsmith's maps of 1814 and 1859, while the Cree and Stoney knew it as o-toos-kwa-na and Mnotha Wapta which translates to 'crackling river' from the sound the water makes when flowing over rock ledges. But what of the name Elbow? Woga Mnoga of the Sarcee Nation has come up with an explanation involving a Sarcee brave called Chaba Mani (Walking Beaver) who was bucked off his horse and fractured his elbow. More likely it's named after a curve in the river about 8 km from Calgary.

D River Terraces

During the last ice age, glaciers and melt streams deposited layer upon layer of gravel and rock debris which filled the valley floor almost to the level of the highway. After the last glacier

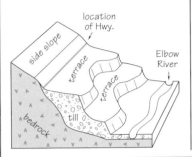

had receded up valley the main melt stream — our Elbow River — started cutting down through the layers. Naturally, the most rapid erosion occurred during warm climatic trends when there was more water released from the ice. So it's these periods of rapid erosion which has resulted in stepped terraces, each terrace indicating the location of the former river.

The drawing on the left shows only two terraces, whereas in actual fact you can count about five, each one occupied respectively by Highway 66, A Loop, B Loop, C, D and E Loops, and by this stretch of interpretive trail. As you will have read, the river has finally reached bedrock.

C Bear's Scratching Posts

Slanting claw marks on aspens indicate a black bear climbed up the tree shown below. Usually it's only the lighter-weight cubs and females who resort to climbing. Vertical claw marks low down the trunk indicate the tree is used for marking territory.

At a small creek crossing stay on the main trail (right trail short-cuts). This marks the start of a gorgeous stretch of sandy bays alternating with resistant sandstone ledges over which the river riffles into deep blue pools.

Turn right (the well-worn trail upstream is worth following farther to Silvester Creek). The official trail, though, heads uphill into the trees.

Keep right (Riverview hiking trail to left). Keep right (left trail leads to E Loop). You're now following a forested terrace. Along this stretch watch for claw marks on aspen trunks.

Keep right (left trail leads to D Loop). Keep right (left trail leads to the amphitheatre and the campground access road). Recross the small creek and descend alongside through damp forest.

Keep left on the main trail (right trail descends to the Elbow River). Keep right (left trail leads to C Loop). Turn left. Climb the hill back to B Loop.

E *Baneberry (Actaea rubra) left and above, is beautiful and highly poisonous.*

E *Twisted stalk (Streptopus amplexifolius), above and below is also called scootberry which is why you want to savour only one juicy berry!*

Elbow Falls Loop
0.8 km

early spring
summer
late fall

A short safe loop on a paved trail with numerous viewpoints of Elbow Falls. Suitable for young children when supervised by adults.

Start: Elbow Falls Trail (Hwy. 66) at Elbow Falls parking lot.

From the far end of the parking lot the signposted trail heads out towards the Elbow River.

Keep right, then straight twice. Arrive at a viewing platform upstream of the falls.

Return to the last junction and go right. A paved trail, stepped and railed, rises to different levels with different viewpoints for the falls. The highest viewpoint looks downstream through the canyon. Here, the main trail turns left (trail to right above the cliffs not recommended) and traverses the hillside to join the outgoing trail.

Turn right. Return to the parking lot.

Above the falls, looking towards the trail.

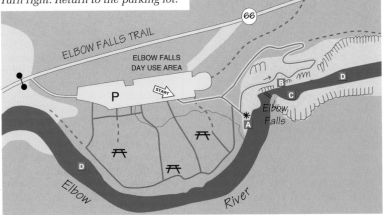

A Close Call

Luckier than most rivers, the Elbow is allowed to run free almost to its confluence with the Bow in Calgary. But it had a close call in 1914 when the Water Power Branch of the Department of the Interior advocated building a dam between Elbow Falls and Canyon Creek. In another report of 1916 the Commission of Conservation of Canada suggested the dam be moved east of Canyon Creek, presumably to add Canyon Creek's spring runoff to the flow. Had it happened (drawing to left): a power house would be sitting in the valley bottom not too far from Paddy's Flat campground. The storage reservoir would have flooded the flats east of Cobble Flat day-use area, in the process inundating Elbow Falls and covering up the magnificent gorge below the falls.

B How the Falls formed

What happened is that a layer of harder Rundle strata lay directly across the river's course. That's the rock you are standing on. Over time, the softer rock downstream of the harder layer was more quickly eroded by the force of the water than the hard rock, thus forming a drop. Ultimately, as the hard rock erodes, the fall will retreat upstream and become just another rapid.

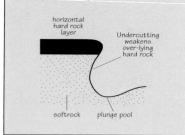

horizontal hard rock layer

Undercutting weakens over-lying hard rock

softrock   plunge pool

D Harlequin Ducks

Look for pairs of *Histrionicus histrionicus* both upstream and downstream of the falls during the springtime (unless you're a whizz at sorting out one drab-coloured female diving duck from another). These birds are sea diving ducks from the west coast who migrate every spring to the turbulent streams of the Canadian Rockies for courting, mating and breeding. The male doesn't hang around. After the female has produced the eggs he's off, leaving his mate to bring up the young. So come before June if you want to see the male, a bluish-black beauty with a

Elbow Falls in spate.

Photo: Don Beers.

smart pattern of white crescents, spots, and stripes; the overall effect reminiscent of the pantomime character harlequin. When harlequins dive underwater they turn the stones looking for a light summer diet of larvae from mayflies, craneflies, stoneflies and caddisflies.

ⓒ Keepers are forever
The pool below the fall is technically called the plunge pool which doesn't mean you can swim in it. Don't even think of it. Ominously, canoers refer to this re-circling hydraulic as a keeper, meaning once the current's caught you you're trapped. After plunging over the step, the water boils up to the surface, then flows back *upstream* to the drop to begin the process all over again.

Lives lost in the past have prompted Kananaskis Country to erect walls, railings and warning signs.

Beaver Lodge
1.3 km one way

spring
summer
fall

An interesting stroll past a string of beaver ponds to picnic tables near the Elbow River. A good chance to observe the work of beavers, including their latest mission to flood the trail.

Start: Elbow Falls Trail (Hwy. 66) at Beaver Flat campground. The trail is also accessible from Beaver Lodge parking lot. This stretch of road is open from May 15th to December 1st.

Walk to the junction of A and B campground Loops. Follow A loop for a few metres.

Turn right. The trail passes the biffy, crosses a beaver canal and a bridge between ponds. Rising water levels have necessitated a new trail to be built around the lower pond on higher ground. Continue past a string of dams and ponds fed by mossy springs. An interpretive sign marks a beaver lodge built into the bank of an exceptionally large pond. From here the trail crosses a bridge and divides.

Turn right (the main left trail climbs past picnic tables to Beaver Lodge parking lot).

The largest beaver pond.

Prairie

ford

Creek

BEAVER
LODGE

P

Powderface Creek

P

POWDERFACE

ford

C

B

D

Elbow ~ River

66

trail
under
water

ELBOW FALLS TRAIL

A

START

A

C

B

BEAVER
FLAT
CAMPGROUND

The secondary trail descends to the bank of the Elbow River and turns left. Cross a creeklet.

Turn left. The trail loops past picnic tables, the soggy ground on your left enclosing more beaver ponds where you're sure to see someone trying their luck at fishing.

Turn right (the rough left trail later divides, both forks leading to fords). Turn left and return the same way to the main trail.

A small anticline seen from across the Elbow River at **D**.

About Beavers

ᴄ Dams Beavers control their own environment, a trait they share with *Homo sapiens*.

Dams are built for security from predators. A beaver starts off by placing willow twigs at the edge of the stream lengthways and with his front feet lays either a rock or mud on it to stop it floating away. The next layer is lain crosswise, and so on. A beaver always starts on the side where the current is least strong. For variety, a beaver will start from both sides, then fill in the middle bit last or build a foundation right across the stream and keep adding willows. On the lower side of the dam lots of sticks are placed lengthwise to serve as braces. Finally, the whole thing is sealed with mud often several feet deep at the base of the construction. Notice how dams are often curved to resist water pressure better. If water levels rise too high and the lodge becomes flooded, beavers lower the level by opening the dam.

Eating preferences Beavers love aspen above all, followed by balsam poplar, willow and then spruce. Don't be surprised at toppled spruce trees. It's a good building material and the bark and the needles don't taste half bad either. Some authorities say that spruce is only eaten by mothers-to-be with strange cravings. Sharp incisor teeth chisel easily through three-foot thick tree trunks to expose delicious sap-line layers.

Drawing from Indian Days of Long Ago, Tamarack Press.

ᴀ Canals are built between the pond and a source of food to facilitate transportation of the food back to the lodge. Usually they are deep enough to hold 15 to 30 centimetres of water.

The size of this house merits a Stoney name Chabti siyan, meaning 'old beaver lodge'.

Marvellous adaptations The incisor teeth never stop growing, so beavers must be constantly gnawing on trees to keep them worn down. Knowing this, you won't be so quick to condemn the little critters. After all, who wants vampire teeth. Lips located behind the teeth mean beavers can gnaw underwater with their mouth shut. Nostrils have flaps which close automatically underwater (beavers can remain under water for 15 minutes at a time, beaver watchers note). Eyes have a transparent membrane over the eyeball for underwater work. The tail is used as a rudder, as a warning device when danger beckons and as a prop when working upright gnawing trees. While front feet are adapted to land i.e. walking, grasping sticks and digging, hind feet are webbed for swimming. A preening toe acts like a comb when beavers preen themselves.

B Lodges During dam building and while waiting for the pond to fill up, the beaver lives in one-roomed apartments in the bank. When the time comes to upscale, the animals pile up a mound of sticks and mud, often over the air vent of their burrow, in effect building a grandiose extension which is what happened here. After all, it makes sense to use existing underwater openings and underwater driveways. Mud is then plastered all over the outside except at the top to leave room for a ventilation hole. The beaver then gnaws and chews his way up through the middle of the mound and when above water level excavates a large room divided up into sleeping quarters, a living-dining area plus pantry, and a bathroom. This underwater entrance keeps the lodge safe from predators, like coyotes, especially in winter.

Ford Knoll
4.5 km loop

late spring
summer
fall

After leaving colourful Forget-menot Pond the trail climbs steeply up a small hill where you are rewarded with an exceptional view of surrounding mountains. The height gain of 235 m makes this a strenuous outing.

Start: Elbow Falls Trail (Hwy. 66). Start from Forgetmenot Pond day-use area near Little Elbow Recreation Area. This stretch of road is open between May 15th and December 1st.

From opposite the first parking lot take the trail which heads away from the pond towards Highway 66.

Cross the highway. Pass through the cattle fence.

Turn right. Cross an old road. The trail climbs through trees to a junction with Powderface Ridge Trail.

Keep left, then right on the main trail. A winding climb through pine forest brings you to a flat saddle and T-junction.

Turn left. What follows is the steepest climb of the day. Persevere.

Near the summit cross an old road at a 4-way junction (no signpost, logs are laid across the road to right). A faint narrow trail leads to the summit ridge.

View from Ford Knoll summit of Forgetmenot Ridge beyond the Elbow River.

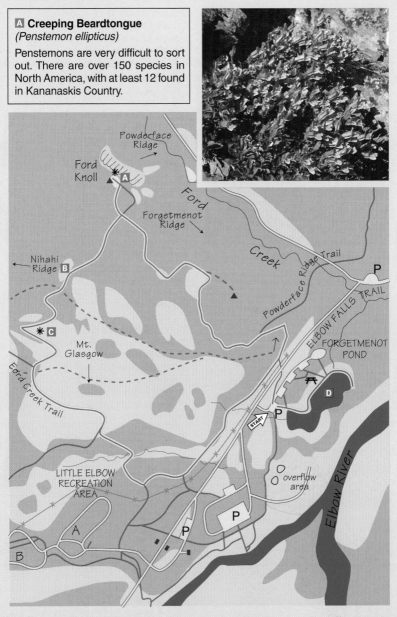

A Creeping Beardtongue
(Penstemon ellipticus)

Pensemons are very difficult to sort out. There are over 150 species in North America, with at least 12 found in Kanananskis Country.

Powderface Ridge

Ford Knoll
A

Forgetmenot Ridge

Ford Creek

Powderface Ridge Trail

P

Nihahi Ridge B

ELBOW FALLS TRAIL

C

Mt. Glasgow

FORGETMENOT POND

Ford Creek Trail

D

P

START

P

overflow area

LITTLE ELBOW RECREATION AREA

Elbow River

A

P

P

B

Descending the west slope.

▣ A Mountain View Story

The 1st of November 1914. Two German armoured cruisers, Scharnhorst and Gneisenau, and three light cruisers, Dresden, Leipzig and Nurnberg under command of Vice-Admiral Graf Maxmilian von Spee had sailed across the Pacific to the west coast of Chile where their job was to disrupt British shipping. Alerted to what was going on, a flotilla based in the Falkland Islands under command of Rear Admiral Sir Christopher Cradock had taken off in pursuit of von Spee. Cradock's squadron was greatly inferior to von Spee's but rather than wait for reinforcements in the shape of the battleship Canopus, Cradock, disregarding orders, left the Falklands before she arrived. He would pay for his mistake and have a mountain named after him in BC. Von Spee, hearing that the British light cruiser Glasgow was coaling up at Coronel, a Chilean port 200 miles south of Valparaiso, moved in to attack. The two forces met 50 miles off Coronel just before 5 pm and as expected Cradock's squadron was outnumbered and out-gunned. Cradock's flagship blew up at 8 pm. Only the Glasgow and Otranto escaped to tell the tale. Stunned, the British sent two battle cruisers to find and sink the German squadron which resulted five weeks later in the First Battle of the Falkland Islands.

In the event, it was the Germans who found the British. What happened was that the British squadron was coaling up at Port Stanley in the Falkland Islands; the Glasgow plus the armoured cruisers Cornwall, Carnarvon and Kent, and the two battle cruisers Invincible and Inflexible, all under the com-

Bluerock Mtn.

Threepoint Mtn.

Mt. Burns

Cougar Mtn.

mand of Admiral Frederick Charles Doveton Sturdee who didn't care a hang about security since it was common knowledge that the English were bent on revenge. Strangely, von Spee was completely in the dark. But not for long. By incredible coincidence, the German squadron, on the move again, had rounded Cape Horn and was approaching the islands believing them to be unprotected when they saw masts and funnels sticking up above a low ridge. Turning tail they were pursued (after completing coaling) by the British battle cruisers which had greater speed and range. First away was the 'dashing little Glasgow' under Captain John Luce, his job to remain in touch with von Spee while avoiding shell fire. At 13.20, von Spee ordered Dresden, Nurnberg and Leipzig to escape while the Scharnhorst and Gneisenau turned to face the enemy like cornered animals. Leaving them to the mercy of the battle cruisers, Glasgow, Cornwall and Kent sped after the fleeing ships, ultimately sending the first two to the bottom. Dresden's escape was temporary; she was scuttled 3 months later by Glasgow and Kent in the South Pacific.

B The Seven Hills of Nihahi
East of Nihahi Ridge are seven hills evenly spaced. Ford Knoll just happens to be the southernmost one with a name. Water running off the eastern escarpment of Nihahi Ridge has taken the path of least resistance: soft shales over bands of hard Cardium sandstone. Over time, the streams have cut into the shales making valleys, leaving between 'summits' of harder rocks.

HMS Glasgow.

Mt. Glasgow

slopes of Mt.Cornwall

Banded Peak

Turn left at the red marker (to right is the faint outline of the old road). Though the summit lies in trees, grassy ledges above the eastern cliff allow views of Forgetmenot and Powderface Ridges. Among the rocks grow big clumps of purple creeping beardtongue.

RETURN

Retrace your steps to the 4-way junction. Turn right. The road climbs initially, then starts descending the west flank through young pines and meadows. Expect a couple of steep downhills. Off to the west is Nihahi Ridge and all the peaks of the Front Ranges.

Cross an old road. Below the zigzags, turn left. You're now on Ford Creek Trail which continues winding down the hill.

Forgetmenot Pond.

Turn left (right trail leads to B Loop). Cross a small creek.

Turn left (right trail leads past the amphitheatre area to the equestrian campgrounds access road). Turn left before the fence. Walk parallel to Highway 66 and jump two tiny creeks which feed into Forgetmenot Pond.

Turn right. Pass through the fence.

Cross the highway. Arrive back at the parking lot.

What better way to end the walk than with a barbecue? From all four parking lots, trails lead to picnic tables and the shoreline trail around colourful Forgetmenot Pond. This erstwhile gravel pit is stocked annually with Rainbow trout.

D The astounding colour of the pond, even on a cloudy day, is thought to come from minute particles of limestone suspended in the water. Particles of a certain size reflect in the blue/green parts of the spectrum. Colour is best in late summer when bigger particles have sunk to the bottom.

Nihahi Ridge Loop
9.6 km loop

summer
fall

A scenic but strenuous walk in its middle stages as it climbs up a rocky ridge. The views of the Front Range are something you will never forget. The loop uses well-signed trails and ends with a forest walk past old beaver ponds.

Start: Elbow Falls Trail (Hwy. 66) at Little Elbow Recreation Area. Turn second left into a very large parking lot. Lucky campers can pick up the trail en route. After Labour Day, a hunters' parking lot opens up at the end of the campground access road. Starting here, you may as well cut out the loop, thus reducing the walk to 6 km. This stretch of road is open between May 15th and December 1st.

Find the trail leaving the far left-hand corner of the parking lot to the left of the biffy.

Straightaway, cross a trail. Turn right. Little Elbow River interpretive trail follows the gravelly bank of the Little Elbow upstream.

Keep left. Keep left (right trail up the bank leads to the equestrian campground). As you climb to the suspension bridge watch for Butterworts and Elephantheads on the calcareous flat.

At the 4-way junction keep straight (left trail crossing the bridge is Big Elbow Trail, right trail accesses the campground access road. Keep left (right trail leads to C Loop). Pass the interpretive sign.

A Grizzly!

Occasionally this trail is closed after a grizzly sighting in the meadows. Possibly it's the same bear on his annual tour of favourite eateries. After wintering, bears lose up to 40% of their body weight so they have quite a bit of catching up to do. Plant-wise they prefer growing green plants which are high in protein. As green-up progresses, so the bears move ever higher into alpine meadows where much of their favourite food grows on moist south and west-facing meadows and along the forest edge. They also have a yen for hedysarum roots before green-up and after flowering in the fall. Again, as summer progresses the bears move onto east and north slopes where hedysarum is still dormant. They probably give the avalanche slopes a look-over, too, for winter killed sheep and goats.

Photo Don Beers.

Keep left of trails heading out to the road. The trail now climbs to a viewpoint looking out across the Little Elbow River to Mt. Glasgow with more interpretive signs, then runs close to the campground access road. Join the road at E Loop (interpretive sign).

Turn left. Walk up the road to the bend.

Keep straight. Leaving the road, go through the gate and down the hill into the hunter's parking lot. Follow the ongoing Little Elbow Trail which was built as a fire road.

Straightaway, keep left on the main trail (grassed trail to right). At the next signpost turn right. The trail climbs to a T-junction.

Turn left. Follow the horse trail from the equestrian campground.

Turn right at the top of a hill. This is the start of the Nihahi Ridge Trail proper.

The trail wriggles uphill through pines, the angle gradually easing as it enters the meadow. From the top of the rib is a useful view of Nihahi Ridge. Here the trail turns left and traverses a steep slope to gain the ridge at a viewpoint. The initial climb up the rocky ridge is a muscle-wrenching exercise and you'll be glad to reach a flat area with cairn. One final effort up the last (orange) hill brings you to the saddle, a stoney wasteland devoid of any shelter from the wind. Your reward is a tremendous view up the Little Elbow towards the Opal Range.

Though unofficial trails climb higher up the steepening ridge, most people end the walk here.

Retrace your steps to the T- junction on the horse trail.

If starting from the hunters' parking lot return the way you came.

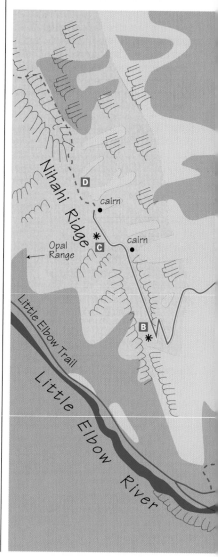

The name Nihahi means rocky or 'steep cliff mountain' in Stoney.

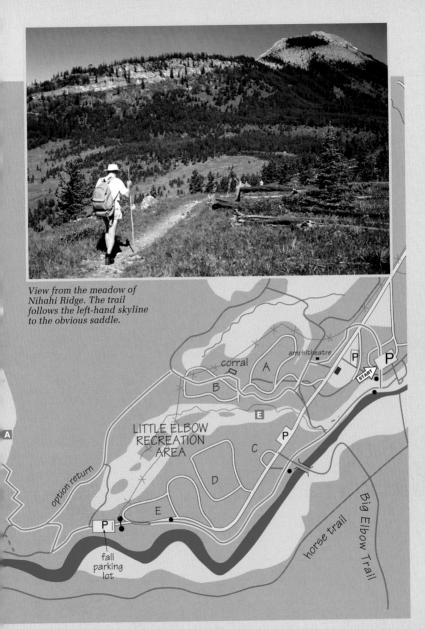

View from the meadow of Nihahi Ridge. The trail follows the left-hand skyline to the obvious saddle.

LITTLE ELBOW
RECREATION
AREA

corral

amphitheatre

START

option return

fall
parking
lot

horse trail

Big Elbow Trail

B Goat Transplant

Diminished from over-hunting due to government mismanagement and with numbers not increasing, K-Country's Mountain goats *(oreamnos ameri–canus)* are having to be replenished from herds in British Columbia. In 1993, 20 goats were flown into this area. The journey was traumatic: having nets shot over them from helicopters, being tranquillized, crated and flown in a Dash 8 to Alberta, trucked into Kananaskis Country, and finally slung in nets below helicopters to the release site.

Photo Don Beers.

Above: the million dollar view at C. *Follow the windings of the Little Elbow to its source in the Opal Range. The flat-topped summit at right is Mt. Romulus which overtops the nearer Mt. Remus. In Roman legends, Romulus killed his twin Remus and reigned alone in the city which became Rome. Photo Leon Kubbernus.*

Right: The upper saddle, showing the steepening ridge in the background.

D High Altitude Flowers Above timberline, summer is very short with most flowers blooming within a 6 week period. If you want to search for alpines among the rocks, hike this trail in July.

Above left: Double bladder pod (Physaria didymocarpa) with diamond-shaped leaves.
Above right: Roseroot (Sedum roseum).

THE LOOP

If not, keep left on the horse trail. Stay left. The horse trail winds through pine forest with little in the way of views.

Turn right. Pass through the drift fence into the equestrian campground between sites #4 and #5 on Loop B.

Cross Loop B road. And again. Keep right. The trail keeps to the right of the corral.

Turn right near the ramp. Cross the main equestrian campground access road at the 4-way junction. The trail restarts kitty corner and climbs into the pines. A lovely stretch follows the bank of a small creek notable for its succession of out-of-use beaver ponds.

Turn left. Cross the equestrian campground access road. Turn right on the trail to the amphitheatre. Keep left at the amphitheatre. Keep right and cross Highway 66. Cross the parking lot loop road. Arrive back at the parking lot.

E Beaver Dam Succession
Having used up most of the available food like willows, the beavers in this valley have moved elsewhere. With no maintenance the ponds have silted up and been invaded by grasses and sedges. The dams are mostly earthen now, fertile beds for a new generation of willows as shown in the photo above. One day the beavers will return to this second-hand dam.

Jumpingpound Trail East
5 km loop

early spring
summer
late fall

This all-season loop has two distinct sections: an easy riverside walk alongside Jumpingpound Creek and a more strenuous hilly section which crosses aspen hillsides and view meadows behind Jumpingpound Ranger Station.

Start: Sibbald Creek Trail (Hwy. 68) at Pine Top day-use area.

From opposite the biffy a trail heads out to the highway.

Cross the highway. The trail climbs aspen hillside, then heads west.

Cross an old road starting behind Jumpingpound Ranger Station. The trail continues traversing aspen hillsides with patches of meadow, then descends to Bellyache Valley and crosses a small stream among spruce trees. A more strenuous uphill climb brings you to larger meadows bright with buffalo beans and shooting stars in early spring. Here is your finest view: Moose Mountain and the Jumpingpound valley extending to Sibbald Flat with the peaks of the Front Ranges poking up above Cox Hill. Continue traversing to a junction.

Turn left. Descend aspen hillside to the highway.

A *Jumpingpound Ranger Station.*

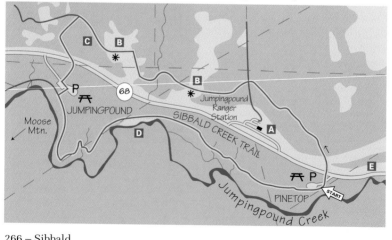

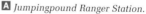

A buffalo bean meadow. Moose Mountain in the distance.

B The buffalo are coming

Buffalo bean *(Thermopsis rhombifolia)* looks rather like a bright yellow lupine with its similar pea-like flower. It is in fact sometimes called the false lupin. One of our earliest spring flowers (together with dandelions), its flowering was used as an indicator by the Blackfoot and other Indian tribes to tell when buffalo bulls were about to leave their winter range for summer grazing on the prairie. The Blackfoot call it wudzi-eh-kay 'buffalo flower'. Toxic alkaloids make the flower and especially the bean-like seeds exceptionally poisonous. Fortunately, it's unpalatable to grazing cattle.

◙ Pin Cherry
(Prunus Jumpingpound)
is a dainty shrub with the usual cherry leaves. It's easy to distinguish the pin from the chokecherry with which it is often confused. In the pin, the flowers are clustered, each white flower attached to the same point on the twig by a long stem. Berries are bright red. On the other hand, choke cherry flowers hang in cylindrical clusters about 10 cm long, each flower attached to a central stalk which in turn attaches to the twig. The deep red berries look almost black. Both 'drupes' are extremely sour (where do you think the name choke-cherry comes from?), but with plentiful sugar make excellent jellies, jams and pie fillings. Warning: stones, twigs and wilted leaves are extremely poisonous, producing hydrocyanic acid when ingested.

Cross the highway. The trail continues, short-cutting through to Jumpingpound day-use area access road at the parking lot.

Turn left. Cross the lot. At the trail sign the trail continues to a T-junction.

Turn left. Your trail heads east, following the bank of Jumpingpound Creek. It joins a cutline as it makes a sharp turn to the left.

Keep right. Forgoing the meadow, the trail keeps to the trees, crossing a tiny stream, then climbing rather sharply. Gradually you move further away from the river, and cross another side stream.

Cross a cutline. Arrive at Pine Top day-use area parking lot beside the biffy.

◙ The name Jumpingpound
refers to a buffalo jump near the confluence of the creek with the Bow River.

⊡ *Sio Tida*

'Prairie Chicken Plains' is the big meadow you drove through just outside of the Kananaskis Country boundary. Before the land was fenced it was a popular camping area for the nomadic Stonies and a traditional spring dancing ground for prairie chickens, now long gone from overhunting. Head down, neck feathers held vertically, yellow neck sacs inflated to bursting point, wings lowered, tail erect, the males strutted about stamping their feet and snapping their tails in fan-like movements, all the while making boom-like sounds. As the females came closer to see what all the fuss was about, the males quickened the pace, finally bowing with wings outspread, the bill almost touching the ground. What female could resist?

Indian dancing evolved from observing the mannerisms of birds and animals. In the difficult prairie chicken dance the male dancer emulates the birds by bending over at the waist, spreading out his wings and moving back and forth stomping his legs. Drum rhythms came by listening to grouse drumming which is why the music quickens towards the end.

The NW-SE Indian trail passing through this way was known as Prairie Chicken Trail and was likely the wagon trail used by Thomas Blakiston of the Palliser Expedition in 1858 to get from Morley to the Crowsnest. You bet this was a convoluted route. But to travel the flat prairies in the vicinity of Highway 2 was to risk running foul of the Blackfoot.

Sarcee Indian contest dancer at Redwood Meadows Powwow.

Prairie chicken (Tympanuchus). Tympanon is Greek for a drum.

Jumpingpound Trail West
5.2 km loop

spring
summer
fall

Another walk with two distinct sections: a flat forest stroll alongside Jumpingpound Creek and a much hillier section traversing the ridge above the highway through aspen and spruce forest. Occasional meadows give fine views across to Sibbald Flat. Watch for red markers on trees.

Start: Sibbald Creek Trail (Hwy. 68) at Jumpingpound day-use area. The trail can also be picked up from Pine Grove Group Campground.

From Jumpingpound day-use area parking lot a trail heads out to a T-junction on the bank top.

The trail just west of Jumpingpound day-use area. A typical scene.

Turn right. Initially, the trail follows the bank top with occasional views of Jumping pound Creek down below, then cuts inland towards Pine Grove group campground. Come to the day-use area access road. (The campground road leaves the access road a few metres to your right.)

DETOUR
Turn left at the access road and walk to the group day-use area. Located on a grassy point rimmed with sandstone outcroppings overlooking Bryant Creek near its confluence with the Jumpingpound, it's the ideal spot for lunch. If it's raining, an enclosed picnic shelter and small cabin will keep you dry.

Map labels:
- road
- access road
- SIBBALD CREEK TRAIL
- 68
- Bryant Creek
- D
- C
- C
- ✳
- PINE GROVE GROUP CAMP
- JUMPINGPOUND
- START
- option
- Jumpingpound Creek
- B
- A

A Bryant Creek

honours Alfred Harold Bryant, forest ranger for the Jumpingpound area between 1916 and his death in 1934. "A good ranger, for he scared everyone and arrested no one".

B Pine Grove Meadow

Telephone ski trail at West Bragg is the original telephone trail between forestry cabins. If, in the 1930s, you had followed that trail northwards you would have come to a forestry station in the meadow west of Bryant Creek. From here, it continued up Bryant Creek to Morley, following the Stoney pack trail Sawin Ahnibi Chagu, meaning 'where Blackfoot squaw was brought trail'. Stonies called Bryant Creek Sawin Waptan 'Where they brought the Blackfoot woman creek', while the meadow was known as Sawin Ahnibi Sna 'where Blackfoot woman was brought home clearing'. Jumpingpound Creek has also been known as Sawin Ahnibi 'where Blackfoot woman was brought home' though its more usual Stoney name is Tokijarhpabi Wapta 'where Blackfoot camped river'.

Ranger Bryant on Highway 68 at Bryant Creek, September 1924. Photo J.A. Hutchison. Courtesy Forest Technology School.

The cabin on the point.

🄲 Violets

The early blue is equally at home in the open or in aspen woods. In common with some of the other earlies (crocus, buttercups, dandelions), the violet occasionally blooms again in the fall after a hard frost is followed by weeks of sunny warm weather when presumably it becomes the late blue. It's worth lying down to sniff the fragrance. Flowers are used as a fragrance in perfumes, crystallized as toppings for violet cream chocolates and used in cough syrups! The Romans theorized that garlands of violets worn around the head would cure headaches.

Cross the day-use area access road. The trail enters a large meadow—view of Moose Mountain and Cox Hill to your left—and circles around right through a young pine plantation to Hwy. 68.

Cross the highway. Turn right, then left up the grassy bank. The trail continues to a clearing.

Turn right. For a short distance follow a cutline.

Turn right. A gradual climb through a stand of white spruce brings you to a meadow view of Moose Mountain. Wind downhill to cross a tiny creek.

Cross a cow trail in the valley bottom, then a reclaimed access road to a former gas well. Climb through another grove of white spruce followed by meadow patches. The trail wanders past Douglas firs, instantly recognisable by their deeply grooved bark.

Turn right at the T-junction. Descend to the highway.

Cross the highway. The trail continues, short-cutting through forest to Jumpingpound day-use area.

◨ About White Spruce

You know the trees are spruce because (if you can reach a branch low enough) you can roll the 4-sided needles between your fingers. Fir needles are flat and won't roll. Then compare spruce needles with pine needles which are a lot longer. Having established these trees as spruce, how do you know they're not Engelmann spruce? Think smooth. Twigs are relatively free of hairs; Engelmann twigs are hairy. Cones have smooth margins whereas Engelmann's are somewhat ragged. Odds are it's white spruce growing at low elevations like here.

White spruce.

Engelmann spruce.

Courtesy University of Washington Press.

Spruce in Straight Lines Spruce seeds have a difficult time germinating. Conditions on the forest floor have to be just right, not too much nor too little moisture. Generally, seedlings do best when confined to well-decayed logs which retain moisture. If you come on a group of saplings look to see if they line up. When small, the trees are vulnerable to browsing for many years. Should they survive, it takes 10 years to attain a height of only two metres.

The Uses of Spruces Once upon a time Indians boiled surface roots and macerated them to make a cord used in sewing. Specifically, for sewing together canoes. Spruce gum was then rubbed into the seams to make the canoes waterproof. Spruce wood is used for contemporary paddles and oars. It's said a broth of spruce bark saved Jacques Cartier (who did a lot of canoeing) from scurvy. Spruce beer is definitely an acquired taste akin to the Greek wine Retsina.

Pine Woods Loop
4 km return

early spring
summer
late fall

An easy walk with one long uphill which takes you through aspen forest and meadows to a young pine plantation above Coxhill Creek. In season a flower walk.

Start: Sibbald Creek Trail (Hwy. 68). Turn off onto the one-way Demonstration Forest Loop. Park at Spruce Woods day-use area.

A Meadow

At this spot Jumping Pound Creek overflowed its banks and laid down layers of gravel. Grass grew here and flowers like old man's whiskers. Then in the 1950s, the ground was levelled for a sawmill. After the mill was removed, salt licks attracted cattle that kept down the vegetation.

At the trail sign, follow the stepped trail down the bank to Jumpingpound Creek. Cross the bridge.

Turn right at the T-junction. A short stint through a meadow, then damp old spruce forest brings you to an old exploration road.

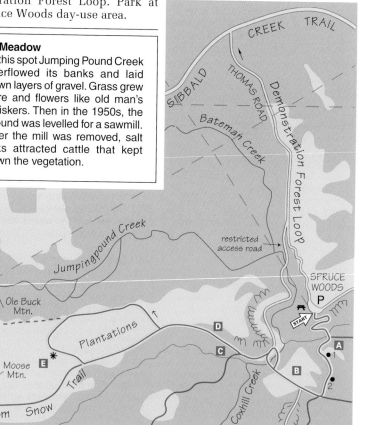

Showy locoweed
(Oxytropis splendens)

*The meadow at **B** with showy locoweeds.*

A Old Man's Whiskers

(Geum triflorum)

Nodding rose-coloured flowers appear in triplicate at the end of a long rose-coloured stem and seem closed when they are actually fully mature. If you look closely during the pollination phase, the five red sepals are open just wide enough to disclose five tiny yellow petals inside. Everything about this plant is rose-coloured including the rhizome which was used for making rose-coloured tea by Indians. This flower's also called three-flowered avens, prairie smoke, torch flower, and long-plumed avens because after pollination the flowers are replaced by fluffy heads of silvery plumes.

Right: Old man's whiskers.

Oxytropis has some poisonous species like early yellow loco weed which contains the habit-forming chemical selenium attractive to cattle who become addicted to the stuff. Not this plant, though. When massed together, the effect is brilliant. The whole plant — the silvery stalk, leaflets, and flower cluster are covered with silky hairs which colour-coordinate beautifully with the spike of purple flowers.

D Indian Paint Brush

This a gorgeous flower. Excuse *me*... the flowers are actually green! It's the bracts which are coloured the full range of lipsticks and nail polishes, plus yellow and white. To see them in their full glory you have to climb to alpine meadows. In lowland woods you mostly seem to get this low-altitude red shade, though pink is a possibility. There are so many species even the experts have a hard time in sorting them out. Parasitic, their roots attach to other plants to gain some nutrients which is why they won't transplant to the garden.

Lonicera dioica

C Twining Honeysuckle
is actually a vine. The flowers, which change from yellow to orange-red as they mature, are clustered in a saucer of two leaves joined at the base. The perfume is heavenly. Each flower is trumpet-shaped with a swollen knob near the base where the nectar accumulates and is available to hummingbirds and swallow tail butterflies who both have long 'tongues'.

At the 4-way junction turn right. You are now on Tom Snow Trail, a long distance equestrian and hiking trail between Dawson day-use area on Powderface Trail and Station Flats on Elbow Falls Trail.

Keep straight. In a meadow join Husky's exploration access road to gas wells on the north side of Moose Mountain. Follow the muddy swath across a large flowery meadow extending almost to Coxhill Creek.

Go right. A narrow trail crosses Coxhill Creek by a footbridge. (At the time of writing you can also cross using the road bridge.)

Turn left. This new road, which comes in from the right, is called Thomas Road and has been used and reclaimed innumerable times.

Keep right twice (Thomas Road goes left). Still following the Tom Snow Trail you climb a long hill below aspen forest to a sandy bank top.

Turn right at the trail sign A narrower trail loops around a young pine plantation planted in 1974. At the viewpoint is a 360 degree view of Ole Buck Mountain round to Moose Mountain and its satellites.

Turn left. Back on the Tom Snow Trail, you head east along the road on the bank top above Coxhill Creek. At the next junction you join your outgoing trail.

Return the same way to the parking lot.

E *The viewpoint in the plantation. Moose Mountain behind.*

Moose Creek Loop
2.4 km

spring
summer
late fall

A slightly more strenuous trip than Pine Woods with some short steep hills in both directions. Overall, it's mainly a forest walk ending with an beautiful stretch alongside Moose Creek through Balsam poplars and pine forest festooned by lichen. Numbered posts refer you to the official brochure which is available at the trailhead.

Start: Sibbald Creek Trail (Hwy. 68). Turn off onto the one-way Forest Demonstration Loop. Park at Spruce Woods day-use area.

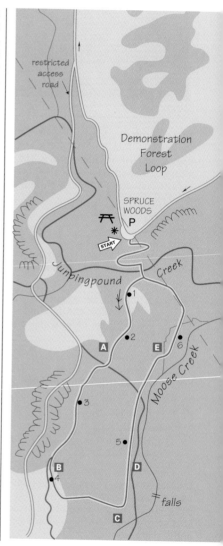

At the trail sign, follow the stepped trail down the bank to Jumpingpound Creek. Cross the bridge.

At the T-junction turn right. You pass a meadow on the left, then wind through old damp spruce forest.

At the 4-way junction, cross the old Moose Creek exploration road. The trail (also Tom Snow Trail) climbs above a small valley occupied by Husky's exploration road. A clearing at interpretive sign 4 marks the turnaround point of your trail.

Go left (Tom Snow Trail carries on). A pleasant stretch above the bank ends when you make a steep descent to Moose Creek which rises from the north face of Moose Mountain. At valley bottom the trail turns left and runs between a high bank and the creek.

Cross the old valley road. A narrower trail continues downstream through damp forest with balsam poplars telling you this is what is called a flood

A Burls

are giant-sized galls. Just past interpretive sign 2 is a spruce with swellings all the way up the trunk. These are caused by accelerated growth in the cambium layer, thought to be a defence mechanism against invading insect or fungal parasites which are walled off from the rest of the tree.

plain. Cross a bridge over an overflow channel. Close to the confluence with Jumpingpound Creek, the trail turns left onto a cutline which is soon left when the trail veers left again. Note intersecting game trails and dead poplars lining the trail, a perfect place to spot woodpeckers and sapsuckers.

Turn right at the T-junction and return the way you came.

B Hillside

This hillside became a clearing in 1970 when pine and spruce were logged for posts and poles. At the time the pine was heavily infested with dwarf mistletoe which spreads like wildfire through the rest of the forest unless infected trees are removed. The area's been artificially seeded with pine. White spruce seem to be regenerating naturally.

The hillside at 4.

ⓒ Northern Bedstraw *(Galium boreale)* grows in snowy profusion on the bank. Now here's a *really* interesting plant! In the late summer the flowers are replaced by small round burs which cling to your pants, socks and your dog's fur. While wearily picking the burs, you have to admit the plant's method of relocating takes some beating. In the natural way of things the fruits (the burs) clings to the fur of small animals and are handily conveyed to another location, hence its other names: cleavers and catchweed.

In the old days dried plants were mixed with straw to stuff mattresses—hence its common name. Young leaves rich in vitamin C were used as seasoning in soups and stews. Dried leaves also made tea. The lotion from steeped leaves faded freckles and treated psoriasis. Powdered roots sprinkled on wounds halted bleeding and promoted healing. Roots when boiled yielded a red/magenta dye called madder which was used by our native Indians to stain porcupine quills. Even today, the roasted seeds make the best coffee substitute of any plant in Canada.

Right: Balsam poplar at **E**
Below: Northern bedstraw.

E Floodplains

This is a very damp spot in the spruce forest, especially in Spring when runoff escapes the banks of Moose Creek and runs in shallow channels through the forest. The vegetation of flood plains is very distinctive and includes white spruce, willows of many species, red osier dogwood, sedges and balsam poplars like the magnificent specimen on the page facing.

In fact, the latter depend on floods for their very survival. Silt deposited by floods would appear to be necessary for germination of new trees like balsam poplar and cottonwoods which is why environmentalists are screaming about dams like the Oldman. Downstream of the dam is a marvellous floodplain forest which could well be in its last generation. And it's not only the trees which are lost but also an important bird habitat.

Moose Creek running over its banks.

D Old Man's Beard

Often a damp forest results in trees festooned with, not moss, but lichen matching the paintwork on the bridge and looking a lot like tinsel on a Christmas tree. Already you've seen a lot of lichen on this loop. The pale green stuff is *Usnea alpina* (photo below) which has a central cord stronger than the sheath. The black wispy lichens *(bryoria)* are called hair lichens. The fluorescent lime green lichen growing on dead wood is wolf lichen *(Letharia vulpina)*.

Sibbald Flat Viewpoint
4.2 km return

early spring
summer
late fall

A very easy walk along the Sibbald Forestry Exhibit Trail to a viewpoint overlooking Sibbald Flat where the buffalo once grazed.

Start: Sibbald Creek Trail (Hwy. 68). Take the access road signed Sibbald Lake campground. For Sibbald Lake picnic area take the middle fork at the 3-way junction. From Sibbald Lake Campground (right fork) many trails both official and unofficial join the trail.

Alternatively, the trail can be reversed by starting from Sibbald Viewpoint day-use area just east of the turn-off to Sibbald Lake Campground.

From the parking lot the trail starts at an interpretive sign 'Sibbald Forestry Exhibit Trail'.

Keep left (trail to right leads back to the campground access road and B Loop at sites #84 and #86). Turn left at the 4-way intersection (trail to right leads to E Loop near site #14). Detour to the south shore of Sibbald Lake where rafting and watching for the Bateman Creek beavers are popular pastimes.

Return to the last junction. Turn left. The main trail leaves the lakeshore and enters pine forest.

Keep left (two trails to right lead to E Loop at sites #19 and #22). Go straight. You intersect a trail between A Loop and a bench overlooking the Bateman Creek beaver ponds.

Sibbald Lake, looking
towards Ole Buck Mountain.

A White Earth Lake

In 1859 Sibbald Lake was called White Earth Lake by James Hector of the Palliser Expedition who came close to the Stoney Indian name Umsiyathkan Eyagubin meaning 'where one can obtain the white clay'. The clay was apparently used for facial make-up during festive and religious occasions like the Sun Dance ceremony and was gouged from the lake bed rather than from the shoreline. The lake's shallow nature means that 90% of fish are winter-killed. Though lots of people try, fishing is not the greatest.

B The name "Sibbald"

Frank Sibbald, son of the more famous Andrew, grew up with the Stonies at Morleyville who called him Tokun 'The Fox' in recognition of his hunting skills. Naturally, he was an excellent horseman and as skilful as any Indian at tracking stray horses. Among his many jobs: guide and packer for the CPR survey crew in 1882/3, and packer in 1893 to Professor Lucius Coleman on the famous trip to find Mt. Brown which at that time was reputed to be the highest peak in the Canadian Rockies. But that's another story. In later years he became a rancher and homesteaded on Jumpingpound Creek just outside the Kananaskis Country Boundary, running his cattle on the meadow which was later to bear his name.

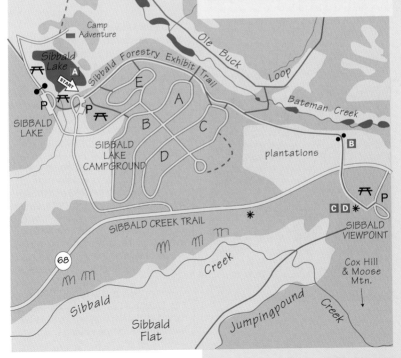

Look to the right where there's a good example of a squirrel midden. Pass another bench.

Keep left (trails to right lead to C Loop at sites #95 and #96, and a biffy). Stay right. This is an important junction, since you don't want to follow the descending trail to left which is Ole Buck Loop. All is now straightforward. Your trail shortly enters cutblocks at two interpretive exhibits which mark the demarcation of two young pine plantations. Here the trail makes a right turn and leads straight to Sibbald Creek Trail (Hwy. 68). Moose Mountain is straight ahead.

Cross the highway. The trail curves left along the top of a steep bank and is supplied with a bench at the viewpoint for Sibbald Flat. It's not far now to Sibbald Viewpoint day-use area at a trail sign.

Walking between two young Lodgepole pine plantations. Moose Mountain in the background,

■C Sibbald Flat

used to be called Sibbald Park. Because it's very often snow free in winter months, this extra large meadow has in the past attracted ungulates like elk and buffalo in great numbers, and obviously, where there were many animals you got many hunters congregating, ranging in time from prehistoric ancestors of the Indians to the Stonies of the late 19th century. Unlike today's hunters who must camp in paved crescents away from all the action, the old people got a grandstand view of what was going on from the bench above the flat. Nowadays you're far more likely to see cattle.

■B Deadly Infection

Dwarf mistletoe, a conifer loving parasite causing witches broom, has rootlike structures which penetrate the bark and feed yellowish shoots clustered around infection points. The flower is superseded by a dark green berry whose single seed is shot, as from a cannon, as far as 18 metres, likely onto another unsuspecting tree. The generation of pines before these were chopped due to mistletoe infection, those to left in 1962 and those to right 12 years later in 1974. During burning of the slash, it was hoped the heat would melt resin bonds in the pine cones and release seed into the ground but not enough seeds took, so lodgepole pine and Douglas fir seeds were sown in 1965 and again in 1970. All the Douglas firs died. Pines flourished and were thinned in 1981 by the Christmas tree cutting method.

Sibbald Flat. Note the highway running right to left below Deer Ridge.

D What happened when they rebuild Highway 68

That the bench was a prehistoric winter campground with extremely important artifacts only came to light in 1979 when road construction nearly demolished the whole lot. In a spirit of cooperation, the highway engineer not only delayed construction so the archeologists could get their noses to the ground for a year (the road was constructed from east to west instead of the other way around), but he also realigned the road to a lower elevation so at least part of the campground was left undisturbed.

Gravel and rocks exposed on the steep bank were handy for manufacturing tools of amazing quantity and range: projectile points (arrowheads), bifacially flaked cutting and scraping tools, gravers (for carving), drills, perforators, choppers, hammers and anvil stones. Most important, the Sibbald Flat campground was the first site in western Canada found to contain artifacts of the Fluted Point Tradition in good stratigraphic context.

The people of the Fluted Point Tradition who lived over 10,000 years ago were the first visitors and there has been almost continuous occupation since then with excavations at the grass roots level revealing 18th century pipe stems and glass beads, not to mention a lot of 20th century rubbish, like brass tacks, beer bottles and shotgun shells which haven't been covered with enough dirt to be truly interesting yet. We'll have to wait another few thousand years for that to happen. It's interesting to note that in all the bones dug up, there was not one buffalo bone marked by a steel knife which suggests that the historic as opposed to the prehistoric occupation took place after the near extinction of the animals.

Ole Buck Loop
3 km

early spring
summer
fall

A short rather strenuous walk which leaves Sibbald Lake Campground and climbs onto a spur of Ole Buck Mountain giving views of the entire Sibbald Lake area. This walk is especially worthwhile in spring flowers and fall colours.

Start: Sibbald Creek Trail (Hwy. 68). Turn off to Sibbald Lake Campground. The nearest access is Loop C opposite site #96 at the biffy. Also accessible via Sibbald Forestry Exhibit Trail from Loop E, Loop A or Sibbald Lake picnic area, or from Sibbald Viewpoint day-use area on Hwy. 68 (see previous walk).

Start from Sibbald Lake Campground at C loop near site #96.

Downhill of the biffy the trail connects with Sibbald Forestry Exhibit Trail.

Turn right. Turn left. Descend and cross willowy Bateman Creek.

Keep right at the T-junction. Walk up a meadow into a small side valley filled with aspens. After crossing the stream, you're into pine forest where the trail steepens considerably, offering some hard work en route to the high point on a spur of Ole Buck Mountain.

At the high point turn right A short spur trail leads to a rocky point with bench. Since the trail was built, growing pines have eclipsed the view which has been narrowed to Moose Mountain in line with the trail.

Return to the junction.

B Why Aspens turn yellow in fall
It's simple really. Thanks to substances called carotenoids which do not need sunlight for synthesis, aspen leaves are yellow all their life, only the yellow is hidden in summer by the green pigment chlorophyll which needs so many hours of daylight and warm temperatures to synthesize. In fall, the rate at which the chlorophyll is synthesized slows down and allows the yellow colouring to show through.

A So why do Willows turn red?

The colour comes from pigments called anthocyanins which develop in a totally different way from chlorophyll, being neither affected by hours of sunlight nor by temperatures, but by a change in the metabolic breakdown of sugar over the summer. Anthocyanins also colour strawberries, raspberries and rose hips.

The Drink which refreshes

Got a headache or feeling weary after walking all day? If you've left your pain killers at home, you can always chew on a bit of willow bark. A better way is to make Willow Tea. Strangely, the taste is not bitter like aspirin but nutty like cashew nuts!

1. Gather a few short lengths of willow twigs, preferably the new shoots. Peel off the outer bark and use the soft green cambium layer inside.

2. Boil the scrapings in a cup or two of water, then steep for 15 minutes. Add honey or lemon.

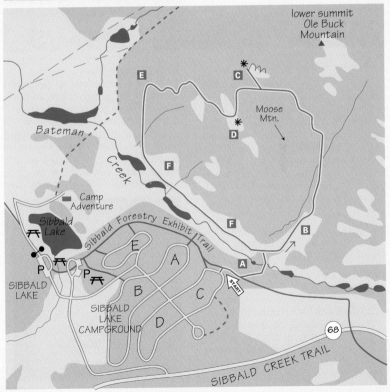

C The high point. View back down the trail of Moose Mountain.

Turn right. The trail descends the other side of the spur to patches of meadow and another bench. Watch for a glimpse of Sibbald Lake at the first bend. From this lower viewpoint some peaks of the Fisher Range are visible above Cox Hill and sundry nameless foothills. Continue zigzagging downhill through pine forest, then aspen forest, to Bateman Creek meadows.

Turn left. The main trail returns to the bridge alongside Bateman Creek. This can be a slow walk when spring flowers are in full bloom.

Turn right over the bridge. Return the way you came.

D **Ole Buck** was named by A.O. Wheeler around the turn of the 20th century, probably after some old deer they were hunting. The Stoney call it Chapta Baha taga, 'big pine hill'.

E **Wild Sweet Pea**
Lathyrus ochroleucus is the wild version of the garden sweet pea but comes in only one colour. A distinguishing feature is the coiling tendrils which enable it to climb up trees and bushes. The creamy-coloured flowers lack the fragrance of the cultivated variety. Look for it in aspen forests.

Shooting Star meadows.

▣ *Spring Flowers*

Yellow Puccoon
(Lithospermum ruderale)
Very often it's the plain-looking plants which prove to be the most interesting. So it is with the puccoon. Mind you, the leaves are quite eye-catching, being stiff and sharply pointed like lances. While other flowers may be swaying in the strong west wind, not so the puccoon which in addition to having a thick, stiff stem, is anchored by a thick tap root. In the old days the roots were used by Indians for food and as a source of red dye used in staining animal skins and as body paint. The yellow flowers are followed by hard shiny white fruits called nutlets. Powdered nutlets mixed with hot water, or better still wine, act as a diuretic, a laxative and contraceptive. The Assiniboine used puccoon tea as a birth control method apparently. It's actually been proved that natural estrogens in the plant suppress the release of certain hormones required for ovulation.

Shooting Stars
Dodecatheon pulchellum have nodding magenta flowers and look rather like cyclamens. They do in fact belong to the same family. As the seeds mature, the flower stalk straightens with the result that the capsules becomes stiffly erect, thus aiding in seed dispersal.

Sibbald Flat
1.5 km loop

early spring
summer
fall

A moderate walk through typical foothills countryside of aspen woods and meadows to a viewpoint on top of a ridge. On your return make a detour to Moose Pond and a Sun Dance Lodge built by the Stoney Indians.

Start: Sibbald Creek Trail (Hwy. 68). Take the road to Sibbald Lake Campground. At the three-way junction take the left-hand fork into Sibbald Lake parking lot. The gated road beyond leads to Camp Adventure and is private.

The trail starts from the parking lot at the trail sign and rises through mixed forest past interpretive sign 1.

Turn right. Continue climbing past 2.

Turn right. The trail winds up a ridge through aspen forest, ultimately arriving in a meadow with a bench; a very fine viewpoint. Have the flower book handy. The trail continues a little higher up the ridge to a second bench looking northwest to Deer Ridge.

Return down the trail to the junction.

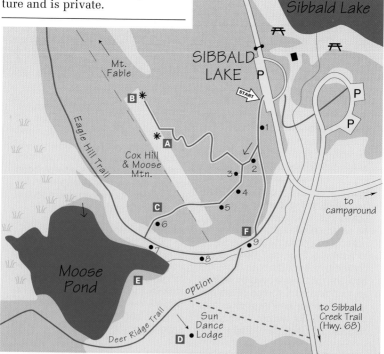

A The view of Moose Pond, the Sun Dance Lodge, Moose Mountain (left) and Cox Hill.

B Cougars

Wherever there are lots of deer, you'll find cougars and that means the Sibbald Lake area. I count myself lucky when a few years ago I inadvertently flushed a cougar out of a thicket less than a kilometre upstream of Moose Pond. He (or she) happened to be a bright rust colour, but could equally well have been gray, brown, yellow-ish and all shades in between. Its given length of two and a half metres is a bit misleading, because its incredibly long tail takes up nearly half of that. Well padded paws and back feet which step into front paw prints make it a stealthy stalker after deer which is its favoured dinner. This brings us to the problem of attacks on pets and livestock.

Understand that the hunting range is dictated by the abundance or scarcity of game in an area. For instance, if many deer have been killed by hunters the previous fall and/or if the winter is long, cold and snowy, cougars are going to extend their range, driven by hunger, coming out of Kananaskis Country into farms and subdivisions which are encroaching into the forest.

from "Indian Days of the Long Ago."

Aspen Clones

Aspen forests are delightful to walk through. They face the sun, the ground underfoot is usually dry unless there's a horse trail passing through, the ground below grows grass and all manner of flowers and, though not quite in the same league as maples, the leaves turn yellow in the fall. They are also quite noisy. Due to stalks that are flattened, the leaves quiver and rattle in the slightest breeze. Growing in pure stands, they cover whole hillsides. This is because reproduction is via cloning. The tree propagates along its roots. So you can see that each tree in a clone grove has the same genetic make-up as its neighbour. In the fall it's easily to differentiate the different clone groves because trees of one clone all turn colour at the same time.

Morningstar

"In the beginning Great Mystery sang into being the stars which are really persons living up in sky." Brothers Blue Star and White Star journeyed to the land of the Stonies on Earth to spread the teachings of the Great Mystery. While there, they fell in love with the two daughters of Starlight the Stoney chief, Little-Striped Wing and Fisher-Calling Woman, and took them back to their lodges in the sky. After a while the two sisters got bored from staying in one position and lonely, too, for the life of the Stonies. The Great Mystery spoke "Let your wives return for 40 days, but you, my sons, must remain in your star lodges where your brilliance serves as a skyroof, beauty and direction to the Stonies". Well, wouldn't you know, when the 40 days were up the sisters ran and hid in some rocks. When the brothers realized what had happened, they abandoned their lodges and descended to earth to search for them. Unsuccessful, they returned to the sky country to be reprimanded by Great Mystery, "You have given your word lightly. You shall no longer sit in the great council of stars. You shall go to a shallow place and remain there for all time". To White Star he added, "However, you may sit close to Earth so that you may watch over your Stoney wife. You may visit Little-Striped Wing every night before Sun rakes his great fires. And you shall be the lowest of all stars. I name you Morning Star."

The Sun Dance Lodge. The centrepiece has four poles symbolizing the four corners of the Earth. 12 upright poles refer to the 12 virtues in the Indian religion. Bolts of cloth signify prayer.

D Ti Jarubi chubi

means 'make-a-lodge-for-sacred-ways'. A sacred aspen/Balsam poplar is cut down and used as the centre pole. Aspen boughs make a fence around the centre pole, with a gap left for the entrance which faces east towards the rising sun. For four days the Stonies dance and sing songs honouring Sun, Thunder, Great White Buffalo and Great Eagle. Offerings such as pipes, animal hides and medicine bundles are made in order to receive the spirit of the Great Mystery. The vowing spirit woman is the keeper of the spirit bundles. At one time, much to the horror of the first white men, the vowing man used to offer up his life as a physical sacrifice to Sun. Bound at the wrist and ankles he was hung upside down and raked by bear claws.

Balsam poplar at Moose Pond.

E Useful Aspen Bark

The bark of young trees is a smooth, unblemished greenish white, turning grey and furrowed in old age, more like that of balsam poplars lining Moose Pond. Trunks are popular scratching posts for black bears who also climb the trees. Animals mark their territory like mule deer who leave scent from glands located near the base of their antlers. Bark is sometimes used as emergency food in hard winters and by the size and shape of the strips torn off you can tell whether it was moose, deer or an elk passing by. On the other hand aspen to the beaver is definitely gourmet, which is why aspens near active beaver ponds are all trimmed.

Indian health tip: If you run out of suncream try rubbing some of the grey powder from the bark onto your skin.

Turn right. The trail crosses a cutline and descends to meadows bordering Moose Pond. Join Eagle Hill Trail.

Turn left. Follow alongside the small creek issuing from Moose Pond.

Scabiosa.

F Scabious

You won't find the family *dipsacaceae* in any of the flower books covering the Canadian Rockies or Alberta. You'll need a flower guide to Europe where there are both wild and cultivated varieties. Dipsacus is a Greek name for 'thirst' and relates to the leaves which are opposite and fused around the stem in such a way they collect water. The common name arises from the Latin 'scabies'. Rubbing yourself with the leaves is supposed to relieve the itch.

DETOUR *Between interpretive signs #8 and #9 turn right.* Follow Deer Ridge Trail across the small creek into the big meadow. About halfway across are one or two Sun Dance Lodges. You may find a Sweat Lodge close to the forest edge.

Return to the main trail.

Turn right. Just past #9 interpretive sign, turn left. Climb uphill.

Turn right. Follow your outgoing trail back to the parking lot.

Field Guides

Acorn, John & Sheldon, Ian **Butterflies of Alberta** Lone Pine Publishing, 1993.

Cormack, R.G.H. **Wild Flowers of Alberta** McClealland and Stewart, 1977.

Droppo, Olga **Alberta Berries** Calgary Field Naturalists' Society, 1988.

Gadd, Ben **Handbook of the Canadian Rockies** Corax Press, 1995.

Hallworth, Beryl & Chinnappa C. C. **Plants of Kananaskis Country** University of Alberta Press, University of Calgary Press, 1997.

McDonald, Joan F. (Ed.) **The Birdfinding Guide to the Calgary Region.** Calgary Field Naturalists' Society, 1993.

McGillivray, W. Bruce & Semenchuk, Glen P. **Field Guide to Alberta Birds** Federation of Alberta Naturalists 1998.

Russell, Anthony P. **Amphibians & Reptiles of Alberta** University of Calgary Press, 1993.

Scotter, George W., Ulrich, Tom J. & Jones, Edgar T. **Birds of the Canadian Rockies** Douglas & McIntyre, 1990.

Scotter, George W. & Flygare, Halle **Wildflowers of the Canadian Rockies** Hurtig, 1986.

Wilkinson, Kathleen **Trees and Shrubs of Alberta** Lone Pine Publishing, 1990.

Wilkinson, Kathleen **Wildflowers of Alberta** University of Alberta Press & Lone Pine Publishing, 1999.

Willard, Terry **Edible and Medicinal Plants of the Rocky Mountains and Neighbouring Territories** Wild Rose College of Natural Healing, 1992.

Witt, Dale H., Marsh, Janet E. & Bovey, Robin B. **Mosses, Lichens and Ferns of Northwest North America** Lone Pine Publishing, 1988.

Books about the Area

Birrell, Dave **50 Roadside Panoramas in the Canadian Rockies** Rocky Mountain Books, 2000.

Daffern, Gillean **Kananaskis Country Trail Guides vol 1 & vol 2** Rocky Mountain Books, 1996.

Eastcott, Doug **Backcountry Biking in the Canadian Rockies** Rocky Mountain Books, 1999.

Gowland, J. S. **Smoke over Sikanaska** Werner Laurie, 1955, out of print.

Gowland, J. S. **Sikanaska Trail** Werner Laurie, 1956, out of print.

Hanisch, Ernst **Kananaskis Ram** Rocky Mountain Books, 1996

Kane, Alan **Scrambles in the Canadian Rockies** Rocky Mountain Books, 2003.

Martin, John & Jones, Jon **Sport Climbs in the Canadian Rockies** Rocky Mountain Books, 2000.

Perry, Chris & Josephson, Joe **Bow Valley Rock** Rocky Mountain Books, 2000.

Appleby, Edna **Canmore. The Story of an Era** 1979.

Oltmann, Ruthie **My Valley the Kananaskis** Rocky Mountain Books, 1997.

Patterson, R. M. **The Buffalo Head** Horsdal & Schubart, 2000.

Patterson, R. M. **Far Pastures** Horsdal & Schubart, 2000.

Index of Walks